Olderr's Fiction Subject Headings

A Supplement
and Guide to
the LC Thesaurus

Olderr's Fiction Subject Headings

A Supplement
and Guide to
the LC Thesaurus

Steven Olderr

American Library Association
Chicago and London 1991

Text and cover design by Ophelia Chambliss-Jones

Composed by Alexander Typesetting, Inc. in Times Roman with Palatino display type on Datalogics

Printed on 50-pound Glatfelter, a pH-neutral stock, and bound in Holliston Roxite vellum cloth by Braun-Brumfield, Inc.

The paper used in this publication meets the minimum requirements of American National Standard for Information Sciences — Permanence of Paper for Printed Library Materials, ANSI Z39.48-1984. ∞

Library of Congress Cataloging-in-Publication Data

Olderr, Steven.
   Olderr's fiction subject headings : a supplement and guide to the LC thesaurus / by Steven Olderr.
     p. cm.
   Includes bibliographical references.
   ISBN 0-8389-0562-5
   1. Subject headings—Fiction. 2. Fiction—Abstracting and indexing. I. Title.
Z695.1.F4704 1991
025.4'980883—dc20
                                      91-8679

Copyright © 1991 by the American Library Association. All rights reserved except those which may be granted by Sections 107 and 108 of the Copyright Revision Act of 1976.

Printed in the United States of America.

95 94 93 92 91   5 4 3 2 1

For Frederick D. Donnelly, Jr., 1928–1976

A dedicated bookman of the old school, who made library work fun. We still miss you, Fred.

Contents

Preface   ix
Acknowledgments   xi
Theory and Practice of Cataloging Fiction   xiii
The Purpose and Use of This Supplementary Thesaurus   xvii
Thesaurus of Fiction Subject Headings   1
Appendix A: Guidelines on Subject Access to Individual Works of
    Fiction, Drama, Etc.   133
Appendix B: Subject Headings   139
  Fictitious Characters   139
  Fiction   141
Selected and Annotated Bibliography   145

Preface

The purpose of this thesaurus is to supplement and explain the *Library of Congress Subject Headings*[1] so that the subject headings therein may be used with works of fiction. The new entries consist of additional cross references, scope notes, and, when necessary, new headings needed for the cataloging of fiction.

This thesaurus had its beginning in 1986 while I was compiling *Mystery Index* (American Library Association, 1987). Over 10,000 mysteries were cataloged in this work using a thesaurus that was made up mostly for my own convenience. Many of the terms were based on Library of Congress headings, but if I didn't care for a heading, I simply made up another. *Professors,* for example, seemed to fit into a mystery context better than the Library of Congress's *College teachers.* The term *College teachers* included mere instructors, and in my mind's eye, I couldn't see an adjunct faculty member as a detective. Detectives were full professors with glasses, briar pipes, and high foreheads.

Mystery Index met with such a good response that the concept was extended to current general fiction, and I compiled the first edition of *Olderr's Fiction Index* for St. James Press in 1987. This experience changed my ideas on thesauruses somewhat. No longer operating within the narrow confines of mystery fiction, I found that some of the Library of Congress (LC) terms started to look better. I used them in many cases, although often clipped because of the limitations of my computer program. In 1988, St. James also began publishing *Olderr's Young Adult Fiction Index,* and outside indexers had to be hired. It became obvious that having an idiosyncratic thesaurus was just going to make it difficult to train the new help and get consistent catalog-

---

[1]*Library of Congress Subject Headings,* 13th ed. (Washington, D.C.: Library of Congress, 1990). All references to the *Library of Congress Subject Headings (LCSH)* refer to this edition. All of the headings used in OLDERR'S FICTION SUBJECT HEADINGS are current with this edition of *LCSH*.

ing, so a new computer program was designed to accommodate full LC headings.

Finally, while I was working at the St. James Press booth at the 1988 American Library Association (ALA) convention in Dallas, several enthusiastic users told me they were borrowing my cataloging for their own in-house catalogs. I was both flattered and horrified. When I got home, I promptly set about changing whatever remaining headings I could into LC form, and the ones that had to be different were marked with a backslash (\) so librarians would be alerted.

It was at this point that Tina MacAyeal, the ALA Books editor who had worked with me on *Mystery Index,* discovered the existence of my thesaurus and thought it would be useful for libraries. Even though librarians can simply borrow the cataloging for current fiction from *Olderr's Fiction Index* and *Olderr's Young Adult Fiction Index,* a thesaurus is still needed for foreign or older works.

This thesaurus has been designed to be fully congruent with the Library of Congress subject headings. Even terms that had to be made up will interfile in an LC-style catalog with no confusion and no contradiction. This thesaurus has evolved over the period of three years and has been field-tested in the cataloging of more than 20,000 works of fiction.

The terms included in this thesaurus are the ones that caused problems or raised questions in the work on *Mystery Index, Olderr's Fiction Index,* and *Olderr's Young Adult Fiction Index.* My intention is to provide help where needed for catalogers of fiction; there is no intention of duplicating the *Library of Congress Subject Headings*.

New problems will inevitably occur as other catalogers work with other books at other times. Questions and comments from users will be of great help in honing and refining future editions.

Acknowledgments

Particular thanks to Mary K.D. Pietris and Jane Martin of the Library of Congress, who took time from their busy schedules to explain to me many terms and practices that applied to the nonfiction use of the LC headings. Kay Sodowsky and Candy Smith, my colleagues in producing *Olderr's Fiction Index* and *Olderr's Young Adult Fiction Index,* made many suggestions for improvements to the thesaurus. The Oak Park (Ill.) Public Library reference service helped clarify many murky definitions. And last, but certainly not least, thanks to Tina MacAyeal, formerly of the American Library Association, through whose efforts this book has come to print.

Theory and Practice of Cataloging Fiction

Why Catalog Fiction?

In 1977, when everybody was reading Colleen McCullough's *Thorn Birds*, eager readers started asking at our library if we had any other "big novels on Australia." We didn't have fiction indexed in our card catalog and didn't get very far with Wilson's *Fiction Catalog*, which listed a few books but none that we owned in spite of having a healthy fiction collection. Polling the staff members didn't help much either.

It is never easy to answer questions as "Do you have any mysteries set in Iowa?" or "Are there any contemporary novels about death and dying?" or "Can you suggest a novel about the home front in World War II?"

Librarians spend a lot of time selecting fiction they think will interest their communities, but the only time readers have a good chance of finding the books is while they're sitting on the new book shelves. It's disheartening to watch a good novel get transferred to the general collection and know that it's unlikely to circulate well unless the author writes another book that gets attention. If it has the misfortune to be shelved on the very top shelf or the bottom two shelves, it's almost sure to be weeded in a few years. Patrons don't browse on their tiptoes and only the young browse while sitting on the floor.

The Reverend Robert Fulghum says that "imagination is stronger than knowledge. That myth is more potent than history. That dreams are more powerful than facts."[1] We can't survive materially in our modern world without knowledge, history, and facts, but our souls still thrive on the ingredients of fiction: imagination, myth, and dreams.

We've taught our patrons not to ask too much about fiction. "Another big book on Australia? Gee, too bad Martha's not on duty today. Her husband was stationed there during the war; she might know." We can't retrieve fic-

---

[1] Robert Fulghum, *It Was on Fire When I Lay Down on It* (New York: Villard, 1989).

tion in this kind of unsystematic fashion and still call our profession library science.

We can find the facts about Australia easily enough, but what does it feel like to live there? We wouldn't dream of sending someone off to the stacks to browse blindly for hard facts, but fiction is considered "soft" information—if we consider it as information at all. Is it true that a thriller set in Ireland cannot convey any useful knowledge about what it feels like to be Irish or to live in Ireland? Is it impossible to learn anything about the human condition from an animal fantasy set in a mythical kingdom at some undefined time in the distant past?

With nonfiction you can do a reasonable amount of directed browsing on a topic simply by getting near the right Dewey number, but if you liked Raymond Chandler's mysteries set in Southern California, you'd have to browse through a lot of Agatha Christie and foggy English moors before getting back to the sunny West Coast again with Ross Macdonald. If a library doesn't have good fiction cataloging, then it's operating on folklore, not library science.

The Problem of Cataloging Fiction

Cataloging fiction requires imagination. A nonfiction work, even if it does not have Cataloging in Publication (CIP) information on the verso of the title page, has a table of contents, an index, topical chapter headings, and other features that will help the cataloger. Even the title is usually an accurate reflection of content. If the book is about envy, it will say so; if it is about jealousy, then it will say that. A fiction work, on the other hand, may be about envy or jealousy and never even use the word in the text. Once the cataloger figures out the theme, there is still the problem of remembering the difference between envy and jealousy. This is not something everyone knows well to begin with, and it is no easier to recall when you've been on duty since 9 AM and students are pouring in and the phone is ringing off the hook.

The *Library of Congress Subject Headings (LCSH)* have grown too huge to include many scope notes, and, anyway, the difference between, say, envy and jealousy, is not something likely to arise in the cataloging of nonfiction works, for which *LCSH* was primarily designed.

There are no expanded scope notes hidden away in the basement of LC. Those that are printed in *LCSH* and the explanatory notes in the *Subject Cataloging Manual: Subject Headings*[2] are all that exist. These are the two prime sources for the scope notes added in OLDERR'S FICTION SUBJECT HEADINGS. They will usually yield an answer if one is willing to spend enough time reading, analyzing cross references, and looking up definitions in standard reference books.

The only other guide to usage is what was done in the past. In a manner similar to common law, you may find authorization from precedent. Examine works cataloged with a particular heading and deduce the general way in which the heading has been used. If enough LC catalogers have used a term in a certain fashion, then that's what it means in a de facto sort of way. This

---

[2]*Subject Cataloging Manual: Subject Headings,* 3rd ed. (Washington, D.C.: Library of Congress, 1988). All references are to the 1988 edition with updates current through 1990.

approach is not extraordinarily precise, and it's easy to spend an hour or two analyzing a single term.

The Importance of Library of Congress Terms

Library of Congress subject headings are the most commonly used headings in American libraries. The advent of MARC (Machine-Readable Cataloging) tapes and CIP has brought more libraries than ever into the fold. As complex or awkward as LC headings may sometimes be, most librarians are familiar with them and nothing comes close to replacing them. A good way to gain respect for LC headings is to try to invent a system on your own. There have been some amusing articles written about silly LC headings, but it's no easy thing to consistently come up with better ones.

This present thesaurus varies from Library of Congress headings only when absolutely necessary. Using it will make your fiction catalog consistent with your nonfiction catalog, and there will be no major new system to learn. Even the alphabetization follows Library of Congress rules; if you locate a term in the LC headings, you can easily locate the additional information in this supplement.

Although fiction is cataloged more broadly than nonfiction, most other LC cataloging rules and practices are unchanged.

Subject Analysis Committee Guidelines

The fiction cataloging guidelines given in *Guidelines on Subject Access to Individual Works of Fiction, Drama, Etc.* (American Library Association, 1990) are included in Appendix A. The hope of those involved in this project is that the Library of Congress will formally adopt these guidelines for its own use and for CIP. The Subject Analysis Committee of the Association for Library Collections and Technical Services (ALCTS) urges adoption of these guidelines even if LC is not able to use them in its cataloging.

Also contained in the *Guidelines* is a brief thesaurus of suggested genre headings. Unfortunately, in the actual practice of cataloging, I found that many of them either conflicted with LC headings or raised other problems.

For example, the *Guidelines* suggest the use of the heading *Gothic novels* for those romantic horror stories with women in diaphanous gowns running away from Victorian mansions on dark and stormy nights. This heading could obviously not be used for collections of "gothic" short stories. It is also misleading, because LC uses the apparently related term *Gothic literature* to mean literature written by Goths. LC uses *Gothic revival (Literature)* only for nonfiction works on the history and criticism of the literature of dark and stormy nights. Hence, my thesaurus uses the term *Gothic revival fiction*, which can be used for both short stories and novels, and will not conflict with catalogs which list historical and critical works on the genre.

Annotated Card Headings

Annotated Card headings were created by LC for use with children's literature. They are published in a separate section in the front of the annual editions of the *Library of Congress Subject Headings*. Annotated Card headings are selected LC headings which have been nominally simplified for use in cataloging children's materials. They are a separate system and not included here since they conflict with other LC headings and would thus require their own separate supplement. I have created such a supplement in manuscript, and hope to have it published.

The Purpose and Use of This Supplementary Thesaurus

This thesaurus has been produced to make possible good quality, consistent cataloging of fiction using the *Library of Congress Subject Headings*. This is accomplished in three primary ways: (1) differentiating and explaining confusing LC terms, (2) adding cross references where needed, and (3) adding new terms where LC has not provided them.

Because this thesaurus is a supplement, it is expected that catalogers will normally use the *Library of Congress Subject Headings (LCSH)* first and only turn to this thesaurus when there is a problem.

Entries in this thesaurus may not carry all of the cross references found in *LCSH,* because it is pointless to repeat what is already adequately covered elsewhere. Nevertheless, some very common terms are reproduced for the sake of convenience. You will find, for example,

    Blackmail
        USE Extortion

because it was found to be one of those headings that cause continual confusion.

Another convenient feature is the inclusion of a number of headings for geographic and government bodies which are common or which might require reference to LC's name authorities list.[1] *LCSH* does not tell you, for example, specifically how to enter the Soviet army, or even Harlem in New York City.

How to Begin Cataloging

Before you begin cataloging, decide how far you want to go with your fiction cataloging and decide on your local policy. Current Library of Congress prac-

---

[1]*CDMARC Names* (Washington, D.C.: Library of Congress, 1990; three CD-ROM disks).
    Name Authorities Cumulative Microform Edition (Washington, D.C.: Library of Congress, 1990; 48X microfiche). There are two separate editions: 1977–1986 and 1987–1990. Both of these versions have the same coverage.

tice is fairly restrictive; headings are applied mostly to collections or the most salient features of individual works. See the Appendix B for the current LC guidelines.

You should also review Appendix A, which contains the fiction cataloging guidelines from *Guidelines on Subject Access to Individual Works of Fiction, Drama, Etc.* These guidelines are recommended by the ALCTS Subject Analysis Committee (SAC) as the new national standard. The *Guidelines* provide for a greater number of subject headings for each work than does LC policy. The *Guidelines* should be adopted by all libraries as the minimum standard.

Olderr's Fiction Index and *Olderr's Young Adult Fiction Index* go beyond the *Guidelines* and catalog the specific chronological setting (*1963\\; 1941–1944*, etc.), ages of protagonists (*Teenage girls—16\\; Young men—24*, etc.), and other special items of interest (*Melodramatic fiction\\; Sexually explicit fiction\\; Literary fiction*, etc.).

The basic headings to consider are these:

>   Topics
>   Genres
>   Geographical settings
>   Chronological settings
>   Characters
>   Treatment.

The Library of Congress usually expects at least 20 percent of a work to be about a certain topic to have that topic noted in the cataloging.[2] It's often difficult to tell just how much of a work of fiction is concerned with any particular topic, but it's a good benchmark to keep in mind. The SAC *Guidelines* suggests a "superficial review of the publication in hand" and stipulates that the cataloger make "no attempt to discern topics which have not been made explicit by the author or publisher."[3] Most libraries will want to follow these guidelines as a practical matter. Two of the strong points of the *Olderr's* indexes[4] are comprehensiveness and the large number of access points, but they make use of reviews and other sources and these would be impractical in most library cataloging. That is not to say, however, that you cannot catalog any additional information that you have access to, either from reviews, personal knowledge, or sources such as the *Olderr's* indexes.

Genre Fiction

If you shelve a particular genre separately in your library, then the heading for that genre may be superfluous for your catalog. This may not be the case if you share a computerized or microform catalog with other libraries that do not separate their genres in the same fashion.

---

[2]*Subject Cataloging Manual: Subject Headings*, Section H-180 (rev. 5/4/88), p.1
[3]*Guidelines on Subject Access to Individual Works of Fiction, Drama, Etc.*, p. 33.
[4]*Olderr's Fiction Index* (Chicago: St. James Press, 1987–). Issued annually.
Olderr's Young Adult Fiction Index (Chicago: St. James Press, 1988–). Issued annually.

To gain a quick familiarity with the range of genre headings available, see the entry under *Fiction* in this thesaurus to find a complete list of genres together with brief definitions. For a fuller explanation, turn to the heading for each separate genre.

Topics

As with nonfiction, topical headings are assigned as appropriate for subjects that are dealt with in a substantive way. If a protagonist is a banker but this has no bearing on the action of the work, and if there is nothing to be learned about how a banker might respond or feel, then there is probably no reason to include this information.

Geographical Settings

Books such as Tom Wolfe's *Bonfire of the Vanities* that have a strong sense of place are always worth a geographic heading. Books such as Gabriel Garcia Marquez's *One Hundred Years of Solitude,* however, have very little concrete sense of place. It could be almost anywhere in Latin America. You may choose to list a geographic setting any time it can be identified or only when it is important.

Chronological Settings

At present, the only mechanism *LCSH* or SAC *Guidelines* provides for conveying a chronological setting is through use of historical headings such as *Great Britain—History—Henry VIII, 1509–1547* or *World War, 1939–1945* and a few general headings such as *Middle Ages*. You may find it very useful to be able to retrieve fiction by chronological settings such as *1923–1927*. If you are tempted to omit a common heading such as *1980–1989,* remember that in a few years many of these books may be weeded out, and the heading will gain a greater importance.

Characters

The *Guidelines* suggest cataloging only fictional characters who appear in at least three works.[5] However, if the choice is between having fewer catalog headings or not cataloging fiction at all, then eliminating characters would be a logical choice. Users will not search by character as much as they will by subject, setting, or genre.

Treatment

Some people may consider terms such as *Melodramatic fiction\\, Sexually explicit fiction\\,* or *Violent fiction* to be subjective labeling and, as such, offensive. However, publishers often cheerfully advertise these features to attract the readership they seek. If these types of headings are used in a factual way, they can be very helpful. If they are used to promote the librarian's point

---

[5]Section II, p. 28, or see Appendix A herein.

of view, they do indeed become subjective value judgments and, at the same time, useless to staff and patrons alike.

Users of the *Olderr's* indexes seem to like the labels. Anyone doing reader's advisory work in fiction has been asked for such things as "a mystery without all the gore" or "a juicy novel like the *Dynasty* TV show." If you have problems with time, space, or philosophy, these headings could be excluded. Since they're not widely used in libraries, patrons won't be expecting them. You may be wise to check with your reader's advisory librarians, however, before you dismiss these headings entirely. Nobody wants to offer a novel of sex and violence to a patron seeking an innocent drawing room melodrama, or vice versa.

Unauthorized Headings

Headings not authorized by the Library of Congress which appear in this thesaurus are marked with a backslash (\). The backslash is not intended to be part of the heading; it is only included to identify non-LC headings for the cataloger. The new headings are in large part derived from other existing thesauruses or *LCSH* itself, and are used only when there is no viable LC alternative. To avoid using these headings, you usually have the option of using authorized related, narrower or broader terms, even though they may not be as accurate. For example, the LC term *Interpersonal relations* may be substituted for the non-standard term *Female-female relationships*\. Obviously, there may be many readers interested in female-female relations who are not necessarily also interested in female-male relations or male-male relations which are also included under *Interpersonal relations*. The use of the unauthorized headings suggested will avoid this type of problem. The obvious reason that LC does not have all the headings that one needs for fiction cataloging is that LC does not do in-depth fiction cataloging.

Fiction Subdivision

Most of the terms in this thesaurus should have the subdivision —*Fiction* added to them for use in a general catalog. This would not be necessary in a separate fiction catalog. Some terms, such as *Science fiction* or *Detective and mystery stories,* are obviously complete as shown. The subdivision —*Juvenile fiction*[6] can be used with works intended for children up to ninth grade or age 15. There is no separate subdivision for young adult fiction. See also the note on the Annotated Card headings on page xv.

A Final Note

As with any thesaurus, do not catalog from cross reference terms. Although the scope notes in this thesaurus often explain broader, narrower, and related headings, it is still necessary to go to the specific entry for a heading to get full information. Failure to read through thesaurus entries is one of the biggest reasons for misapplied subject headings.

---

[6]*Subject Cataloging Manual,* Section H-1690, p.1

Thesaurus of Fiction Subject Headings

Abandoned ships
  USE Derelicts
ABBESSES, CHRISTIAN
  RT Nuns
ABDUCTION [Here are entered works dealing with a female, usually below the age of consent, who is carried off with or without her permission, for purposes of marriage, seduction, or rape. Works dealing with a person seized and detained against his or her will or that of his or her legal guardian are entered under *Kidnapping*.]
  RT Kidnapping
ABNORMALITIES, HUMAN
  RT Mentally handicapped
      Physically handicapped
ABORTION
  BT Fetus
      Pregnancy
ABSURD (PHILOSOPHY) IN LITERATURE [Here are entered works of nonfiction dealing with the history and criticism of the absurd in literature.]
ABSURDIST FICTION\ [Here are entered works that represent the absurdity of man's existence by bizarre or fantastic means. Examples include Samuel Beckett's *Malone Dies* and Thomas Berger's *Neighbors*.
    Works that use the device of desperate, sardonic humor to induce laughter as the appropriate response to the apparent meaninglessness and absurdity of existence are entered under *Black humor fiction*\. Black humor is a frequent device in absurdist fiction.]
  BT Experimental fiction
      Fiction
  RT Black humor fiction\
      Existential fiction\
      Magic realistic fiction\
      Nihilistic fiction\
Abuse of power
  USE Corruption (in politics)
       Police corruption
       Power (Social sciences)
ACCIDENTS
  NT Survival (after airplane accidents, shipwrecks, etc.)
ACCOUNTANTS AS DETECTIVES\
ACROBATS
  RT Circus
ACTIONS AND DEFENSES [Here are entered works dealing with a suit brought in court. Works dealing with a judicial examination and determination of issues between parties to an action are entered under *Trials*.]
  RT Trials
ACTORS
  BT Theater
ACTORS AS DETECTIVES\
  BT Motion picture actors and actresses

ACTRESSES
- BT Entertainers
- Theater

ACTRESSES AS DETECTIVES \
- BT Motion picture actors and actresses
- Women detectives

ADELAIDE (S. AUST.)
- BT South Australia

ADOPTION
- RT Foster children
- Guardian and ward
- Orphans

Adult fiction for young adult readers
- USE Young adult accessible fiction \

ADULTERY
- UF Wife swapping
- BT Problem marriages \
- RT Love affairs \
- Love stories

ADVENTURE STORIES [Here are entered novels and stories characterized by an emphasis on physical and often violent action, exotic locales, and danger, generally with little character development. Examples include Daniel Defoe's *Robinson Crusoe*, C.S. Forester's *African Queen,* and Percival Christopher Wren's *Beau Geste*.

Works of fiction whose primary purpose is to produce true fright and that focus on the supernatural and occult and generally lack romantic involvement are entered under *Horror tales*. Works of fiction characterized by supernatural horror, a heroine with threatened sanity, isolated settings (frequently ruined or haunted castles or large old houses), and elements of romantic love are entered under *Gothic revival fiction* \. Works of fiction dealing primarily with ghosts are entered under *Ghost stories*. Works of fiction whose prime purpose is the depiction of the detection and solution of crimes are entered under *Detective and mystery stories*. Works of fiction that offer excitement and may combine elements of adventure stories, suspense, detective and mystery stories, sea stories, spy stories, and so forth, and which often involve elaborate schemes and some romantic interest are entered under *Thrillers* \.]
- UF International intrigue
- BT Fiction
- RT Escapes
- Terrorism
- Thrillers \
- NT Detective and mystery stories
- Fantastic fiction, Sword and sorcery \
- Ghost stories
- Gothic revival fiction \
- Horror tales
- Spy stories
- War stories

ADVENTURE STORIES, AMERICAN (Australian, etc.) [Here are entered collections of adventure stories written by American (Australian, etc.) authors.]

AFRICA

AFRICANS [Here are entered works dealing with people of Africa regardless of race.]
- NT Blacks

AFRICANS—UNITED STATES [Here are entered works dealing with Africans visiting or living in the United States.]
- NT Afro-Americans

AFRO-AMERICAN DETECTIVES \ [Here are entered works dealing with black American detectives. Works dealing with black detectives who are not American are entered under *Black detectives*.]
- BT Black detectives

AFRO-AMERICANS [Here are entered works dealing with Americans of African ancestry.]
- BT Africans—United States
- RT Slavery

AGED
- UF Old people

AGED—DWELLINGS
- RT Apartment houses

AGED DETECTIVES \

AGED MEN

AGED WOMEN

AGNOSTICISM
- RT Religion

AGRICULTURE [Here are entered works dealing with the art or science of cultivating the soil, producing crops, and raising livestock. Works dealing with farms and the manners and customs thereupon are entered under *Farm life*.]
- RT Farm life

AIDS (DISEASE)

Air Force life [Use the subdivision *Military life* under names of individual air

forces, for example, *United States. Air Force—Military life*.]
AIR PILOTS [Here are entire works dealing with aircraft pilots whether civilian or military.]
    UF Airplane pilots
          Fliers
    SA United States. Air Force—Officers [and similar headings for air pilots in different air forces]
AIR PILOTS AS DETECTIVES \
    RT Airmen as detectives \
AIR RAID SHELTERS
    UF Air raids
    BT Bombing, Aerial
Air raids
    USE Air raid shelters
           Bombing, Aerial
AIR TRAVEL
    UF Airplane travel
          Airplanes—Travel
AIRCRAFT HULKS
    RT Airplanes—Salvaging
Airmen
    USE Subdivision *Airmen* under the names of individual air forces, for example, *United States. Air Force—Airmen*
           [The subdivision *Airmen* is used for works dealing with members of an air force, whether they are men or women, officers or enlisted personnel. The subdivision *Officers* is used for works dealing primarily with officers. The subdivision *Non-Commissioned Officers* is used for works dealing primarily with non-commissioned officers.]
    SA United States. Air Force—Military life
          United States. Air Force—Non-commissioned officers
          United States. Air Force—Officers
AIRMEN AS DETECTIVES \ [Here are entered works dealing with air force members as detectives, whether they are men or women, officers, or enlisted personnel.]
    RT Air pilots as detectives \
Airplane hijacking
    USE Hijacking of aircraft
Airplane pilots
    USE Air pilots
Airplane salvaging
    USE Airplanes—Salvaging
Airplane travel
    USE Air travel
Airplanes, Hijacking of
    USE Hijacking of aircraft
AIRPLANES—SALVAGING
    UF Airplane salvaging
    RT Aircraft hulks
Airplanes—Travel
    USE Air travel
ALABAMA
    NT Mobile (Ala.)
ALASKA
    RT Arctic regions
    NT Anchorage (Alaska)
ALBERTA
    BT Canada
    NT Edmonton (Alta.)
ALBUQUERQUE (N.M.)
    BT New Mexico
ALCOHOLIC DETECTIVES \
ALCOHOLICS
ALCOHOLISM
Alien beings
    USE Extraterrestrial beings \
ALIENATION (SOCIAL PSYCHOLOGY) [Here are entered works dealing with estrangement and loss of or lack of adjustment between an individual and his or her social or intellectual environment. Works dealing with a state of society in which normative standards of conduct and belief have weakened or disappeared, or with a similar condition in an individual, commonly characterized by personal disorientation, anxiety, and isolation, are entered under *Anomy*. Works dealing with detachment from others, either because of one's own wish or from causes beyond one's control, are entered under *Social isolation*. Works dealing with a situation where there are no others of one's kind with whom to associate, or with a mental state in which, by wish or compulsion, one is cut off from normal contacts with family, friends, colleagues, or neighbors are entered under *Solitude*. Works dealing with a lack of intimate association with others and the resultant sadness therefrom are entered under *Loneliness*.]
    UF Social alienation
    RT Anomy
          Loneliness

Social isolation
Solitude
ALIENS, ILLEGAL
  UF Illegal immigrants
        Immigrants, Illegal
Aliens from space
  USE Extraterrestrial beings \
ALLEGORIES [Here are entered works in which the persons and objects represented have a meaning that lies outside the narrative itself. Allegories attempt to evoke an interest in their characters, setting, and events as well as in the ideas that they represent. Examples include John Bunyan's *Pilgrim's Progress* and George Orwell's *Animal Farm*.
    Works that suggest other levels of meaning without making the structure of ideas a formative influence on the narrative are entered under *Symbolic fiction* \. Works in which the allegory is short and simple and which deal with a familiar occurrence in life or nature that by analogy conveys a spiritual truth are entered under *Parables*. Works in which the allegory is short and simple, using animals acting as humans and illustrating the follies and weaknesses of people, are entered under *Fables*. Works dealing with nonexistent, incredible, or unreal worlds, characters, or physical principles are entered under *Fantastic fiction*.]
  BT Fiction
  RT Fantastic fiction
        Good and evil
        Improbable fiction \
        Science fantasy \
        Science fiction
        Symbolic fiction \
  NT Fables
        Parables
Allegories—Animals
  USE Fables
ALMA-ATA (KAZAKH S.S.R.)
  BT Kazakh S.S.R.
Alternate history
  USE Imaginary histories
Alternate worlds
  USE Imaginary histories
Alumni reunions
  USE Class reunions

ALZHEIMER'S DISEASE
  RT Senile dementia
AMATEUR THEATER
  UF High school theater
        School theater
        Student theater
AMAZON RIVER
  RT Brazil
AMBITION
  UF Self-made men
  RT Capitalists and financiers
        Success
AMERICAN FICTION [In a library with a large collection of American fiction this heading would not normally be used since there would be too many entries for it to be of any practical value.]
AMERICAN FICTION—INDIAN AUTHORS [Here are entered collections of works written by American Indians in non-Indian languages. Collections of works written by American Indians writing in their native language are entered under *Indian literature*. Works written by American Indians of a specific tribe are entered under the corresponding heading for the literature, for example, *Navajo literature*.]
  UF Indian fiction
        North American Indian fiction
  RT Indian literature
AMERICAN FICTION—MEXICAN AMERICAN AUTHORS
  UF Mexican American fiction (English)
American-Russian relations
  USE Soviet Union—Foreign relations—United States
        United States—Foreign relations—Soviet Union
AMERICANIZATION
  BT Immigrants—United States
AMERICANS—ENGLAND
  BT Americans—Great Britain
AMERICANS—FRANCE
AMERICANS—GERMANY
AMERICANS—GREAT BRITAIN [Here are entered works dealing with Americans in Great Britain. Works dealing with Britons in the United States are entered under *British—United States*. Works dealing with Americans who are of British extraction are entered under *British Americans*.]
  NT Americans—England

Americans—Ireland
Americans—Northern Ireland
Americans—Scotland
Americans—Wales
AMERICANS—IRELAND
   BT Americans—Great Britain
   NT Americans—Northern Ireland
AMERICANS—NORTHERN IRELAND
   BT Americans—Great Britain
       Americans—Ireland
AMERICANS—SCOTLAND
   BT Americans—Great Britain
AMERICANS—SOVIET UNION
AMERICANS—VIETNAM
AMERICANS—WALES
   BT Americans—Great Britain
AMNESIA
   UF Loss of memory
       Memory loss
AMUSEMENT PARKS
   RT Fairs
       Festivals
Analysts
   USE Psychoanalysts
ANARCHISM
   BT Political fiction
   RT Radicalism
ANCHORAGE (ALASKA)
   BT Alaska
ANDROIDS [Here are entered works dealing with robots in the shape of a human being. Works dealing with machines that perform tasks normally associated with human beings or that seem to possess intelligence similar to that of a human are entered under *Robots*. Works dealing with humans altered with artificial parts are entered under *Cyborgs\.*]
   RT Cyborgs\
       Robots
Anglican bishops
   USE Church of England—Bishops
ANGLICAN COMMUNION—CLERGY
   NT Church of England—Clergy
       Episcopal Church—Clergy
Anglican priests
   USE Church of England—Clergy
ANGLO-INDIANS [Here are entered works dealing with persons of mixed British and Indic heritage.]
   BT British—India
ANGLO-SAXONS
   NT Great Britain—History—Anglo Saxon period, 449-1066

Animal abuse
   USE Animal welfare
ANIMAL WELFARE
   UF Animal abuse
       Animals, Treatment of
   BT Cruelty
ANIMALS
   SA headings for specific kinds of animals such as *Cats, Dogs, Pets,* etc.
   NT Fables
ANIMALS, MYTHICAL
   UF Fantastic fiction—Animals
   RT Monsters
Animals, Treatment of
   USE Animal welfare
ANNAPOLIS (MD.)
   BT Maryland
   RT United States Naval Academy
ANOMY [Here are entered works that deal with a state of society in which normative standards of conduct and belief have weakened or disappeared, or with a similar condition in an individual, commonly characterized by personal disorientation, anxiety, and isolation. Works dealing with detachment from others, either because of one's own wish or from causes beyond one's control, are entered under *Social isolation*. Works dealing with a situation where there are no others of one's kind with whom to associate, or with a mental state in which by wish or compulsion one is cut off from normal contacts with family, friends, colleagues, or neighbors are entered under *Solitude*. Works dealing with a lack of intimate association with another or others, and the resultant sadness therefrom are entered under *Loneliness*. Works dealing with estrangement and loss or lack of adjustment between an individual and his social or intellectual environment are entered under *Alienation (Social psychology)*.]
   RT Alienation (Social psychology)
       Loneliness
       Social isolation
       Solitude
ANTARCTIC REGIONS
   RT Arctic regions
ANTHROPOLOGICAL FICTION [Here are entered works dealing with the cultural and physical life and development of

people from prehistory to the present, especially as concerns primitive or folk societies.]
- UF Ethnological fiction
- BT Fiction

ANTIQUARIANS AS DETECTIVES \

ANTIQUITIES
- RT Art objects
- NT Mummies

ANTISEMITISM
- BT Jews
  - Judaism
  - Social problems
- RT National socialism
- NT Holocaust, Jewish (1939-1945)

ANXIETY [Here are entered works dealing with apprehensive uneasiness of mind, often involving self-doubt and doubt concerning the nature and reality of the uneasiness. Anxiety involves the anguish of fear with the anticipation or uncertainty of failure. Anxiety may have physiological symptoms. Works dealing with fretting or stewing over a problem as a mental activity are entered under *Worry*. Works dealing with a loss of courage that may amount to cowardice are entered under *Fear*.]
- RT Fear
  - Worry

APARTHEID
- BT South Africa—Race relations

APARTMENT HOUSES
- RT Aged—Dwellings
  - Hotels, taverns, etc. [Includes boarding houses]
  - Lodging-houses [This term is used for rooming houses]
  - Public housing

APOCALYPTIC FICTION \ [Here are entered works dealing with a massive holocaust destroying, or having destroyed, civilization.]
- UF Destruction of the earth
  - Earth, Destruction of the
  - End of the world
  - Postapocalyptic fiction
- RT Gloomy fiction \
  - Science fiction
- NT Survival after nuclear warfare \

APOCALYPTIC LITERATURE [Here are entered nonfiction works on the apocalypse.]

Appalachian dialect fiction
- USE Dialect fiction—Mountain Whites (Southern states) \

APPALACHIAN MOUNTAINS
- NT Great Smoky Mountains (N.C. and Tenn.)

APPETITE DISORDERS
- RT Obesity

Arab fiction
- USE Arabic fiction

ARABIC FICTION
- UF Arab fiction

ARCHAEOLOGISTS

ARCHAEOLOGY

ARCTIC REGIONS
- RT Alaska
  - Antarctic regions
  - Greenland

ARGENTINA
- NT Patagonia (Argentina and Chile)

ARGENTINE FICTION

Arguments
- USE Quarreling

ARISTOCRACY [Here are entered works dealing with persons of an ideally superior caste. It does not invariably apply to a fixed or definite group. Works dealing with persons whose rank is inferior to royalty but superior to all others, and whose rank is either directly granted by a ruler or inherited, are entered under *Nobility*. Note that *Nobility* includes baronets even though they would be excluded in British popular usage. Works dealing with persons who are not nobility but who are entitled to bear a coat of arms, and hence, are considered gentlemen or ladies in the technical sense, and are landed proprietors, are entered under *Gentry*. Works dealing with persons of the highest class of people, either because of wealth or prestige, are entered under *Upper classes*.]
- RT Gentry
  - Knights and knighthood
  - Nobility
  - Upper classes

ARISTOCRACY IN LITERATURE [Here are entered nonfiction works on the history and criticism of the aristocracy as portrayed in literature.]

ARISTOCRATS AS DETECTIVES\
   RT Knights as detectives\
       Nobles as detectives\
ARIZONA
   NT Tucson (Ariz.)
ARKANSAS
   NT Little Rock (Ark.)
ARMENIAN S.S.R.
   BT Soviet Union
   NT Yerevan (Armenian S.S.R.)
Army life
   USE subdivision *Military life* under names of individual armies, for example, *United States. Army—Military life*
ARSON
   RT Forest fires
ART
   NT Painting
ART—FORGERIES
   UF Forgery of works of art
   BT Forgery
ART DEALERS
ART GALLERIES, COMMERCIAL
ART METAL-WORKERS
   RT Artisans
ART MUSEUMS
ART OBJECTS
   UF Statuettes
   RT Antiquities
       Figurines
   NT Porcelain
Arthur, King
   USE Arthurian romances
ARTHURIAN ROMANCES
   UF Arthur, King
       King Arthur
   BT Legends
       Romances
ARTIFICIAL INSEMINATION, HUMAN
   RT Sperm banks
ARTISANS
   RT Art metal-workers
Artist life
   USE Artists
ARTISTS
   UF Artist life
ASHKHABAD (TURKMEN S.S.R.)
   BT Turkmen S.S.R.
ASIA
   RT East and West
ASSASSINATION
   RT Execution and executioners
ASSASSINS
   UF Hit men

ATLANTA (GA.)
   BT Georgia
ATLANTIC CITY (N.J.)
   BT New Jersey
ATLANTIC OCEAN
   NT Caribbean Sea
       Gulf Stream
       North Sea
ATLANTIC PROVINCES
   BT Canada
ATLANTIC STATES [Here are entered works dealing with the region that includes Connecticut, Delaware, Florida, Georgia, Maine, Maryland, Massachusetts, New Hampshire, New Jersey, New York, North Carolina, Rhode Island, South Carolina, and Virginia.]
   UF United States—East
       United States—Northeast
   BT United States
ATONEMENT
   RT Guilt
       Reconciliation
       Shame
ATROCITIES
   NT Holocaust, Jewish (1939-1945)
Attorneys general
   USE Legal stories
Au pairs
   USE Child care workers
AUCKLAND (N.Z.)
   BT New Zealand
AUGUSTA (ME.)
   BT Maine
AUNTS
   BT Domestic fiction
   RT Nephews\
       Nieces
AUSTRALIA [For use with geographical headings, the states and territories are abbreviated as follows:

Australian Capital Territory	A.C.T.
New South Wales	N.S.W.
Northern Territory	N.T.
Queensland	Qld.
South Australia	S. Aust.
Tasmania	Tas.
Victoria	Vic.
Western Australia	W.A.

Do not add any geographic identifier to the name of an Australian state or territory. For further information see 23.4C in *AACR2R*.]
   NT Australian Capital Territory

New South Wales
Northern Territory
Queensland
South Australia
Tasmania
Victoria
Western Australia
AUSTRALIAN CAPITAL TERRITORY
 BT Australia
 NT Canberra (A.C.T.)
AUSTRALIAN FICTION
Australian outback
 USE Country life—Australia
AUSTRIA
 NT Vienna
AUSTRIA—HISTORY—1867-1918
 UF Austria-Hungary
Austria-Hungary
 USE Austria—History—1867-1918
AUTHORS [Here are entered works dealing with writers. Works dealing with men and women of letters, literature, or general literary pursuits are entered under *Litterateurs*.]
 UF Literary life
 BT Intellectual life
 RT Books
  Litterateurs
  Plagiarism
AUTHORS AS DETECTIVES \
AUTOBIOGRAPHICAL FICTION [Here are entered works written by an author about his or her own life, even if the main character is given another name. Note that this heading is not given to works dealing with fictional events in the author's life even though the author appears as a character. Examples of this genre include James Joyce's *Portrait of the Artist as a Young Man* and Marcel Proust's *Remembrance of Things Past*. Works in which a true or manipulated account of the author's life serves some sort of didactic purpose are entered under *Confession stories*.
  Works in which real people and real events have been disguised for literary purposes are entered under *Livres á clef*. Works in which people who actually exist or existed and who appear in minor roles are entered under *Real people*\. Works dealing loosely with actual occurrences are entered under *Real events*\. Works of factual representation having the objective quality and authority of the real event are entered under *Nonfiction novels*.]
 UF Documentary fiction
 BT Biographical fiction
  Fiction
  Nonfiction novels\
 RT Livres á clef
  Real events\
  Real people\
 NT Confession stories
AUTOBIOGRAPHICAL FICTION, AMERICAN (English, etc.) [Here are entered collections of autobiographical fiction written by American (English, etc.) authors.]
AUTOMOBILE TRAVEL
 UF Automobiles—Touring
 BT Voyages and travels
 NT Road fiction\ [Works in which a journey is a central part of the action]
Automobiles—Touring
 USE Automobile travel
AVALANCHES
 BT Natural disasters
 RT Snowstorms
AVARICE [Here are entered works dealing with an excessive desire for gain or wealth. Works dealing with the economic effects of the amassment of money or capital in an unreasonable fashion are entered under *Hoarding of money*. Works dealing with persons who live wretched lives in order to hoard their wealth are entered under *Misers*.]
 RT Hoarding of money
  Misers
  Prodigals
AZERBAIJAN (IRAN)
AZERBAIJAN S.S.R.
 BT Soviet Union
 NT Baku (Azerbaijan S.S.R.)

BABYSITTERS
BACK—ABNORMALITIES
 UF Hunchbacks
BAJA CALIFORNIA (MEXICO)
 UF California, Lower
 BT Mexico
BAKU (AZERBAIJAN S.S.R.)
 BT Azerbaijan S.S.R.

BALKAN PENINSULA [Includes Bulgaria, Greece, Romania, Yugoslavia, and the European part of Turkey]
   BT Europe
BALTIMORE (MD.)
   BT Maryland
BANDS (MUSIC)
BANK ROBBERIES
   BT Crime
BANKS AND BANKING
Barbarians
   USE Huns
        Paganism
        Rome—History—Germanic invasions, 3d-6th centuries
Baronets
   USE Nobility
Barons
   USE Nobility
BASEBALL STORIES [Here are entered novels and stories dealing with baseball.]
   BT Fiction
BASKETBALL STORIES [Here are entered novels and stories dealing with basketball.]
   BT Fiction
BATTLES [Here are entered works dealing with battles in general, unspecified actual battles, or battles imagined by the author. Works of nonfiction on the history and criticism of imaginary battles are entered under *Imaginary wars and battles*.]
   BT War stories
   NT Imaginary wars and battles
BEAT FICTION\ [Here are entered works marked by a feeling of ennui, formlessness, exotic philosophizing, uncommitted spontaneity of thought, unconventionality, and a strong rejection of middle class values. This literary movement began in the United States in the 1950s and is epitomized by the work of Jack Kerouac.]
   BT Fiction
   RT Existential fiction\
Beheading
   USE Dismemberment, Bodily
        Execution and executioners
BEIJING (CHINA)
   BT China
BELFAST (NORTHERN IRELAND)
   BT Northern Ireland
BELGRADE (SERBIA)
   BT Serbia

BENEDICTINES
   BT Catholic Church
BEREAVEMENT [Here are entered works dealing with loss, especially by death. Works dealing only with the deep distress caused by bereavement are entered under *Grief*.]
   NT Grief
BERKSHIRE HILLS (MASS.)
   BT Massachusetts
BERLIN (GERMANY)
   BT Germany
BETRAYAL\
   UF Traitors
   RT Treason
   NT Informers
BETROTHAL
   UF Romance
   RT Honeymoon
        Love stories
        Weddings
BEVERLY HILLS (CALIF.)
   BT Los Angeles Suburban Area (Calif.)
BIBLE—HISTORY OF BIBLICAL EVENTS
   UF Bible fiction
        Biblical fiction
   BT Christian fiction
        Religious fiction
   RT Christianity
        Religion
   NT Jesus Christ
        Mary, Blessed Virgin, Saint
        Moses
BIBLE—HISTORY OF CONTEMPORARY EVENTS
   UF Bible fiction
        Biblical fiction
   BT Christian fiction
        Religious fiction
   RT Christianity
Bible fiction
   USE Bible—History of Biblical events
        Bible—History of contemporary events
BIBLE IN LITERATURE [Here are entered nonfiction works on the history and criticism of the Bible as portrayed in literature.]
BIBLE STORIES [Here are entered works of nonfiction about Bible stories.]
Biblical fiction
   USE Bible—History of Biblical events
        Bible—History of contemporary events

BIGAMY
- BT Problem marriages\

BILDUNGSROMAN [Here are entered nonfiction works on the history and criticism of fiction dealing with the youthful development of the protagonist. Works of fiction dealing with the development of the protagonist are entered under *Maturation (Psychology)*.]
- RT Maturation (Psychology)

Billionaires
- USE Millionaires

BIOGRAPHICAL FICTION [Here are entered works dealing predominately with events in the life of an actual person. Examples include Irving Stone's *Love Is Eternal: A Novel of Mary Todd Lincoln and Abraham Lincoln*, and Gore Vidal's *Burr*.

Works written by an author about his own life, even if the main character is given another name are entered under *Autobiographical fiction*. Works in which real people and real events have been disguised for literary purposes are entered under *Livres á clef*. Works of factual representation having the objective quality and authority of the real event are listed under *Nonfiction novels*\. Works in which people who actually exist or existed and who appear in minor roles are entered under *Real people*\. Works dealing loosely with actual occurrences are entered under *Real events*\.]
- UF Documentary fiction
- BT Fiction
  Nonfiction novels\
- RT Livres á clef
  Real events\
  Real people\
- NT Autobiographical fiction

BIOGRAPHICAL FICTION, ENGLISH (Korean, etc.) [Here are entered collections of biographical fiction written by English (Korean, etc.) authors.]

BIOLOGICAL WARFARE
- UF Germs
- BT Epidemics
- RT Gases, asphyxiating and poisonous

BIRMINGHAM (ALA.)
- BT Alabama

BIRTH CONTROL [Here are entered works dealing with the larger social, legal, population or religious aspects of preventing impregnation. Works dealing with the methods of preventing impregnation are entered under *Contraception*.]
- RT Contraception

Birthday parties
- USE Birthdays

BIRTHDAYS
- UF Birthday parties
  Parties, Birthday
- BT Entertaining

BISEXUALITY
- RT Gay men
  Gays
  Lesbians

BLACK DETECTIVES\ [Here are entered works dealing with black detectives who are not Americans. Works dealing with American black detectives are entered under *Afro-American detectives*\.]
- BT Blacks
- NT Afro-American detectives

BLACK HUMOR (LITERATURE) [Here are entered nonfiction works dealing with literature characterized by a desperate, sardonic humor intended to induce laughter as the appropriate response to the apparent meaninglessness and absurdity of existence.]

BLACK HUMOR FICTION\ [Here are entered fictional works that use the device of desperate, sardonic humor to induce laughter as the appropriate response to the apparent meaninglessness and absurdity of existence. Examples include Joseph Heller's *Catch 22* and Evelyn Waugh's *The Loved One*.

Works that represent the absurdity of man's existence by bizarre or fantastic means are entered under *Absurdist fiction*\. Black humor is a frequent device in absurdist fiction. Works that use humor to expose or discredit human vice or folly is entered under *Satirical fiction*\.]
- BT Fiction
  Humorous stories
- RT Absurdist fiction\
  Satirical fiction\

Black magic
- USE Witchcraft
  Wizards

Blackmail
- USE Extortion

BLACKS
- BT Africans [Includes all people of Africa, regardless of race]
- NT Black detectives \
  Interracial marriage
  Race relations
  Slavery

BLIND

Blitz
- USE Bombing, Aerial—England, 1940-1941

BLIZZARDS
- BT Snowstorms

BLOOD ACCUSATION [Here are entered works dealing with the ritual killing of a human being.]
- BT Human sacrifice

Boarding houses
- USE Hotels, taverns, etc.

BOATS AND BOATING [Here on entered works dealing with smaller craft operated on inland bodies of water or near the shore on oceans, usually powered by oars, paddles, poles, or outboard motors. Works dealing with boats using sail power are entered under *Sailboats*. Works dealing with large sailboats or powerboats with closed cabins, built for pleasure or private cruising are entered under *Yachts and yachting*. Works dealing with large seagoing vessels are entered under *Ships*.]
- BT Sea stories
- RT Ships
  Yachts and yachting
- NT River boats
  Sailboats
  Tugboats

Bodice rippers
- USE Love stories, Historical \
  Melodramatic fiction \

BODY SNATCHING
- UF Bodysnatching
  Grave robbing
- BT Dead
- RT Cemeteries

Bodysnatching
- USE Body snatching

Boer War
- USE South African War, 1899-1902

BOHEMIA
- BT Czechoslovakia

BOISE (IDAHO)
- BT Idaho

BOMBING, AERIAL
- UF Air raids
- RT Air raid shelters

BOMBING, AERIAL—ENGLAND, 1940-1941
- UF Blitz
- BT World War, 1939-1945—England

BOOK COLLECTORS
- RT Rare books

Book reviewers
- USE Critics

BOOKS [Here are entered works dealing with actual books or books imagined by the author. Works of nonfiction on the history and criticism of imaginary books and libraries are entered under *Imaginary books and libraries*.]
- UF Literary life
- RT Authors
  Intellectual life
  Literacy
- NT Booksellers and bookselling
  Imaginary books and libraries

Books in series
- USE Series (Publications)

BOOKSELLERS AND BOOKSELLING
- BT Books
- RT Rare books

BOOKSELLERS AS DETECTIVES \

Bootlegging of alcoholic beverages
- USE Distilling, Illicit
  Prohibition

BOSNIA AND HERCEGOVINA
- UF Bosnia and Herzegovina
- BT Yugoslavia
- NT Sarajevo (Bosnia and Hercegovina)

Bosnia and Herzegovina
- USE Bosnia and Hercegovina

BOSTON (MASS.)
- BT Massachusetts

BOSTON SUBURBAN AREA (MASS.)
- NT Cambridge (Mass.)

BOXERS (ATHLETES) AS DETECTIVES \

BOXING STORIES [Here are entered novels and stories dealing with boxing.]
- BT Fiction

BOY DETECTIVES \
- BT Boys

Boy into man
- USE Maturation (Psychology)

BOYS [Here are entered works dealing with male children generally and with males up to and including 12 years of age in particular. The age of the boy may be added to this heading (for example,

Boys—10; *Boys—11*, etc.) although this is not a Library of Congress practice.]
- RT Men
  - Young men [18 to 25 years of age, inclusive]
- NT Boy detectives\
  - Maturation (Psychology)
  - Teenage boys [13 to 17 years of age, inclusive]

BRAZIL
- RT Amazon River

BRAZILIAN FICTION

BRIBERY
- NT Corruption (in politics)

BRIGANDS AND ROBBERS [Here are entered works dealing with persons who commit robbery. Works dealing with persons who commit theft or burglary are entered under *Thieves*. Works dealing with persons who steal, profiteer, or kill, especially in a merciless manner, are entered under *Outlaws*. Works dealing with taking another's property using violence or the threat of violence are entered under *Robbery*. Works dealing with breaking and entering for the purpose of theft or robbery are entered under *Burglary*. Works dealing with stealing as a crime are entered under *Larceny*. Works dealing with the ethical and psychological aspects of theft are entered under *Stealing*. Works dealing with robbery committed on the street and involving a beating or other physical assault are entered under *Mugging*.]
- BT Criminals
  - Robbery
  - Thieves
- RT Burglary
  - Larceny
  - Outlaws
  - Stealing
- NT Mugging

BRISBANE (QLD.)
- BT Queensland

Britain
- USE Great Britain

BRITISH
- NT Irish [Includes the Northern Irish]
  - Orangemen [A secret pro-Protestant society formed in Northern Ireland in 1795]
  - Scots
  - Scots-Irish [Scottish settlers in Northern Ireland, and their descendants]
  - Welsh

BRITISH—AUSTRALIA

BRITISH—CANADA

BRITISH—FRANCE

BRITISH—INDIA
- Anglo-Indians [Persons of mixed British and Indic ancestry]
- India—History—British occupation, 1765-1947

BRITISH—ITALY

BRITISH—SOVIET UNION

BRITISH—SPAIN

BRITISH—UNITED STATES [Here are entered works dealing with Britons living in or visiting the United States.]
- NT British Americans

BRITISH AMERICANS [Here are entered works dealing with Americans of British ancestry.]
- BT British—United States

BRITISH COLUMBIA
- BT Canada
- NT Vancouver (B.C.)

British fiction
- USE English fiction

British-Russian relations
- USE Great Britain—Foreign relations—Soviet Union
  - Soviet Union—Foreign relations—Great Britain

BRITISH VIRGIN ISLANDS
- BT Virgin Islands
- NT Road Town (V.I.)

BRONX (NEW YORK, N.Y.)
- BT New York, N.Y.

BROOKLYN (NEW YORK, N.Y.)
- BT New York, N.Y.)

BROTHERS
- BT Domestic fiction
  - Male-male relationships\
- RT Triplets
  - Twins
- NT Fratricide
  - Half brothers\
  - Stepchildren

BROTHERS AND SISTERS
- BT Domestic fiction
  - Female-male relationships\
- NT Stepchildren

BROTHERS-IN-LAW
- UF In-laws

Brutality
   USE Violence
BUREAUCRACY
   UF Government employees
   RT Civil service
BURGLARY [Here are entered works dealing with breaking and entering for the purpose of theft or robbery. Works dealing with taking another's property using violence or the threat of violence are entered under *Robbery*. Works dealing with persons who commit theft or burglary are entered under *Thieves*. Works dealing with persons who steal, profiteer, or kill, especially in a merciless manner, are entered under *Outlaws*. Works dealing with stealing as a crime are entered under *Larceny*. Works dealing with the ethical and psychological aspects of theft are entered under *Stealing*. Works dealing with persons who commit robbery are entered under *Brigands and robbers*. Works dealing with robbery committed on the street and involving a beating or other physical assault are entered under *Mugging*.]
   BT Stealing
      Thieves
   RT Brigands and robbers
      Larceny
      Mugging
      Outlaws
      Robbery
      Thieves
BURGUNDY (FRANCE)
   BT France
BURLESQUES [Here are entered comic works characterized by ridiculous exaggeration. Works that attack authors or another particular work for comic effect through exaggeration of traits are entered under *Parodies*. Burlesques are broader and stronger than parodies.]
   RT Parodies
   NT Drolls [Short dramatic compositions or stage presentations of a comic or farcical nature]
BURLINGTON (VT.)
   BT Vermont
BUSINESS [Here are entered works dealing with business in general. Works dealing with a specific company or companies are entered under *Business enterprises* or *Corporations*.]
   SA specific types of businesses, such as *Automobile industry and trade*; *Gold mines and mining*, etc.
   NT Business enterprises
      Corporations
      Retail trade
Business depressions
   USE Depressions
BUSINESS ENTERPRISES
   UF Businesses
   BT Business
   NT Stores, Retail
BUSINESS ENTERPRISES—CORRUPT PRACTICES
   BT Commercial crimes
   NT Corporations—Corrupt practices
BUSINESS INTELLIGENCE
   UF Espionage, Industrial
   RT Factories
      Spy stories
Businesses
   USE Business enterprises
BUSINESSMEN
   RT Women in business
   NT Executives
BUSTS [Here are entered works dealing with a sculpted image of the upper part of the human body. Works dealing specifically with a sculpted, cast, or modeled image of an entire figure are entered under *Statues*. Works dealing with an image of a person engraved on a coin or sculpted for a sepulchral monument or with a crude representation of a particular person, such as a stuffed dummy, are entered under *Effigies*. Works dealing generally with the art of sculpting as well as with pieces of art that have been sculpted are entered under *Sculpture*.]
   BT Sculpture
      Statues
   RT Effigies
BYELORUSSIAN S.S.R.
   BT Soviet Union
   NT Minsk (Byelorussian S.S.R.)

C.I.A.
   USE United States. Central Intelligence Agency

CAJUNS [Here are entered works dealing with the French Acadian people of Louisiana and their descendants.]
   RT Louisiana
CALIFORNIA
   NT Hollywood (Los Angeles, Calif.)
      Los Angeles (Calif.)
      San Francisco (Calif.)
California, Lower
   USE Baja California (Mexico)
CALIFORNIA, NORTHERN
CALIFORNIA, SOUTHERN
CAMBRIDGE (ENGLAND)
   BT England
   RT University of Cambridge
CAMBRIDGE (MASS.)
   BT Boston Suburban Area (Mass.)
   RT Harvard University
Cambridge University
   USE University of Cambridge
CAMPS
   UF Summer vacations
   RT Resorts
      Summer resorts
      Vacations
Campus life
   USE College stories
      Schools
      Students
CANADA [When used as parenthetic identifiers for cities or other geographic locations, the provinces and territories are listed as follows:

Alberta	Alta.
British Columbia	B.C.
Manitoba	Man.
New Brunswick	N.B.
Newfoundland	Nfld.
Northwest Territories	N.W.T.
Nova Scotia	N.S.
Ontario	Ont.
Prince Edward Island	P.E.I.
Quebec (Province)	Not abbreviated
Saskatchewan	Sask.
Yukon Territory	Yukon

Do not add any geographic identifier to the name of a Canadian province or territory. For further information, see 23.4C in *AACR2R*.]
   NT Alberta
      Atlantic provinces [Includes New Brunswick, Newfoundland, Nova Scotia, and Prince Edward Island]
      British Columbia
      Manitoba
      Maritime provinces [Includes New Brunswick, Nova Scotia, and Prince Edward Island]
      New Brunswick
      Newfoundland
      Northwest Territories
      Nova Scotia
      Ontario
      Prairie provinces [Includes Alberta, Manitoba, and Saskatchewan]
      Prince Edward Island
      Quebec (Province)
      Saskatchewan
      Yukon Territories
Canada. Royal Canadian Mounted Police
   USE Royal Canadian Mounted Police
CANADIAN FICTION
   NT French-Canadian fiction
CANADIAN FICTION—INDIAN AUTHORS \ [Here are entered collections of works written in non-Indian languages by Canadian Indians (not to be confused with East Indians) living in Canada. Works written by Canadian Indians in their native language are entered under the corresponding heading for that literature, for example, *Eskimo literature*. Collections of works written by Canadian Indians in their native languages are entered under *Indian literature*.]
   UF Indian fiction
      North American Indian authors
   RT Indian literature
CANARY ISLANDS
   BT Spain
CANBERRA (A.C.T.)
   BT Australian Capital Territory
CANCER
CANCER—PATIENTS
   RT Terminally ill
Capers (Criminal)
   USE Larceny
CAPITALISTS AND FINANCIERS
   UF Financial intrigue
      Rich people
      Robber Barons
      Self-made men
      Tycoons
   RT Ambition
      Executives
      Industrialists

Money
Success
CARAVANS [Here are entered works dealing with vehicles or pack animals traveling in a group.]
- UF Wagon trains
- RT Overland journeys to the Pacific
  Western stories

CARGO SHIPS
- BT Ships

CARIBBEAN SEA
- BT Atlantic Ocean
- NT Islands of the Caribbean

CARNIVAL
- RT Masquerades

CARNIVALS [Here are entered works dealing with traveling amusement enterprises consisting of sideshows, games of chance, merry-go-rounds, etc. Works dealing with amusement enterprises featuring feats of physical skill, wild animal acts, clowns, and jugglers are entered under *Circus*. Works dealing with a program of cultural events or entertainment are entered under *Festivals*. Works dealing with public gatherings at which goods are exhibited and sold are entered under *Fairs*.]
- RT Circus
  Fairs
  Festivals

CASTRATION
- BT Dismemberment, Bodily \

CATERERS AND CATERING
- RT Cooks
  Restaurants, lunch rooms, etc.

CATHOLIC CHURCH
- SA Names of religious orders, popes, saints, etc.
- NT Benedictines
  Inquisition
  Jesuits
  Monastic and religious life
  Nuns
  Popes
  Vatican City

CATHOLIC CHURCH—BISHOPS
- BT Catholic Church—Clergy

CATHOLIC CHURCH—CLERGY
- UF Catholic Church—Priests
- RT Nuns
- NT Catholic Church—Bishops
  Monks

CATHOLIC CHURCH—CLERGY AS DETECTIVES \
- RT Monks as detectives \
  Nuns as detectives \

Catholic Church—Priests
- USE Catholic Church—Clergy

CAVE-DWELLERS
- UF Cave men

Cave men
- USE Cave-dwellers

CELIBACY [Here are entered works dealing with not marrying.]
- RT Chastity [Refraining from sexual relations]
  Virginity [Never having had sexual intercourse]

CEMETERIES
- RT Body snatching
  Funeral rites and ceremonies

CENTRAL AMERICA [Here are entered works dealing with the region that includes British Honduras, Costa Rica, El Salvador, Guatemala, Honduras, Nicaragua, and Panama.]
- BT Latin America
- RT South America

Central American Indians
- USE Indians of Central America

Central Intelligence Agency
- USE United States. Central Intelligence Agency

CENTRAL PARK (NEW YORK, N.Y.)
- BT Manhattan (New York, N.Y.)
  New York (N.Y.)

CHANCE [Here are entered works dealing with the incalculable, uncontrollable, and irrational element in existence. Works dealing with the outcome of an event whose success is problematical are entered under *Fortune*. Works dealing with a predetermining agency or agent such as a law of nature or a deity whose decision is inevitable or immutable, are entered under *Fate and fatalism*.]
- RT Fate and fatalism
  Fortune

CHANGELINGS \
- BT Imposters and imposture
  Kidnapping

CHANNEL ISLANDS [If a place is located in the British Channel Islands, use the identifier (*Channel Islands*), for example,

Jersey (Channel Islands). For further information, see 23.4D2 in *AACR2R.*]
  BT Great Britain
  RT England
CHARITIES
  RT Fundraising
CHARLESTON (W. VA.)
  BT West Virginia
CHARLOTTE AMALIE (V.I.)
  BT Virgin Islands
    Virgin Islands of the United States
CHARLOTTE (N.C.)
  BT North Carolina
CHARLOTTETOWN (P.E.I.)
  BT Prince Edward Island
CHARWOMEN AND CLEANERS
  BT Domestics
CHASTITY [Here are entered works dealing with refraining from sexual relations.]
  RT Celibacy [Not marrying]
    Virginity [Never having had sexual intercourse]
CHAUFFEURS
  BT Domestics
CHEERFUL FICTION [Here are entered lighthearted works characterized by the absence of explicit sex, violence, or language.]
  BT Fiction
  RT Gloomy fiction\
    Humorous stories
Cheerless fiction
  USE Gloomy fiction\
CHEYENNE (WYO.)
  BT Wyoming
CHICAGO (ILL.)
  BT Illinois
CHICAGO SUBURBAN AREA (ILL.)
CHILD ABUSE
CHILD CARE WORKERS
  UF Au pairs
    Mother's helpers
    Nannies
    Nursemaids
  NT Governesses
CHILD MOLESTERS
CHILD MOLESTING
CHILDBIRTH
  RT Pregnancy
CHILDREN
  NT Grandparent and child
    Juvenile delinquents
    Maturation (Psychology)
    Students
    Teenagers [13 to 17 years old]
    Young adults [18 to 25 years old]
    Youth [13 to 25 years old]
CHILDREN—EMPLOYMENT
  BT Working class
Children, Gifted
  USE Gifted children
Children, Mentally handicapped
  USE Mentally handicapped children
Children, Mentally ill
  USE Mentally ill children
CHILDREN OF DIVORCED PARENTS
  BT Divorced parents
CHILDREN OF HOLOCAUST SURVIVORS
CHILDREN'S STORIES [Here are entered collections of fiction for children, especially in the general age range from birth through 5th grade. Collections of fiction for children from 6th grade through high school are entered under *Young adult fiction.*]
  BT Fiction
  NT Young adult fiction
CHILDREN'S STORIES, AFRIKAANS (Albanian, etc.) [Here are entered collections of children's stories by Afrikaans (Albanian, etc.) authors.]
CHILE
  NT Patagonia (Argentina and Chile)
CHINA
  RT Taiwan
  NT Beijing (China)
    Tibet (China)
CHINESE FICTION
CHIROPRACTORS
  RT Physicians
CHIVALRY [Here are entered works dealing with the elaborate medieval system of manners and morals. Works of adventure produced in the Middle Ages that deal with knights, kings, and ladies in distress, acting under the impulse of love, religion, or the desire for adventure are entered under *Romances.*]
  RT Knights and knighthood
    Romances
Choose-your-own-adventure fiction
  USE Plot-your-own stories
CHRISTCHURCH (N.Z.)
  BT New Zealand
CHRISTIAN FICTION [Here are entered works written from a Christian religious point

of view, dealing with Christian topics and themes.]
- BT Christianity
  Fiction
  Religious fiction
- NT Bible—History of Biblical events
  Bible—History of contemporary events

CHRISTIAN FICTION, AMERICAN (Brazilian, etc.) [Here are entered collections of Christian fiction written by American (Brazilian, etc.) authors.]

Christian-Jewish relations
- USE Christianity and other religions—Judaism *and* Judaism—Relations—Christianity

CHRISTIANITY
- RT Bible—History of Biblical events
  Bible—History of contemporary events
- NT Christian fiction

CHRISTIANITY AND OTHER RELIGIONS
- BT Religions—Relations

CHRISTIANITY AND OTHER RELIGIONS—JUDAISM [Note that if this heading is used the parallel heading *Judaism—Relations—Christianity* must also be used.]
- UF Christian-Jewish relations
  Jewish-Christian relations
- RT Judaism—Relations—Christianity

CHRISTMAS STORIES [Here are entered novels and short stories dealing with Christmas.]
- BT Fiction

CHRISTMAS STORIES, AMERICAN (Chilean, etc.) [Here are entered collections of Christmas stories written by American (Chilean, etc.) authors.]

CHURCH OF ENGLAND—BISHOPS
- UF Anglican bishops

CHURCH OF ENGLAND—CLERGY
- UF Anglican priests
- BT Anglican Communion—Clergy

CHURCH OF JESUS CHRIST OF LATTER DAY SAINTS
- BT Mormon church

CHURCH SCHOOLS [Here are entered works dealing with general education in schools run under the auspices of a religion. Works dealing with religious instruction given in schools, churches, and private life are entered under *Religious education*.]
- RT Religious education

CHURCHES [Here are entered works dealing with buildings used for worship.]
- BT Religions
- RT Religion
  Synagogues

CINCINNATI (OHIO)
- BT Ohio

Ciphers
- USE Code and cipher stories

CIRCUS [Here are entered works dealing with amusement enterprises featuring feats of physical skill, wild animal acts, clowns, and jugglers. Works dealing with traveling amusement enterprises consisting of sideshows, games of chance, merry-go-rounds, etc., are entered under *Carnivals*. Works dealing with a program of cultural events or entertainment are entered under *Festivals*. Works dealing with public gatherings at which goods are exhibited and sold are entered under *Fairs*.]
- RT Acrobats
  Carnivals
  Clowns
  Fairs
  Festivals

CITIES AND TOWNS [Here are entered works dealing with cities and towns generally. Prefer the name of the specific city or town.]
- RT Metropolitan areas

CITY AND TOWN LIFE [Here are entered works dealing generally with life in any city or town. In most cases, prefer the name of the specific city or town only. Works dealing with villages and small towns in suburban areas are entered under the name of the specific suburban area, for example, *Chicago Suburban Area (Ill.)*. Works dealing generally with life in the suburbs are entered under *Suburban life*.]
- UF Small town life
- RT Suburban life
  Villages

CITY AND TOWN LIFE IN LITERATURE [Here are entered nonfiction works on the history and criticism of city and town life as portrayed in literature.]

CIVIL SERVICE
- RT Bureaucracy
  Diplomatic and consular service
  Postal service

CIVILIZATION
    SA subdivision *Social conditions* under names of countries, classes of persons, and ethnic groups
    NT Social history
        Social problems
Civilizations in space
    USE Extraterrestrial bases
        Extraterrestrial beings \
        Life on other planets
        Space colonies
CLAIRVOYANCE [Here are entered works dealing with the ability to perceive objects hidden from sight.]
    BT Extrasensory perception
CLAIRVOYANTS
    BT Psychics
CLANS—SCOTLAND
    RT Scotland
CLARE (IRELAND)
    UF County Clare (Ireland)
    BT Ireland
Class conflict
    USE Social conflict
CLASS CONSCIOUSNESS [Here are entered works dealing with the awareness of the social class to which a person belongs. Works dealing with conflict that arises because of social classes are entered under *Social conflict*. Works dealing with persons who refuse to associate with persons they feel are beneath their class or attainment are listed under *Snobs and snobbishness*.]
    RT Snobs and snobbishness
        Social conflict
CLASS REUNIONS
    UF Alumni reunions
        College alumni
        College reunions
    BT Universities and colleges—Alumni
CLERGY
    RT Religion
    NT Evangelists
CLERGY AS DETECTIVES \
    NT Monks as detectives \
        Nuns as detectives \
        Rabbis as detectives \
    SA Headings such as *Catholic Church—Clergy as detectives* \ ; *Episcopal Church—Clergy as detectives* \ , etc.
CLEVELAND (OHIO)
    BT Ohio

CLIMACTERIC [Here are entered works dealing with the physical changes that occur as one passes from middle to old age. Works dealing with a period of emotional turmoil occurring in middle age and characterized by a desire for change are entered under *Midlife crisis*.]
    RT Midlife crisis
CLIPPER SHIPS
    BT Sailing ships
CLOCKS AND WATCHES
    RT Time
CLONES \
    RT Doppelgangers \ [A ghostly counterpart of a living person]
        Science fiction
CLOTHING TRADE
    RT Costume designers [Used for fashion designers]
        Dressmakers
        Textile industry
CLOWNS
    RT Circus
COACHING
    UF Stage coaches
    RT Western stories
COAL MINES AND MINING
Cockney dialect fiction
    USE Dialect fiction—Cockneys \
CODE AND CIPHER STORIES [Here are entered novels and stories dealing with codes and ciphers.]
    UF Ciphers
        Codes
        Secret codes
    BT Fiction
CODE AND CIPHER STORIES, JAPANESE (Korean, etc.) [Here are entered collections of works by Japanese (Korean, etc.) authors dealing with codes and ciphers.]
Codes
    USE Code and cipher stories
COHABITATION [Here are entered works dealing with unmarried couples living together as husband and wife. Works dealing with a woman who fornicates with a particular man but does not sell herself are entered under *Mistresses*. Works dealing with couples who are not married are entered under *Unmarried couples*. This last term implies nothing about sexual relationships,

sexual orientation, or living arrangements.]
- RT Mistresses
  Unmarried couples

College alumni
- USE Class reunions
  Universities and colleges—Alumni

COLLEGE AND SCHOOL DRAMA [Here are entered works on drama as a literary form.]

College life
- USE College stories
  College students
  College teachers

College reunions
- USE Class reunions

COLLEGE STORIES [Here are entered novels and stories dealing with college life.]
- UF Campus life
  College life
  Universities and colleges
  University life
- BT Education
  Fiction
- RT Greek letter societies
  Schools
  Students
- NT College students
  College teachers

COLLEGE STORIES, AMERICAN (Australian, etc.) [Here are entered collections of college stories written by American (Australian, etc.) authors.]

COLLEGE STUDENTS
- UF College life
- BT College stories
  Intellectual life
- RT Learning and scholarship
  Scholars

COLLEGE TEACHERS
- UF College life
  Dons
- BT College stories
  Intellectual life
- RT Learning and scholarship
  Scholars

COLLEGE THEATER
- UF School theater
  Student theater

Colonies, Underwater
- USE Underwater colonies

COLORADO
- NT Denver (Colo.)

COMA
- RT Hypersomnia

COMEDIES OF MANNERS \ [Here are entered works that satirically portray the behavior and manners of a particular class or group, generally a sophisticated, artificial society.]
- BT Satirical fiction \

COMIC BOOKS, STRIPS, ETC. [Here are entered works in which characters and scenes are drawn in comic strip fashion. Works in which characters and scenes are photographed with legends inserted either in balloons or in a boxed space in comic strip fashion are entered under *Fotonovela*.]
- UF Graphic fiction
  Graphic novels
- BT Fiction
- RT Illustrated books
- NT Fotonovela

Comic fiction
- USE Humorous stories
  Satirical fiction \

Coming of age
- USE Maturation (Psychology)

COMMERCIAL CRIMES [Here are entered works dealing with crimes in commerce.]
- UF Finance—Corrupt practices
  Financial intrigue
- NT Business enterprises—Corrupt practices
  Financial institutions—Corrupt practices

Common Market
- USE European Economic Community

COMMUNISM
- RT Dictators

COMMUNISM—CHINA

COMMUNISM—UNITED STATES

COMPANIONS \
- BT Domestics

COMPUTERS

CONCENTRATION CAMPS
- RT Holocaust, Jewish (1939-1945)

CONCENTRATION CAMPS IN LITERATURE [Here are entered nonfiction works on the history and criticism of concentration camps as depicted in literature.]

CONCUBINAGE [Here are entered works dealing with the state of being a mistress or the keeping of a mistress. Works dealing with women who habitually fornicate with a particular man but do not

sell themselves are entered under *Mistresses*. Works dealing with women who prostitute themselves to men of high rank and wealth are entered under *Courtesans*. Works dealing with women who sell themselves for fornication are entered under *Prostitutes*. Works dealing with Japanese women trained in lighthearted entertainment primarily for men are entered under *Geishas*. Geishes are not, per se, Japanese prostitutes or courtesans.]
  RT Courtesans
        Geishas
        Mistresses
        Prostitutes

Condemned prisoners
  USE Executions and executioners
         Prisoners

CONDOTTIERI [Here are entered works dealing with professional European mercenary troops during the 14th, 15th, and 16th centuries. Works dealing with troops that serve a country other than their own, primarily or strictly on a wage basis, are entered under *Mercenary troops*. Works dealing with the mercenary troops maintained in former times by Irish chieftains are entered under *Galloglasses*. Works dealing with persons who follow a military career wherever there is the promise of adventure, profit, or pleasure are entered under *Soldiers of fortune*.]
  BT Mercenary troops
        Soldiers of fortune
  RT Galloglasses

CONDUCT OF LIFE [Here are entered works dealing with standards of behavior and works containing moral guidance and advice to the individual. Works dealing with larger philosophical questions and works that apply philosophical viewpoints to a story are entered under *Philosophical fiction\.*]
  BT Didactic fiction
        Philosophical fiction\

CONFEDERATE STATES OF AMERICA

CONFEDERATE STATES OF AMERICA. ARMY—MILITARY LIFE

CONFESSION STORIES [Here are entered novels and stories in which a true or manipulated account of the author's life serves some sort of didactic purpose.]
  BT Autobiographical fiction
        Didactic fiction
        Fiction

Conflict of classes
  USE Social conflict

CONFLICT OF GENERATIONS
  BT Domestic fiction
  RT Parent and child

Conflict of religions
  USE Religions—Relations

Conflict of social classes
  USE Social conflict

Congress
  USE United States. Congress

Congressmen as detectives
  USE Legislators as detectives—United States\

Congresswomen as detectives
  USE Women legislators as detectives—United States\

CONJURING [Here are entered works dealing with entertainment of a type in which a performer does tricks of so-called magic. Works dealing with the use of charms, spells, etc., believed to have a supernatural power to produce or prevent a particular result considered unobtainable by natural means are entered under *Magic*. Works dealing with people who do either magic or conjuring are entered under the heading *Magicians*.]
  RT Magic
        Magicians
        Wizards

CONNECTICUT
  NT Hartford (Conn.)

CONSERVATION OF NATURAL RESOURCES
  UF Environment
        Preservation of natural resources
  BT Nature stories
  RT Historic sites—Conservation and restoration
        Pollution

CONSPIRACIES
  UF Intrigue
  RT Political fiction
        Terrorism
        Thrillers\

CONSTABLES [Here are entered works dealing with peace officers charged with both keeping the public peace and certain

petty judicial matters. Works dealing with marshals serving in American federal courts are entered under *United States marshals*. Works dealing with municipal peace officers are entered under *Police*. Works dealing with peace officers who are elected county officials or work as police in a department headed by such an official are entered under *Sheriffs*. Works that deal with various kinds of law enforcement officers, or law enforcement officers generally, are entered under *Peace officers*. Westerns that deal with law enforcement officers are entered under *Peace officers* if it cannot be readily determined whether the officer is a marshal or sheriff. The heading *Police* is not used with westerns unless specifically so used in the text. Do not use any of the peace officer headings with detective and mystery fiction.]
  BT Peace officers
        Police
  RT Sheriffs
        United States marshals
CONTRACEPTION [Here are entered works dealing with the methods of preventing impregnation. Works dealing with the larger social, legal, population, or religious aspects are entered under *Birth control*.]
  RT Birth control
Convent life
  USE Monastic and religious life of women
CONVENTS
  BT Nuns
  RT Monastic and religious life of women
CONVERSATIONS\ [Here are entered works which are centered on conversations or in which dialogue is heavily relied upon as a literary device. Works of nonfiction on the history and criticism of imaginary conversations are entered under *Imaginary conversations*. Works that contain collections of dialogues are entered under *Dialogues*.]
  RT Dialogues
  NT Imaginary conversations
CONVERSION
  UF Religious conversion
COOKS
  BT Domestics
  RT Caterers and catering
        Restaurants, lunch rooms, etc.
CORN
  BT Grain
Corporate intrigue
  USE Corporations—Corrupt practices
CORPORATIONS
  BT Business
CORPORATIONS—CORRUPT PRACTICES
  UF Corporate intrigue
  BT Business enterprises—Corrupt practices
CORRUPTION (IN POLITICS)
  UF Abuse of power
  BT Bribery
Corruption of juries
  USE Jury—Corrupt practices
Cosa Nostra
  USE Mafia
COSSACKS
  BT Soldiers
        Soviet Union. Rabosche-Krest'îanskaîa Krasnaîa Armiîa [This is the Soviet army.]
COSTUME DESIGNERS
  RT Clothing trade
        Dressmakers
        Models, Fashion
Costume parties
  USE Masquerades
Counterespionage
  USE Spy stories
COUNTERFEITERS
COUNTERFEITERS AND COUNTERFEITING [Here are entered works dealing with forged money and the forging of money.]
  BT Forgery
COUNTRY LIFE [Here are entered works dealing with life in rural areas, including rural villages. Works dealing predominately with rural villages are entered under *Villages*. Works dealing with life in villages and small towns in metropolitan areas are entered under *Suburban life*. Works presenting a generally idealized version of rustic life and expressing complex ideas through supposedly simple characters, such as shepherds who speak in courtly language, are entered under *Pastoral fiction*.]
  UF Provincial and rural life
        Small town life
  RT Suburban life

    NT Pastoral fiction
          Villages
COUNTRY LIFE—AUSTRALIA [Here are entered works dealing with country life in Australia or life in the Australian outback. If a specific province or territory is given, that may be used as well.]
    UF Australian outback
          Outback
COUNTRY LIFE—CANADA
COUNTRY LIFE—ENGLAND
COUNTRY LIFE—FRANCE
COUNTRY LIFE—NEW YORK (STATE)
COUNTRY LIFE—TEXAS
COUNTRY LIFE—UNITED STATES
County Clare (Ireland)
    USE Clare (Ireland)
County Kerry (Ireland)
    USE Kerry (Ireland)
Court life
    USE Courts and courtiers
COURTESANS [Here are entered works dealing with women who prostitute themselves to men of high rank or wealth. Works dealing with Japanese women trained in lighthearted entertainment primarily for men are entered under *Geishas*. Geishas are not, per se, prostitutes or courtesans. Works dealing with women who habitually fornicate with a particular man but do not sell themselves are entered under *Mistresses*.]
    BT Prostitutes
    RT Geishas
          Mistresses
COURTLY LOVE
    RT Courtship
Courtroom fiction
    USE Legal stories
           Trials
COURTS AND COURTIERS [Note that when used as a subdivision with a country, *Court* is singular; for example, *England—Court and courtiers*.]
    UF Court life
          Intrigue
    RT Nobility
COURTS MARTIAL AND COURTS OF INQUIRY
COURTSHIP
    UF Romance
    RT Courtly love
          Love affairs \
          Love stories

COUSINS \
    BT Domestic fiction
Cowardice
    USE Fear
COWBOYS
    RT Cowgirls
          Western stories
COWGIRLS
    RT Cowboys
          Western stories
          Women ranchers
Cozy mysteries
    USE Detective and mystery stories, Genteel \
CRICKET STORIES [Here are entered novels and stories dealing with the sport of cricket.]
    BT Fiction
CRIME
    UF Underworld, Criminal
    BT Social problems
    RT Detective and mystery stories
          Thrillers \
    NT Bank robberies
          Kidnapping
          Mugging
          Murder
          Punishment
          Robbery
          Shoplifting
CRIME PASSIONEL [Here are entered works dealing with killing for sexual motives.]
    BT Murder
    NT Mariticide \ [Wife killing her husband]
          Uxoricide [Husband killing his wife]
Criminally insane
    USE Insane, Criminal and dangerous
CRIMINALS
    NT Brigands and robbers
          Ex-convicts
          Gunfighters \
          Juvenile delinquents
          Quacks and quackery
CRITICS
    UF Book reviewers
          Reviewers
    BT Journalists
CRO-MAGNON MAN
    BT Man, Prehistoric
CROATIA
    BT Yugoslavia
    NT Zagreb (Croatia)

CRUELTY [Here are entered works that deal with the disposition to inflict pain and suffering, or with a person who has no humane feelings. Works that deal with the motivation for or effects of the exertion of physical force to injure or abuse someone are entered under *Violence*. Works dealing with persons taking delight in or receiving sexual gratification from inflicting cruelty are entered under *Sadism*. Works dealing with persons taking delight in or receiving sexual gratification from having cruelty inflicted upon them are entered under *Masochism*.]
  NT Animal welfare
        Masochism
        Sadism
        Violence
        Wife abuse
CRUSADES
  RT Knights and knighthood
        Romances [Works of adventure produced in the Middle Ages]
CULTS
  RT Religion
CULTURE CONFLICT
  NT East and West
Curses, Family
  USE Family curses
CYBORGS [Here are entered works dealing with humans altered with artificial parts. Works dealing with robots in the shape of a human being are entered under *Androids*. Works dealing with machines that perform tasks normally associated with human beings or that seem to possess intelligence similar to that of a human are entered under *Robots*.]
  RT Androids
        Robots
CYCLES (LITERATURE) [Here are entered works that are a collection of romances (medieval adventure stories about knights and their deeds) centering around some outstanding event or character, and which are commonly traditional stories given form by a succession of authors. Works that continue the narrative course of a previous book are entered under *Sequels (Literature)*. Works that have a separate series title and volume number are entered under *Series (Publications)*. Single works of fiction appearing in serial form are entered under *Serialized fiction*.]
  BT Romances
  RT Sequels (Literature)
        Serialized fiction
        Series (Publications)
Czars
  USE Soviet Union—Kings and rulers
CZECH AMERICANS [Here are entered works dealing with Americans of Czechoslovakian ancestry.]
  BT Czechs—United States
CZECH FICTION
CZECHOSLOVAKIA
  NT Bohemia
CZECHS—UNITED STATES [Here are entered works dealing with Czechs visiting or living in the United States.]
  NT Czech Americans

DALLAS (TEX.)
  BT Texas
DALMATIA (CROATIA)
  BT Yugoslavia
DANCERS
  NT Stripteasers
DANES
  BT Denmark
        Northmen
  RT Vikings
DARDANELLES STRAIT (TURKEY)
  BT Turkey
DARWIN (N.T.)
  BT Northern Territory
DAUGHTERS
  BT Women
  RT Parent and child
  NT Filicide [Murder of a son or daughter by their mother or father]
        Parricide [Murder of a mother or father by their son or daughter]
        Stepchildren
DAUGHTERS AS DETECTIVES
  BT Women detectives
  NT Father and daughter detectives\
        Mother and daughter detectives\
DAUGHTERS-IN-LAW
  UF In-laws
DAUGHTERS IN LITERATURE [Here are entered nonfiction works on the history and

criticism of daughters as portrayed in literature.]

DEAD
  NT Body snatching

DEATH
Decapitation
  USE Dismemberment, Bodily \
      Execution and executioners

Deep sea diving
  USE Diving, Submarine

DEFECTORS
  BT Treason
  RT Deserters, Military
      Spy stories

DEGENERATION
  UF Dissipation
      Libertines
      Profligates
      Wastrels
  RT Picaresque fiction \
      Prodigals
      Sexual deviation

DELAWARE
  NT Wilmington (Del.)

DELUSIONS [Here are entered works dealing with deception either by oneself or by others. Works dealing with the perception of visual and occasionally other sensory impressions that have no reality are entered under *Hallucinations and illusions*.]
  RT Hallucinations and illusions

DEMONIAC POSSESSION
  RT Devil
      Horror tales
      Satanism
  NT Exorcism

DEMONOLOGY
  RT Horror tales
      Satanism
  NT Monsters
      Witchcraft

DENMARK
  NT Danes

DENVER (COLO.)
  BT Colorado

DEPRESSION, MENTAL [Here are entered works dealing with an often prolonged disordered psychological state of low spirits and unhappiness whose cause is often internal in origin. Works dealing with a mood of dejection, discouragement, or pensiveness which is of a more transitory nature and which has an external cause are entered under *Melancholy*. Works dealing with an utter loss of hope or confidence are entered under *Despair*. Works dealing with deep distress caused by, or seemingly caused by, bereavement are entered under *Grief*. Works dealing with the atmosphere or effect produced by depression, melancholy, grief, or despair are entered under *Sadness*. *Sadness* can also be used as a general term for low spirits or unhappiness when there is no clear explanation or indication of the cause or extent.]
  RT Despair
      Grief
      Melancholy
      Sadness

DEPRESSIONS
  UF Business depressions

DERELICTS [Here are entered works dealing with derelict and abandoned marine craft. Works dealing with the salvaging of such craft are entered under *Salvage*. Works dealing with wandering, disorderly, or dissolute but not necessarily displeasing persons are entered under *Rogues and Vagabonds*.]
  UF Abandoned ships
      Ships, Abandoned
  BT Ships
  RT Rogues and vagabonds
      Salvage
      Shipwrecks

DES MOINES (IOWA)
  BT Iowa

DESERTERS, MILITARY
  RT Defectors

DESERTION AND NON-SUPPORT
  BT Problem marriages \

DESPAIR [Here are entered works dealing with an utter loss of hope or confidence. Works dealing with deep distress caused by, or seemingly caused by, bereavement are entered under *Grief*. Works dealing with an often prolonged disordered psychological state of low spirits and unhappiness whose cause is often internal in origin are entered under *Depression, Mental*. Works dealing with a mood of dejection, discouragement, or pensiveness which is of a more transitory nature and which has an external cause are entered under

Melancholy. Works dealing with the atmosphere or effect produced by depression, melancholy, grief, or despair are entered under *Sadness. Sadness* can also be used as a general term for low spirits or unhappiness when there is no clear explanation or indication of the cause or extent.]
- RT Depression, Mental
  Grief
  Melancholy
  Sadness

Destruction of the Earth
- USE Apocalyptic fiction\

DETECTIVE AND MYSTERY STORIES [Here are entered genre novels and stories dealing with the detection and solution of crime. Works dealing with the killing of a human being in a situation which is not necessarily a crime, or in a neutral sense with no moral or legal quality, are entered under *Homicide*. Works dealing with the unlawful killing of a human being with malice aforethought are entered under *Murder*. These two terms are used only for fiction about murder per se that deals with law, reasons, effects, philosophy; do not use them with a work of detective and mystery fiction.]
- UF Private detectives
- BT Adventure stories
  Fiction
  Light fiction\
  Thrillers\
- RT Crime
  Detectives
  Homicide
  Murder
  Suspense fiction\

DETECTIVE AND MYSTERY STORIES, AMERICAN (Argentine, etc.) [Here are entered collections of detective and mystery stories written by American (Argentine, etc.) authors.]

Detective and mystery stories, Cozy
- USE Detective and mystery stories, Genteel\

DETECTIVE AND MYSTERY STORIES, GENTEEL\ [Here are entered works of prose fiction in the detective and mystery genre that are characterized by an absence of explicit violence, sex, or language.]
- UF Cozy mysteries
  Detective and mystery stories, Cozy

DETECTIVE AND MYSTERY STORIES, HARDBOILED\ [Here are entered works of prose fiction in the detective and mystery genre that are characterized by an impersonal, stoic, nonjudgmental, and generally unemotional presentation of violent themes or events. In addition to the violence, explicit language and sex are also often present.]
- UF Explicit violence in fiction
  Hardboiled detectives
- BT Gloomy fiction\
  Linguistically profane fiction\
  Sexually explicit fiction\
  Violent fiction\

DETECTIVE AND MYSTERY STORIES, HUMOROUS\
- BT Humorous stories

DETECTIVE AND MYSTERY STORIES, LOCKED ROOM\ [Here are entered works of prose fiction in the detective and mystery genre that deal with crimes that take place in a room locked from the inside or in another location where it is apparently impossible for a murderer to enter.]
- UF Locked room mysteries

DETECTIVE AND MYSTERY STORIES, POLICE PROCEDURAL\ [Here are works of prose fiction in the detective and mystery genre in which there is usually a team of detectives from a police department working together within departmental rules to solve one crime or a series of crimes. Special attention is given to the workings of the department.]
- UF Police procedurals

DETECTIVES [Here are entered only general fictional works centered largely upon the lives and feelings of detectives as human beings. Works centered on the detection or solution of a crime are entered under *Detective and mystery stories*. The heading *Detectives* is not used with the genre heading *Detective and mystery stories*, but works featuring detectives other than mainstream white males are entered under identifying headings such as *Black detec-*

tives\, *Gay men as detectives*\, *Jewish detectives*\, *Women detectives*, etc. Any profession or trade may also be used to form this type of heading, for example, *Actors as detectives*, *Lawyers as detectives*, etc. Compound headings, such as *Bells and bell ringers*, can be clipped for this purpose and become *Bell ringers as detectives*\.]
  UF Private detectives
  RT Detective and mystery stories
DETROIT (MICH.)
  BT Michigan
DEVIL
  RT Demoniac possession
  NT Satanism
DIALECT FICTION\ [Here are entered novels and stories strongly characterized by dialogue written as though someone with a pronounced accent were speaking it.]
  BT Fiction
DIALECT FICTION—AFRO-AMERICANS\
  UF Negro dialect fiction
Dialect fiction—Appalachians
  USE Dialect fiction—Mountain Whites (Southern states)\
DIALECT FICTION—COCKNEYS\
  UF Cockney dialect fiction
  BT Dialect fiction—English\
DIALECT FICTION—ENGLISH\ [Here are entered novels and stories strongly characterized by dialogue written as though someone with a pronounced English accent were speaking.]
  BT Dialect Literature, English
  NT Dialect fiction—Cockneys\
DIALECT FICTION—IRISH\
  UF Irish dialect fiction
DIALECT FICTION—MOUNTAIN WHITES (SOUTHERN STATES)\
  UF Appalachian dialect fiction
      Dialect fiction—Appalachians
  BT Dialect fiction—Southerners\
DIALECT FICTION—NEW ENGLANDERS\
  UF New England dialect fiction
DIALECT FICTION—SCOTS\
  UF Scottish dialect fiction
DIALECT FICTION—SOUTHERNERS\
  UF Southern dialect fiction
  NT Dialect fiction—Mountain Whites (Southern states)\
DIALECT FICTION—SWEDES\
  UF Swedish dialect fiction

DIALECT LITERATURE, AMERICAN [Here are entered collections of dialect literature written by American authors.]
DIALECT LITERATURE, ENGLISH [Here are entered collections of dialect literature written by English authors.]
  NT Dialect fiction—English\
DIALOGUES [Here are entered collections of dialogues in the English language. Works that are centered about conversations or in which dialogue is heavily relied upon as a literary device are entered under *Conversations*. Works of nonfiction on the history and criticism of imaginary conversations are entered under *Imaginary conversations*.]
  RT Conversations\
  NT Imaginary conversations
DIAMONDS
  RT Jewelry
DIARIES [Here are entered works that feature or are about diaries.]
DIARY FICTION\ [Here are entered novels and stories that to a significant extent are presented as transcriptions of diaries.]
  UF Fiction in diary form
  BT Fiction
DICTATORS
  RT Communism
      Fascism
DIDACTIC FICTION [Here are entered works that are primarily intended to teach a lesson. Works in which a true or manipulated account of the author's life serves didactic purpose are entered under *Confession stories*. Works dealing with standards of behavior and works containing moral guidance and advice are entered under *Conduct of life*. Works dealing with larger philosophical questions and works that apply philosophical viewpoints to a story are entered under *Philosophical fiction*\.]
  BT Fiction
      Philosophical fiction\
  NT Conduct of life
      Confession stories
DIDACTIC FICTION, AMERICAN (Chinese, etc.) [Here are entered collections of didactic fiction written by American (Chinese, etc.) authors.]

DIME NOVELS [Here are entered cheap, melodramatic, and exciting novels written in the late 19th century.]
- BT Fiction

DIME NOVELS, GERMAN (Canadian, etc.) [Here are entered collections of dime novels written by German (Canadian, etc.) authors.]

DINNERS AND DINING
- UF Parties, Dinner
- RT House parties\

DIPLOMATIC AND CONSULAR SERVICE
- UF Foreign relations
  Government employees
- BT Political fiction
  World politics
- RT Civil service

DIPLOMATS [Here are entered works dealing with persons engaged in conducting relations between nations. Works dealing with persons engaged in politics are entered under *Politicians*. Works dealing with persons who exercise wise leadership in the best interest of the general public without petty partisanship are entered under *Statesmen*.]
- BT Statesmen
- RT Politicians

Disappearances
- USE Missing persons

DISAPPEARED PERSONS [Here are entered works dealing with persons who have disappeared and are presumed to have been illegally imprisoned or killed for political reasons.]
- BT Missing persons
- RT Kidnapping

DISASTER RELIEF
- UF Survival after disasters
- BT Natural disasters
  Storms

DISASTER VICTIMS
- UF Survival after disasters
- BT Natural disasters
  Storms

DISASTERS
- RT Thrillers\
- NT Epidemics
  Famines

Disfigurement
- USE Face—Wounds and injuries

Disguise
- USE Double identity\
  Impersonation

Impostors and imposture
Masquerades
Mistaken identity\

DISMEMBERMENT, BODILY\
- UF Beheading
  Decapitation
- BT Murder
- NT Castration

Dissipation
- USE Degeneration
  Picaresque fiction\
  Prodigals

DISTILLING, ILLICIT
- UF Bootlegging of alcoholic beverages
  Liquor traffic
- RT Prohibition

DIVING, SUBMARINE
- UF Deep sea diving

DIVORCE
- BT Problem marriages\

DIVORCED FATHERS
- UF Ex-husbands

DIVORCED MEN
- UF Ex-husbands

DIVORCED MOTHERS
- UF Ex-wives

DIVORCED PARENTS
- NT Children of divorced parents

DIVORCED WOMEN
- UF Ex-wives

Djinn
- USE Jinn

Doctor stories
- USE Medical fiction\

Documentary fiction
- USE Autobiographical fiction
  Biographical fiction
  Livres á clef
  Nonfiction novels\
  Real events\
  Real people\

DOMESTIC FICTION [Here are entered works dealing with the life of a nuclear or an extended family in a single household or with several generations reacting together in the span of a single generation. Note that the Library of Congress authorizes only collections of domestic fiction here. Works dealing with the lives and inter-relationships of several generations of the same family over an extended period of time are entered under *Family chronicles*\. Works dealing with psychologically troubled

or dysfunctional families are entered under *Problem families*. Works that deal primarily with the relationship of husband and wife are entered under *Marriage*.]
- UF Domestic relations
  Family
  Family life
  Relatives
- BT Fiction
- RT Conflict of generations
  Guardian and ward
  Husband and wife
  Marriage
- NT Aunts
  Brothers
  Brothers and sisters
  Conflict of generations
  Cousins\
  Family chronicles\
  Family curses\
  Family reunions
  Fathers
  Foster children
  Foster parents
  Grandfathers
  Grandmothers
  Grandparent and child
  Mothers
  Nephews\
  Nieces
  Parent and child
  Problem families
  Problem marriages\
  Single-parent family
  Sisters
  Stepchildren
  Stepfathers
  Stepmothers
  Uncles

DOMESTIC FICTION, AMERICAN (English, etc.) [Here are entered collections of domestic fiction written by American (English, etc.) authors.]

Domestic relations
- USE Domestic fiction

DOMESTICS
- RT Hired men\
- NT Charwomen and cleaners
  Chauffeurs
  Companions
  Cooks
  Governesses
  Servants in literature [Nonfiction history and criticism]
  Stewards

Dons
- USE College teachers

DOPPELGANGERS\ [Here are entered works dealing with the ghostly counterpart of a living person.]
- BT Ghost stories
- RT Clones\

DORMANCY (BIOLOGY)
- UF Suspended animation
- RT Hypersomnia [Extended sleep]

Double agents
- USE Spy stories

DOUBLE IDENTITY\ [Here are entered works dealing with someone who has two separate identities, each of his own invention. Works dealing with persons who are innocently mistaken for someone else are entered under *Mistaken identity*\. Works dealing with who one is or is known as are entered under *Identity*. Works that deal with assuming an identity with the intent to deceive are entered under *Impostors and imposture*. Works that deal with assuming the personality, behavior, or appearance of someone for other than deceitful intent are entered under *Impersonation*. Works that deal with imposture as a legal charge are entered under *False personation*. Works that deal with imposture of a public official as a legal charge are entered under *Impersonating an officer*. Works that deal with trials of someone accused of either false personation or impersonating an officer are entered under *Trials (Impostors and imposture)*.]
- UF Disguise
- BT Identity
- RT False personation
  Impersonating an officer
  Impersonation
  Impostors and imposture
  Mistaken identity\
  Trials (Impostors and imposture)

DOWN'S SYNDROME
- RT Mentally handicapped

DRAMA
- RT Theater

DRAMATISTS
- RT Theater

DRESSMAKERS
  UF Seamstresses
  BT Clothing trade
  RT Costume designers
      Tailors
DRIFTERS [Here are entered works dealing with aimless persons who wander from place to place and job to job. Works dealing with traveling beggars who will not work are entered under *Tramps*. Works dealing with the legal charge of being a tramp are entered under *Vagrancy*. Works dealing with persons who travel as a way of life are entered under *Wayfaring life*. Works dealing with wandering, disorderly, or dissolute but not necessarily displeasing persons are entered under *Rogues and vagabonds*. Works that are episodic in the detailing of the adventures of a rascal, rogue, or vagabond getting by on his or her wits are entered under *Picaresque fiction*\.]
  RT Homelessness
      Picaresque fiction\
      Rogues and vagabonds
      Tramps
      Vagrancy
      Wayfaring life
DROLLS [Here are entered short dramatic compositions or stage presentations of a comical or farcical nature.]
  BT Burlesques
DROUGHTS
  RT Rain and rainfall
DRUG TRAFFIC
  RT Heroin traffic
DRUGS [Here are entered works dealing with medicines. Works dealing with the medical profession are entered under *Medicine*.]
  UF Medicines
  RT Medicine
  NT Vaccines
Dual personality
  USE Multiple personality
DUBLIN (IRELAND)
  BT Ireland
Dukes
  USE Nobility
DUSHANBE (TAJIK S.S.R.)
  BT Tajik S.S.R.
DWARFS

DYSTOPIAS [Here are entered works dealing with an imaginary society where people lead a depressingly wretched existence.]
  BT Gloomy fiction\
  RT Fantastic fiction
      Science fiction
      Utopias

E.E.C.
  USE European Economic Community
E.S.P.
  USE Extrasensory perception
Earls
  USE Nobility
Earth, Destruction of the
  USE Apocalyptic fiction\
EAST AND WEST
  BT Culture conflict
EAST INDIANS [Here are entered works dealing with persons from India.]
  BT India
  RT Indic fiction [Fiction written by persons from India]
EASTER STORIES [Here are entered novels and stories dealing with Easter.]
  BT Fiction
EATING DISORDERS
  RT Obesity
ECCENTRICS AND ECCENTRICITIES
  UF Odd people
ECCENTRICS IN LITERATURE [Here are entered nonfiction works on the history and criticism of eccentrics as portrayed in literature.]
ECOLOGY
  BT Nature stories
  RT Pollution
ECUADOR
EDINBURGH (SCOTLAND)
  BT Scotland
EDITORS
  BT Newspapers
      Periodicals
  RT Publishers and publishing
EDITORS AS DETECTIVES\
EDMONTON (ALTA.)
  BT Alberta
EDUCATION
  NT College stories
      Schools

Edwardian England
   USE Great Britain—History—Edward VII, 1901-1910
EFFIGIES [Here are entered works dealing with an image of a person engraved on a coin or sculpted for a sepulchral monument, or a crude representation of a particular person, such as a stuffed dummy. Works dealing specifically with a sculpted, cast, or modeled image of an entire figure are entered under *Statues*. Works dealing with a sculpted image of the upper part of the body are entered under *Busts*. Works dealing generally with the art of sculpting as well as with pieces of art that have been sculpted are entered under *Sculpture*.]
   BT Sculpture
   RT Busts
       Statues
EGOISM [Here are entered works dealing with self-absorption and concentration on oneself and one's interests. Works dealing with self-love and the overvaluation of oneself are entered under *Narcissism*. Works dealing with selfishness or a concern for oneself at the expense of others are entered under *Self-interest*.]
   RT Self-interest
   NT Narcissism
EGYPT
EGYPT—KINGS AND RULERS
   UF Pharaohs
EL SALVADOR
   NT Salvadoran fiction
ELECTIONS
   BT Political fiction
ELECTRONIC INDUSTRIES
   UF Electronics industries
Electronics industries
   USE Electronic industries
ELEMENTARY SCHOOLS [Here are entered works dealing with schools typically including, but not necessarily confined to, kindergarten through 6th grade, or kindergarten through 8th grade.]
   UF Grammar schools
   BT Schools
Elizabethan England
   USE Great Britain—History—Elizabeth, 1558-1603

EMBEZZLEMENT
   BT Thieves
EMERALDS
   RT Jewelry
Emigres
   USE *Exiles* [Persons banished from their home country]
       Refugees [Persons who have fled their home country for safety]
       for persons who live in another country for other reasons, use their country of residence as a subdivision of their nationality, for example, *Polish—United States; Americans—France,* etc.
Emotionally maladjusted children
   USE Problem children
End of the world
   USE Apocalyptic fiction \
ENGLAND [If a place is located in England, add the identifier *(England)*, for example *Cornwall (England); Stratford-upon-Avon (England)*. This identifier is not added to either the Isle of Man or the Channel Islands. See 23.4D in *AACR2R* for further information.]
   BT Great Britain
   RT Channel Islands
       Isle of Man
   NT Cambridge (England)
       Isle of Wight (England)
       London (England)
       Oxford (England)
ENGLAND—COURT AND COURTIERS
ENGLAND—KINGS AND RULERS
ENGLAND—NOBILITY
   BT Great Britain—Nobility
ENGLAND—SOCIAL CONDITIONS
England, Georgian
   USE Great Britain—History—1714-1837
       Love stories, Georgian
England, Regency
   USE Great Britain—History—George III, 1760-1820
       Love stories, Regency \
ENGLISH FICTION
   UF British fiction
ENGLISH FICTION—IRISH AUTHORS [Here are entered works written in English by Irish authors, or collections of works written exclusively in English by Irish authors. When this heading is used, also use the heading *Irish fiction*.]
   UF Northern Irish fiction

   RT Irish fiction
ENGLISH FICTION—SCOTTISH AUTHORS [Here are entered works written in English by Scottish authors, or collections of works written exclusively in English by Scottish authors. When this heading is used, also use the heading *Scottish fiction*.]
   RT Scottish fiction
ENGLISH FICTION—WELSH AUTHORS [Here are entered works written in English by Welsh authors, or collections of works written exclusively in English by Welsh authors. When this heading is used, also use the heading *Welsh fiction*.]
   RT Welsh fiction
ENTERTAINERS
   NT Actresses
        Singers
        Vaudeville
ENTERTAINING
   NT Birthdays
        House parties \
        Masquerades
        Office parties \
ENTOMOLOGY
   UF Insect study
Environment
   USE Conservation of natural resources
         Nature and nurture [For heredity and environment]
         Nature stories
         Pollution
ENVY [Here are entered works dealing with coveting something which belongs to another. Works dealing with intolerance of a rival for what one regards as one's own are entered under *Jealousy*.]
   RT Jealousy
EPIC LITERATURE [Here are entered broad and lengthy works that recount the deeds of a legendary or historical hero. Works that use the epic formula to overstate something and thus make it ridiculous and which are generally shorter than epic works are entered under *Mock-heroic literature*. German epic literature from the 13th century dealing with the struggles and conquests of the Germanic tribes during the epoch of migrations are entered under *Heldensage*. Medieval Scandinavian heroic adventure literature detailing historical and legendary occurrences, generally of important families, are entered under *Sagas*. Works of traditional narrative that are shorter than epics but still purport to have some basis in reality are entered under *Legends*. Works of traditional narrative that are shorter than epics but deal more with the supernatural and less with the historical are entered under *Mythology*. Works that deal with shorter narratives about common or illiterate people and that are passed on by word of mouth are entered under *Folk literature*. Collections of traditional narratives that are for the most part fictitious and are told primarily for entertainment are entered under *Tales*.]
   RT Folk literature
        Legends
        Mythology
        Tales
   NT Epic novels \
        Heldensage
        Mock heroic literature
        Sagas
EPIC NOVELS \ [Here are entered novels that parallel traditional epics in range and magnitude. Examples include *War and Peace* by Leo Tolstoy, *Moby Dick* by Herman Melville, *The Grapes of Wrath* by John Steinbeck, *Ulysses* by James Joyce, and *Dr. Zhivago* by Boris Pasternak.]
   BT Epic literature
        Fiction
   RT Family chronicles \
EPIDEMICS
   UF Germs
   BT Disasters
   NT Biological warfare
        Plague
EPISCOPAL CHURCH—CLERGY
   BT Anglican Communion—Clergy
EPISODIC NOVELS \ [Here are entered novels that have little or no central plot and/or that detail events that have little or no causal relationship to one another. Works that are episodic in the detailing of the adventures of a rascal getting by on his wits are entered under *Picaresque fiction* \. Collections of a series of stories with a common narrative framework or stories that are contained

within a novel or another story are entered under *Frame-stories*.]
- BT Fiction
- RT Frame-stories
Picaresque fiction \

EPISTOLARY FICTION [Here are entered works of fiction told largely through the use of letters between characters. Works dealing with letters as a theme or a major factor in the action are entered under *Letters*. Poetic narratives in epistolary form that express the sentiments between heroes or heroines and their wives or sweethearts are entered under *Heroid*.]
- UF Letters—Stories told in letter form
- BT Fiction
Letters
- NT Heroid
Imaginary letters

EPISTOLARY FICTION, AMERICAN (English, etc.) [Here are entered collections of epistolary fiction written by American (English, etc.) authors.]

EROTIC LITERATURE [Here are entered collections of several different types of literature whose primary purpose is erotic stimulation.]
- NT Erotic stories

EROTIC STORIES [Here are entered novels and stories whose primary purpose is erotic stimulation. Works of fiction that contain explicit portrayals of sexuality as a subsidiary part of a larger story are entered under *Sexually explicit fiction* \. Works that deal with the production, distribution, or social effects of erotica are entered under *Pornography*. Works of nonfiction that deal with the history and criticism of sex as portrayed in literature are entered under *Sex in literature*.]
- UF Explicit sex in fiction
- BT Erotic literature
Fiction
- RT Pornography
Sex in literature
Sexually explicit fiction \

EROTIC STORIES, AMERICAN (Argentine, etc.) [Here are entered collections of erotic stories by American (Argentine, etc.) authors.]

Escaped convicts
- USE Fugitives from justice

ESCAPES
- UF Manhunts
Prisoners, Escaped
- RT Adventure stories

ESPIONAGE [Here are entered works on the art and techniques of espionage; as such, this is primarily a nonfiction heading. Genre works about the actual operations of spies are entered under *Spy stories*. Works about women operatives are entered under *Women spies*.]
- NT Spy stories
Women spies

Espionage, Industrial
- USE Business intelligence

ESTONIA
- BT Soviet Union
- NT Talinn (Estonia)

Ethnological fiction
- USE Anthropological fiction \

EURASIANS
- UF Mixed bloods

EUROPE
- NT Balkan Peninsula

EUROPEAN ECONOMIC COMMUNITY
- UF Common Market
E.E.C.

EVANGELISTS
- BT Clergy
- RT Spiritual healing

EX-CONVICTS
- BT Criminals

Ex-husbands
- USE Divorced fathers
Divorced men

Ex-Nazis
- USE National Socialists

Ex-wives
- USE Divorced mothers
Divorced women

Exaggeration
- USE Improbable fiction \
Mythomania
Tall tales

EXECUTIONS AND EXECUTIONERS
- UF Beheading
Condemned prisoners
Decapitation
Prisoners, Condemned
- RT Assassination
Lynching

EXECUTIVES
- BT Businessmen
Women in business

RT Capitalists and financiers
EXILES [Here are entered works dealing with persons banished from their own country by vested authority as a punitive measure. For persons who live in another country for other reasons, use their country of residence as a subdivision of their nationality, for example, *Polish—United States*; *Americans—France*, etc. Works dealing with persons who have fled their home country for safety are entered under *Refugees*.]
    UF Emigres
          Expatriates
    RT Refugees
EXISTENTIAL FICTION \ [Here are entered works that represent life as essentially meaningless, absurd, or not explainable by reason or scientific means, but only through concrete experience or as man acts upon it to create meaning, even though such actions only lead to a greater awareness of loneliness or despair. Works that represent the absurdity of man's existence by bizarre or fantastic means are entered under *Absurdist fiction*\. Works that represent life as senseless and useless and that deny the objectivity of moral truth and/or represent social organization as so poor that destruction is desirable for its own sake even if there is no possibility of reform are entered under *Nihilistic fiction*\.]
    BT Experimental fiction
          Fiction
          Philosophical fiction \
    RT Absurdist fiction \
          Beat fiction \
          Nihilistic fiction \
EXISTENTIALISM IN LITERATURE [Here are entered nonfiction works on the history and criticism of existentialism in literature.]
EXORCISM
    BT Demoniac possession
    RT Satanism
Expatriates
    USE Exiles [Persons banished from their home country]
           Refugees [Persons who have fled their home country for safety]
           for persons who live in another country by choice, use their country of residence as a subdivision of their nationality, for example, *Polish—United States; Americans—France*, etc.
Expeditions
    USE Explorers
EXPERIMENTAL FICTION [Here are entered works with a nontraditional style, format, or approach.]
    BT Fiction
    RT Fantastic fiction
          Improbable fiction \
          Literary fiction \
    NT Absurdist fiction \
          Existential fiction \
          Magic realistic fiction \
          Nihilistic fiction \
          Stream of consciousness fiction
          Surrealistic fiction \
          Symbolic fiction \
Explicit language in fiction
    USE Linguistically profane fiction \
Explicit sex in fiction
    USE Erotic stories
           Sexually explicit fiction \
Explicit violence in fiction
    USE Detective and mystery stories, Hardboiled \
           Violent fiction \
EXPLORERS
    UF Expeditions
EXTORTION
    UF Blackmail
EXTORTION IN LITERATURE [Here are entered nonfiction works on the history and criticism of extortion as portrayed in literature.]
EXTRASENSORY PERCEPTION [Here are entered works dealing with the ability to perceive things with the mind that are beyond or outside the ordinary senses. Works dealing with the ability to perceive objects hidden from sight are entered under *Clairvoyance*. Works dealing with the ability to foresee the future with the mind are entered under *Precognition*. Works dealing with the ability to foresee the future by occult or supernatural means are entered under *Fortune-telling*. Works dealing with the communication between one mind and another without the use of ordinary senses are entered under *Telepathy*. Works dealing with communication

with the dead are entered under *Spiritualism*. Works dealing with persons who have extrasensory perception are entered under *Psychics*.]
  UF E.S.P.
  RT Fortune-telling
        Spiritualism
  NT Clairvoyance
        Precognition
        Psychics
        Telepathy

EXTRATERRESTRIAL BASES [Here are entered works dealing with manned installations existing for specific purposes, such as servicing space ships etc., on natural extraterrestrial bodies. Works dealing with manned installations existing for specific functions, such as servicing space ships, etc., in orbit around natural extraterrestrial bodies or the earth are entered under *Space stations*. Works dealing with communities established by man on planets other than Earth are entered under *Space colonies*.]
  UF Civilizations in space
        Galactic empires
        Imaginary planets
        Other worlds
        Space civilizations
  RT Life on other planets
        Science fiction
        Space colonies
        Space stations

EXTRATERRESTRIAL BEINGS\ [Here are entered works dealing with beings on Earth or in a predominantly human society who are from other planets. Works dealing with life forms on other planets that are not of earthly origin are entered under *Life on other planets*.]
  UF Alien beings
        Aliens from space
        Civilizations in space
        Galactic empires
        Imaginary planets
        Martians
        Other worlds
        Space civilizations
        Visitors from outer space
  BT Science fiction
  RT Life on other planets
        Parallel worlds\

Extravagance
  USE Prodigals

F.B.I.
  USE United States. Federal Bureau of Investigation

FABLES [Here are entered works in which the allegory is short and simple, which use animals acting as humans, and which illustrate the follies and weaknesses of people. Works in which the allegory is short and simple, dealing with a familiar occurrence in life or nature that by analogy conveys a spiritual truth are entered under *Parables*. Works in which the persons and objects represented have a meaning that lies outside the narrative itself are entered under *Allegories*. Allegories attempt to evoke an interest in their characters, setting, and events as well as in the ideas that they represent. Works that suggest other levels of meaning without making the structure of ideas a formative influence on the narrative are entered under *Symbolic fiction*\.]
  UF Allegories—Animals
  BT Allegories
        Animals
        Animals, Mythical
        Fiction
  RT Fantastic fiction
        Parables
        Symbolic fiction\

FABLES, AFRICAN (American, etc.) [Here are entered collections of fables written by African (American, etc.) authors.]

FACE—WOUNDS AND INJURIES
  UF Disfigurement

FACTORIES
  RT Business intelligence
        Labor disputes
        Working class

FAILURE (PSYCHOLOGY)

FAILURE (PSYCHOLOGY) IN LITERATURE [Here are entered nonfiction works on the history and criticism of failure as represented in literature.]

Fairies
  USE Fairy tales

FAIRS [Here are entered works dealing with public gatherings at which goods are

exhibited and sold. Works dealing with a program of cultural events or entertainment are entered under *Festivals*. Works dealing with traveling amusement enterprises consisting of sideshows, games of chance, merry-go-rounds, etc., are entered under *Carnivals*. Works dealing with amusement enterprises featuring feats of physical skill, wild animal acts, clowns, and jugglers are entered under *Circus*.]
- RT Amusement parks
  Carnivals
  Circus
  Festivals

FAIRY TALES [Here are entered works of prose fiction centered upon fairies. Works in which fairies appear but are not a prime focus or are only one part of a number of extraordinary or supernatural creatures are entered under *Fantastic fiction*.]
- UF Fairies
  Fantastic fiction—Fairies
- BT Fantastic fiction
  Fiction
- RT Improbable fiction\

False accusation
- USE Malicious accusation

FALSE IMPRISONMENT
- BT Prisoners

FALSE PERSONATION [Here are entered works that deal with the legal charge of imposture. Works that deal with imposture of a public official as a legal charge are entered under *Impersonating an officer*. Works that deal with the trial of someone accused of false personation or impersonating an officer are entered under *Trials (Impostors and imposture)*. Works dealing with someone who has two separate identities, each of his own invention, are entered under *Double identity*\. Works dealing with persons who are innocently mistaken for someone else are entered under *Mistaken identity*\. Works that deal with assuming an identity with the intent to deceive are entered under *Impostors and imposture*. Works that deal with assuming the personality, behavior or appearance of someone for other than deceitful intent are entered under *Impersonation*.]
- BT Impersonation
  Impostors and imposture
- RT Double identity\
  Mistaken identity\
  Trials (Impostors and imposture)
- NT Impersonating an officer

Family
- USE Domestic fiction

FAMILY CHRONICLES\ [Here are entered works dealing with the lives and interrelationships of several generations of the same family over an extended period of time. Examples of this type of work are Pearl Buck's *The Good Earth* and the novels of John Galsworthy's Forsyte Saga, such as *The Man of Property* and *End of the Chapter*. Works dealing with the life of a nuclear or extended family in a single household or with several generations reacting together in the span of a single generation are entered under *Domestic fiction*. Works dealing with psychologically troubled or dysfunctional families are entered under *Problem families*. Works that deal primarily with the relationship of husband and wife are entered under *Marriage*.]
- UF Family sagas
- BT Domestic fiction
- RT Marriage
  Problem families

FAMILY CURSES\ [Here are entered works dealing with a tragic fault, bad luck, or other problem which manifests itself in one generation after another.]
- UF Curses, Family
- BT Domestic fiction
- RT Problem families

Family life
- USE Domestic fiction

Family feuds
- USE Quarreling
  Vendetta

FAMILY REUNIONS
- BT Domestic fiction
  Reunions

Family sagas
- USE Family chronicles\

FAMINES
- BT Disasters

FANTASTIC FICTION [Here are entered works dealing with nonexistent, incredible, or unreal worlds, characters, or physical principles. Works in which fairies are featured but are not a prime focus or are only one part of a number of extraordinary or supernatural creatures are also entered here. Works of fantasy that are centered upon fairies are entered under *Fairy tales*. Works of fantasy that deal with possible, although not necessarily probable, events and which are based approximately on scientific principles as we know them are entered under *Science fiction*. Works that invent a new cosmology, new scientific principles, or new laws of nature and which are a blending of science fiction and fantastic fiction are entered under *Science fantasy*. Works that are essentially realistic but which incorporate extremely unlikely events yet do not fall under other categories of fantastic fiction are entered under *Improbable fiction*.]
  UF Fantasy fiction
       Other worlds
  BT Fiction
       Light fiction\
       Thrillers\
  RT Allegories
       Dystopias [The opposite of utopias]
       Experimental fiction
       Fables
       Fairy tales
       Improbable fiction\
       Science fantasy\
       Science fiction
       Utopias
Fantastic fiction—Animals
  USE Animals, Mythical
Fantastic fiction—Fairies
  USE Fairy tales
FANTASTIC FICTION, AMERICAN (English, etc.) [Here are entered collections of fantastic fiction by American (English, etc.) authors.]
FANTASTIC FICTION, HUMOROUS\
  BT Humorous stories
  RT Science fiction, Humorous\
FANTASTIC FICTION, SWORD AND SORCERY\ [Here are entered works of fantastic fiction that feature epic combat, sorcerers, often dangerous quests, magic, the supernatural, and romance.]
  UF Sorcery
  BT Adventure stories
  RT Magic
       Magicians
       Wizards
Fantasy fiction
  USE Fantastic fiction
Fantasy, Science
  USE Science fantasy\
Farcical fiction
  USE Humorous stories
       Satirical fiction\
FARGO (N.D.)
  BT North Dakota
FARM LIFE [Here are entered works dealing with farms and the manners and customs thereupon. Works dealing with the art or science of cultivating the soil, producing crops, and raising livestock are entered under *Agriculture*.]
  UF Provincial and rural life
  RT Agriculture
       Migrant labor
       Ranch life
  NT Farmers
       Peasantry
       Peonage
       Serfdom
       Villeinage
       Women in agriculture
FARM LIFE IN LITERATURE [Here are entered nonfiction works dealing with the history and criticism of farm life as portrayed in literature.]
FARMERS
  BT Farm life
FASCISM
  RT Dictators
FATE AND FATALISM [Here are entered works dealing with a predetermining agency or agent, such as a law of nature or a deity whose decision is inevitable or immutable. Works dealing with the incalculable, uncontrollable, and irrational element in existence are entered under *Chance*. Works dealing with the outcome of an event whose success is problematical are entered under *Fortune*.]
  RT Chance
       Fortune

FATHER AND DAUGHTER DETECTIVES \
   RT Daughters as detectives \
FATHER AND SON DETECTIVES \
   RT Sons as detectives \
FATHERS
   BT Domestic fiction
      Men
   RT Foster parents
      Single-parent family
   NT Filicide [Murder of a son or daughter by his or her mother or father]
      Parricide [Murder of a parent by his or her son or daughter]
      Paternity
FATHERS AND DAUGHTERS
   BT Female-male relationships \
   RT Parent and child
FATHERS AND SONS
   BT Male-male relationships \
   RT Parent and child
FATHERS-IN-LAW
   UF In-laws
FATHERS IN LITERATURE [Here are entered nonfiction works on the history and criticism of fathers as portrayed in literature.]
FEAR [Here are entered works dealing with a loss of courage that may amount to cowardice. Works dealing with apprehensive uneasiness of mind, often involving self-doubt, and with doubt concerning the nature and reality of the uneasiness are entered under *Anxiety*. Anxiety involves the anguish of fear with the anticipation or uncertainty of failure and may have physiological symptoms. Works dealing with fretting or stewing over a problem as a mental activity are entered under *Worry*.]
   UF Cowardice
   RT Anxiety
      Worry
Federal Bureau of Investigation
   USE United States. Federal Bureau of Investigation
FEMALE-FEMALE RELATIONSHIPS \ [Here are entered works dealing with relations between women or girls. Works dealing with what it means to be friends or the concept of friendship are entered under *Friendship*. Works dealing with the broader concept of relations with others are entered under *Interpersonal relations*.]
   UF Women, Relations between
   BT Interpersonal relations
   RT Friendship
   NT Lesbian couples
      Mothers and daughters
      Sisters
FEMALE-MALE RELATIONSHIPS \ [Here are entered works dealing with relations between men and women or between girls and boys. Works dealing with what it means to be friends or with the concept of being friends are entered under *Friendship*. Works dealing with the broader concept of relations with others are entered under *Interpersonal relations*.]
   UF Male-female relationships
      Men—Relations with women
      Women—Relations with men
   BT Interpersonal relations
   RT Friendship
   NT Brothers and sisters
      Fathers and daughters
      Love stories
      Marriage
      Mothers and sons
FEMALE OFFENDERS
FEMININITY (PHILOSOPHY)
   UF Womanhood
FEMININITY (PSYCHOLOGY)
   UF Womanhood
FEMINIST FICTION \ [Here are entered works of fiction written from a feminist point of view.]
   BT Feminist literature
      Fiction
FEMINIST LITERATURE [Here are entered collections of literature in various forms (fiction, verse, nonfiction, etc.) dealing with feminist themes.]
   NT Feminist fiction \
FENIANS [Here are entered works dealing with a 19th-century group seeking Irish independence from Great Britain.]
   RT Irish Republican Army
FERTILIZATION IN VITRO, HUMAN
   RT Infertility, Female
      Mothers
      Pregnancy
FESTIVALS [Here are entered works dealing with a program of cultural events or entertainment. Works dealing with

public gatherings at which goods are exhibited and sold are entered under *Fairs*. Works dealing with traveling amusement enterprises consisting of sideshows, games of chance, merry-go-rounds, etc., are entered under *Carnivals*. Works dealing with amusement enterprises featuring feats of physical skill, wild animal acts, clowns, and jugglers are entered under *Circus*.]
- RT Amusement parks
  Carnivals
  Circus
  Fairs

FETUS
- BT Pregnancy
- NT Abortion

FEUILLETONS [Here are entered works of fiction that are serialized in newspapers. Works of fiction serialized in magazines or other print media are entered under *Serialized fiction*.]
- BT Fiction
  Serialized fiction

FEUILLETONS, BULGARIAN (French, etc.) [Here are entered collections of feuilletons written by Bulgarian (French, etc.) authors.]

FICTION [This term is not used for a single work of fiction since so many items would be entered here that the heading would become meaningless.]
- SA Headings for national literatures such as *Irish fiction*; *Polish fiction*, etc.
- NT Absurdist fiction\ [Works that represent the absurdity of man's existence by bizarre or fantastic means]
  Adventure stories [Novels and stories characterized by an emphasis on violent action, exotic locales, and danger]
  Allegories [Works in which persons and objects represented have meanings outside the narrative itself]
  Anthropological fiction\ [Works dealing with the cultural and physical development of people, especially from primitive or folk cultures]
  Autobiographical fiction [Works written by an author about his or her own life]
  Baseball stories [Novels and stories dealing with baseball]
  Basketball stories [Novels and stories dealing with basketball]
  Beat fiction\ [Works marked by a feeling of ennui, formlessness, exotic philosophizing, uncommitted spontaneity of thought, unconventionality, and a strong rejection of middle class values]
  Biographical fiction [Works dealing with the life of an actual person]
  Black humor fiction\ [Works that use the device of desperate, sardonic to induce laughter as the appropriate response to the meaningless and absurdity of existence]
  Boxing stories [Novels and stories dealing with the sport of boxing]
  Cheerful fiction\ [Lighthearted works characterized by the absence of explicit sex, violence, or language]
  Children's stories [Collections of fiction for children, especially up through 5th grade]
  Christian fiction [Works dealing with Christian topics or themes]
  Christmas stories [Novels and stories dealing with Christmas]
  Code and cipher stories [Novels and stories dealing with codes and ciphers, or employing codes and ciphers]
  College stories [Novels and stories dealing with college life]
  Comic books, strips, etc. [Includes graphic novels]
  Confession stories [Novels and stories in which an account of the author's life serves a didactic purpose]
  Cricket stories [Novels and stories dealing with the sport of cricket]
  Detective and mystery stories [Novels and stories dealing with the detection and solution of crimes]
  Dialect fiction\ [Works written as though someone were speaking English with an accent]
  Diary fiction\ [Works that are largely presented as diary transcriptions]
  Didactic fiction [Works that are primarily intended to teach a lesson]
  Dime novels [Cheap melodramatic and exciting late 19th century novels]
  Domestic fiction [Works dealing with family life]

Easter stories [Novels and stories dealing with Easter]

Epic novels\ [Novels that parallel traditional epics in their range and magnitude]

Episodic novels\ [Novels that have little or no central plot and/or detail events that have no causal relationship to one another]

Epistolary fiction [Works told largely through the use of letters between characters]

Erotic stories [Novels and stories whose prime purpose is erotic stimulation]

Existential fiction\ [Works that represent life as essentially meaningless, absurd, not explainable by reason or scientific means, but only through concrete experience or as man acts upon it to create meaning]

Experimental fiction [Broad term for works with a non-traditional style, format, or approach]

Fables [Short animal allegories]

Fairy tales [Novels and stories in which fairies play a central part]

Fantastic fiction [Nonexistent, incredible, or unreal worlds, characters, and/or physical principles]

Feminist fiction\ [Fiction on feminist themes]

Feuilletons [Fiction serialized in newspapers]

Fiction in verse\ [Novels and short stories told in verse]

Fishing stories [Novels and stories dealing with the sport of fishing]

Folk literature [Shorter narratives of common or illiterate people passed on by word of mouth]

Football stories [Novels and stories dealing with football (do not confuse with soccer)]

Fotonovela [Fiction with the narrative told in pictures and captions]

Gay fiction\ [Broad term for fiction by male and female gays on gay themes and topics]

Gay male fiction\ [Fiction by gay males on gay topics and themes]

Ghost stories [Novels and stories about ghosts]

Gloomy fiction\ [Broad term for works characterized by cheerlessness; prefer narrower headings such as *Detective and mystery stories, Hardboiled*\, *Dystopias*, etc.]

Golf stories [Novels and stories dealing with golf]

Gothic revival fiction\ [Fiction characterized by supernatural horror, a heroine of threatened sanity, remote or isolated settings, and often elements of romantic love]

Historical fiction [Used for fiction of an unspecified historical period, collections of historical fiction, or nonfiction on the history and criticism of historical fiction.]

Horror tales [Fiction whose primary purpose is to produce fright]

Humorous stories [Includes novels]

Hunting stories [Novels and stories dealing with hunting]

Improbable fiction\ [Broad term for works that are essentially realistic, but which contain extremely unlikely events]

Islamic stories [Novels and stories dealing with Islamic topics or themes]

Jewish religious fiction [Works dealing with Jewish religious topics or themes]

Legal stories [Novels and stories that deal with the law]

Legends [Works of traditional narrative, shorter than epics, which purport to have some basis in fact]

Lesbian fiction\ [Works by lesbians on lesbian topics and themes]

Light fiction\ [Broad term for works that have no serious intent and are written solely for entertainment. Prefer narrower headings such as *Detective and mystery stories*; *Horror tales*, etc.]

Linguistically profane fiction\ [Works characterized by the use of foul or obscene language]

Literary fiction\ [Broad term for works of serious intent done in a literary style. Prefer narrower headings such as *Philosophical fiction*\; *Good and evil*, etc.]

Livres a clef [For romans a clef]

Love stories [Novels and stories in which romantic love is the central element]
Magic realistic fiction\ [Works that use magic, dream, and fantasy combined with realistic elements and that have an emphasis on spontaneity and freshness of language]
Martial arts fiction [Works dealing with the martial arts]
Maturation (Psychology) [Coming of age fiction]
Medical fiction\ [Genre works dealing with the medical world, including doctors, nurses, and hospitals]
Melodramatic fiction\ [Works characterized by sensationalism, extravagant emotional appeal, and the subordination of characterization to plot]
Missionary stories [Children's novels and stories dealing with missionaries]
Motion picture fiction\ [Fiction based on stories originally written for use as motion picture scripts]
Musical fiction [Works dealing with music]
Nature stories [Novels and stories dealing with nature]
Nihilistic fiction\ [Works that represent life as senseless and useless with conditions so bad that destruction is desirable for its own sake even if there is no possibility of reform]
Nonfiction novel [Nonfiction works on the nonfiction novel]
Nonfiction novels\ [Fictional works of factual representation having the objective quality and authority of the real event]
Novellas (Short novels)\ [Novels of less than usual length, usually having the compact structure of a short story together with the fuller development of character, plot, and/or theme of a novel]
Novelle [Nonfiction works about the brief moral or satiric narratives popular in medieval and Renaissance times]
Pastoral fiction [Works dealing with generally idealized rustic life, and expressing complex ideas through supposedly simple characters, such as shepherds who speak in courtly language.]
Philosophical fiction\ [Works dealing with philosophical questions or that apply philosophical viewpoints to the story]
Picaresque fiction\ [Episodic works about the adventures of rascals, rogues, or vagabonds getting by on their wits]
Picaresque literature [Nonfiction works on picaresque literature]
Plot-your-own stories [Novels and stories in which the reader chooses from a number of plot options]
Political fiction [Works dealing with politics]
Proletarian fiction\ [Works with a sympathetic portrayal of the working class and exposure of social injustices and inequalities]
Psychological fiction [Works dealing with the thoughts and psychological motivations of the characters]
Radio stories [Novels and stories based on fiction originally written for radio broadcast]
Railroad stories [Novels and stories dealing with railroads and railroad travel]
Religious fiction [Fiction about religion or dealing with religious topics and themes]
Road fiction\ [Fiction in which a road journey is a major part of the action]
Romances [Works of adventure produced in the Middle Ages dealing with knights, kings, or ladies in distress acting under the impulse of love, religion, or the desire for adventure]
Romantic suspense fiction\ [Works of suspense in which romantic love plays a central part]
Romanticism [Nonfiction works dealing with the movement that began in the 18th century that emphasized feeling and imagination over intellect and reason]
Satirical fiction\ [Fiction that uses humor to expose human vice or folly]

Science fantasy\ [Fiction that combines elements of fantastic fiction and science fiction]
Science fiction [Works of fantasy that deal with possible, though not necessarily probable, events and are based approximately on scientific principles as we know them]
Sea stories [Novels and stories using the sea as a setting or dealing generally with the sea and its environment]
Sequels (Literature) [Works that are complete in themselves, but which continue the narrative course of a previous book]
Serialized fiction [Fiction that first appeared in serial installments in media other than newspapers]
Series (Publications) [Works that have a separate series title and volume number]
Sexually explicit fiction\ [Works marked by explicit description of sex acts]
Short-short stories\ [Short stories of 500 words or less]
Short stories
Sports stories [Novels and stories dealing with sports. Use specific headings for specific sports.]
Spy stories [Novels and stories dealing with espionage and spies]
Stream of consciousness fiction [Works that portray the uninterrupted and uneven flow of the consciousness of characters]
Surrealistic fiction\ [Works of conventional style and technique that juxtapose incongruous objects, characters, and actions]
Suspense fiction\ [Works whose prime purpose is to produce a feeling of frightened anticipation]
Symbolic fiction\ [Works that make heavy use of symbolism]
Tales [Traditional narratives that are for the most part fictitious, and primarily for entertainment]
Tall tales [Works characterized by bragging and exaggeration of the truth]
Television stories\ [Novels and stories based on stories originally written for television broadcast]
Three-decker novels [A single novel published in three separate books]
Thrillers\ [General term for works that hold the interest by swift and continuous action, intrigue, suspense, and adventure]
Unfinished books [Works not completed by the original author]
Violent fiction\ [Work characterized by explicit descriptions of violent acts]
War stories [Broad term for novels and stories dealing with war]
Western stories [Adventure novels and stories that take place in the American West]
Young adult accessible fiction\ [Works originally written for adults, but which are nonetheless suitable for young adults]
Young adult fiction [Collections of fiction for children in the 6th through 12th grades]
Fiction in diary form
  USE Diary fiction\
FICTION IN VERSE\ [Here are entered novels and stories told in verse.]
  UF Novels in verse
    Stories in verse
    Story poems
  BT Fiction
FIGURINES
  RT Art objects
FILICIDE [Here are entered works dealing with the murder of a son or daughter by his or her mother or father. Works dealing with the murder of a mother or father by his or her son or daughter are entered under *Parricide*.]
  BT Daughters
    Fathers
    Mothers
    Murder
    Parent and child
    Sons
  RT Parricide
FINANCE
  RT Wall Street
Finance—Corrupt practices
  USE Commercial crimes

FINANCIAL INSTITUTIONS—CORRUPT PRACTICES
- UF Financial intrigue
- BT Commercial crimes

Financial intrigue
- USE Capitalists and financiers
  Commercial crimes
  Financial institutions—Corrupt practices

FINLAND
- RT Lapland

FINNS
- BT Scandinavians

FIRE IN LITERATURE [Here are entered nonfiction works on the history and criticism of fire as portrayed in literature.]

FIRES
- NT Pyromania [The irresistible impulse to start fires]

FIRES IN LITERATURE [Here are entered nonfiction works on the history and criticism of fires as portrayed in literature.]

FISHERIES
- UF Fishing, Commercial

Fishing
- USE Fishing stories

Fishing, Commercial
- USE Fisheries

FISHING STORIES [Here are entered novels and stories dealing with the sport of fishing.]
- UF Fishing
- BT Fiction
- RT Outdoor life

Fliers
- USE Air pilots

FLOODS
- RT Rain and rainfall
  Rainstorms
  Storms

FLORENCE (ITALY)
- BT Italy

FLORIDA
- NT Key West (Fla.)
  Miami (Fla.)
  Tallahassee (Fla.)

FOLK LITERATURE [Here are entered works passed on by word of mouth that deal with shorter narratives about common or illiterate people. Collections of traditional narratives that are for the most part fictitious and are told primarily for entertainment are entered under *Tales*. Broad and lengthy works that recount the deeds of a legendary or historical hero are entered under *Epic literature*. Works of traditional narrative that are shorter than epics but still purport to have some basis in reality are entered under *Legends*. Works of traditional narrative that are shorter than epics but deal more with the supernatural and less with the historical are entered under *Mythology*.]
- BT Fiction
- RT Epic literature
  Heldensage [13th century German epics]
  Legends
  Mythology
  Tales
- NT Sagas
  Wandering Jew

FOLK LITERATURE, AFRICAN (Albanian, etc.) [Here are entered collections of folk literature by African (Albanian, etc.) authors.]

FOLK MUSIC
- UF Music, Folk
- BT Musical fiction

FOOD IN LITERATURE [Here are entered nonfiction works on the history and criticism of food as portrayed in literature.]

FOOTBALL STORIES [Here are entered novels and stories dealing with football (not to be confused with soccer).]
- BT Fiction

FORCED LABOR
- RT Labor camps [For non-compulsory workers]

Foreign Legion
- USE France. Armée. Légion étrangère

Foreign relations
- USE Diplomatic and consular service
  World politics

FOREST FIRES
- RT Arson

FOREST RANGERS
- BT Forests and forestry

FORESTS AND FORESTRY
- NT Forest rangers

FORGERY
- NT Art—Forgeries
  Counterfeits and counterfeiting [Forged money and the forging of money]

Forgery of works of art
- USE Art—Forgeries

FORTUNE [Here are entered works dealing with the outcome of an event whose success is problematical. Works dealing with a predetermining agency or agent, such as a law of nature or a deity whose decision is inevitable or immutable, are entered under *Fate and fatalism*. Works dealing with the incalculable, uncontrollable, and irrational element in existence are entered under *Chance*.]
   UF Luck
   RT Chance
         Fate and fatalism

FORTUNE-TELLERS [Here are entered works dealing with persons who have the ability or who claim to have the ability to foresee the future by supernatural means. Works dealing with persons who have the ability or who claim to have the ability to foresee the future with their minds are entered under *Psychics*.]
   RT Psychics

FORTUNE TELLERS AS DETECTIVES \
   RT Psychic detectives \

FORTUNE-TELLING [Here are entered works dealing with the ability to foresee the future by occult or supernatural means. Works dealing with the ability to foresee the future with the mind are entered under *Precognition*. Works dealing with the ability to foresee the future because of divine inspiration are entered under *Prophecy*.]
   RT Extrasensory Perception
         Precognition
         Prophecy

FOSTER CHILDREN [Here are entered works dealing with children receiving parental care although not legally or biologically related to the caregiver. Works dealing with legal guardianship of a child are entered under *Guardian and ward*.]
   BT Domestic fiction
   RT Adoption
         Guardian and ward
         Orphans

FOSTER PARENTS
   BT Domestic fiction
   RT Fathers
         Mothers

FOTONOVELA [Here are entered works in which characters and scenes are photographed and legends are inserted either in balloons or in a boxed space in comic strip fashion.]
   BT Comic books, strips, etc.
         Fiction

FOURTH DIMENSION
   RT Parallel worlds [Worlds existing simultaneously in the same location as our own]

FRAME-STORIES [Here are entered stories contained within a novel or another short story and collections of a series of stories with a common narrative framework, such as Sherwood Anderson's *Winesburg, Ohio*. For frame-stories that are collections of short stories, also use the heading *Short stories*.]
   UF Novels with short stories
         Short stories within a novel
         Stories within a novel
   BT Short stories
   RT Episodic novels \
         Picaresque fiction \

Frame-ups
   USE Malicious accusation

FRANCE
   RT Gaul
   NT Burgundy (France)
         Normandy (France)
         Paris (France)
         Riviera (France)
         Strasbourg (France)

FRANCE—COURT AND COURTIERS

FRANCE—KINGS AND RULERS

FRANCE—NOBILITY

FRANCE. ARMÉE
   UF France. Army
   NT France. Armée—Military life

FRANCE. ARMÉE. LÉGION ÉTRANGÈRE
   UF Foreign Legion
         France. Foreign legion
         French Foreign Legion

FRANCE. ARMÉE—MILITARY LIFE
   BT France. Armée

France. Army
   USE France. Armée

France. Foreign Legion
   USE France. Armée. Légion étrangère

Franco-Americans
   USE French Americans

FRATRICIDE [Here are entered works dealing with the murder of a brother by a sibling.]
  BT Brothers
     Murder
FREE LOVE
  BT Sex
FRENCH—CANADA [Here are entered works dealing with French people visiting or living in Canada.]
  NT French-Canadians
FRENCH—UNITED STATES [Here are entered works on French people visiting or living in the United States.]
  NT French Americans
FRENCH AMERICANS [Here are entered works dealing with Americans of French ancestry.]
  UF Franco-Americans
  BT French—United States
FRENCH-CANADIAN FICTION
  BT Canadian Fiction
FRENCH-CANADIANS [Here are entered works dealing with Canadians of French ancestry.]
  BT French—Canada
FRENCH FICTION
French Foreign Legion
  USE France. Armée. Légion étrangère
Friends
  USE Friendship
FRIENDSHIP [Here are entered works dealing with what it means to be friends or with the concept of friendship. Works dealing with the broader concept of relations with others are entered under *Interpersonal relations*. Works dealing with relations between women or girls are entered under *Female-female relationships*. Works dealing with relations between men or boys are entered under *Male-male relationships*. Works dealing with relations between men and women or girls and boys are entered under *Female-male relationships*.]
  UF Friends
  BT Interpersonal relations
  RT Female-female relationships\
     Female-male relationships\
     Male-male relationships\
FRONTIER AND PIONEER LIFE
  UF Prairie life
  RT West (U.S.)
     Western stories
FRUNZE (KIRGIZ S.S.R.)
  BT Kirgiz S.S.R.
FUGITIVES FROM JUSTICE
  UF Escaped convicts
     Manhunts
     Prisoners, Escaped
FUNDRAISING
  RT Charities
FUNERAL RITES AND CEREMONIES
  RT Cemeteries
FUR TRADE
  RT Trappers
FUTURE [Here are entered works that take place at an unspecified time in the future. If a specific date is available, use that instead.]
  RT Science fiction
FUTURE IN LITERATURE [Here are entered nonfiction works on the history and criticism of the future as portrayed in literature.]
FUTURE LIFE [Here are entered works dealing with life after death.]

Galactic empires
  USE Extraterrestrial bases
     Extraterrestrial beings\
     Life on other planets
     Science fiction
GALLOGLASSES [Here are entered works dealing with the mercenary troops maintained in former times by Irish chieftains. Works dealing with European professional mercenary troops of the 14th, 15th, and 16th centuries are entered under *Condottieri*. Works dealing with troops that serve a country other than their own primarily or strictly on a wage basis are entered under *Mercenary troops*. Works dealing with persons who follow a military career wherever there is the promise of adventure, profit, or pleasure are entered under *Soldiers of fortune*.]
  BT Mercenary troops
     Soldiers of fortune
  RT Condottieri
GAMBLING
  NT Sweepstakes

GANGS
  NT Organized crime
GASES, ASPHYXIATING AND POISONOUS
  RT Biological warfare
GAUL
  RT France
GAY FICTION\ [Here are entered works on gay topics and themes by male and female gay authors.]
  BT Fiction
     Gays
  NT Gay male fiction\
     Lesbian fiction\
GAY MALE COUPLES
  UF Homosexual love affairs
     Love affairs, Homosexual
  BT Male-male relationships\
GAY MALE FICTION\ [Here are entered works on gay male topics and themes by gay male authors.]
  BT Fiction
     Gay fiction\
GAY MEN
  BT Gays
  RT Bisexuality
GAY MEN AS DETECTIVES\
GAYS [Here are entered works dealing with both male and female gays. Works dealing only with male gays are entered under *Gay men*. Works dealing only with female gays are entered under *Lesbians*.]
  RT Bisexuality
     Gay fiction
  NT Gay men
     Lesbians
GEISHAS [Here are entered works dealing with Japanese women trained in light-hearted entertainment primarily for men. Geishas are not, per se, prostitutes or courtesans. Works dealing with women who sell themselves for fornication are entered under *Prostitutes*. Works dealing with women who prostitute themselves to men of high rank or wealth are entered under *Courtesans*. Works dealing with women who habitually fornicate with a particular man but who do not sell themselves are entered under *Mistresses*.]
  RT Concubinage
     Courtesans
     Mistresses
     Prostitutes

GENERALS [If the general featured in the work is a member of a particular armed force, use the appropriate heading for that service, for example, *United States. Army—Officers*.]
GENEVA (SWITZERLAND)
  BT Switzerland
Genies
  USE Jinn
GENTRY [Here are entered works dealing with persons who are not nobility but who are entitled to bear a coat of arms, and hence, are considered gentlemen or ladies in the technical sense, and are landed proprietors. Works dealing with persons of an ideally superior caste, not invariably a fixed or definite group, are entered under *Aristocracy*. Works dealing with persons whose rank is inferior to royalty but superior to all others, and whose rank is either directly granted by a ruler or inherited are entered under *Nobility*. Note that *Nobility* includes baronets even though British popular usage does not. Works dealing with persons considered of the highest class of people either because of wealth or prestige are entered under *Upper classes*.]
  RT Aristocracy
     Knights and knighthood
     Nobility
     Upper classes
GEOGRAPHICAL MYTHS
  UF Imaginary countries
GEORGE TOWN (PINANG)
  UF Pinang (Pinang)
  BT Pinang
GEORGIA
  NT Atlanta (Ga.)
Georgian England [This term most often applies to the reign of the first four King Georges of Great Britain who reigned from 1714 to 1830. Use the heading *Great Britain—History, 1714-1837* [sic] if the specific king is not known. Works of love fiction are entered under *Love stories, Georgian*. The term "Georgian" may also apply to the reign of King George V, which lasted from 1910 to 1936; if this is the case, use the heading *Great Britain—History—George V, 1910-1936*.]
  USE Great Britain—History—1714-1837

Great Britain—History—George V, 1910-1936
Love stories, Georgian\

GEORGIAN S.S.R.
- BT Soviet Union
- NT Tbilisi (Georgian S.S.R.)

GERMAN AMERICANS [Here are entered works dealing with Americans of German ancestry.]
- BT Germans—United States

GERMANS—UNITED STATES [Here are entered works dealing with Germans visiting or living in the United States.]
- NT German Americans

GERMANY
- NT Berlin (Germany)

GERMANY—NOBILITY

GERMANY (EAST) [Here are entered works dealing with the communist Democratic Republic (1949-1990) and with the eastern part of Germany before and after that time.]

GERMANY (WEST) [Here are entered works dealing with the Federal Republic (1949-1990) and with the western part of Germany before and after that time.]

Germany. Air Force
- USE Germany. Luftwaffe

Germany. Army
- USE Germany. Heer

GERMANY. GEHEIME STAATSPOLIZEI
- UF Germany. Gestapo
  Gestapo

Germany. Gestapo
- USE Germany. Geheime Staatspolizei

GERMANY. HEER
- UF Germany. Army
  Germany. Wehrmacht
  Wehrmacht

GERMANY. KRIEGSMARINE
- UF Germany. Navy

GERMANY. LUFTWAFFE
- UF Germany. Air Force
  Luftwaffe

Germany. Navy
- USE Germany. Kriegsmarine

Germany. Wehrmacht
- USE Germany. Heer

Germs
- USE Biological warfare
  Epidemics

Gestapo
- USE Germany. Geheime Staatspolizei

GHOST STORIES [Here are entered novels and stories featuring ghosts. Works that may also have ghosts and which are characterized by supernatural horror, a heroine with threatened sanity, remote or isolated settings which are frequently ruined or haunted castles or large old houses, and often with elements of romantic love are entered under *Gothic revival fiction*\. Works that may also use ghosts and often the occult but which generally lack romantic involvement and whose purpose is primarily to produce true fright are entered under *Horror tales*. Works that deal primarily with the supernatural, but of which ghosts are only a small part and whose prime purpose is not fright are entered under *Supernatural*. Works dealing with haunted houses centered upon the structure itself are entered under *Haunted houses*.]
- BT Adventure stories
  Fiction
  Supernatural
- RT Gothic revival fiction\
  Haunted houses
  Horror tales
- NT Doppelgangers\

GHOST STORIES, AMERICAN (Canadian, etc.) [Here are entered collections of ghost stories by American (Canadian, etc.) authors.]

GHOSTS IN LITERATURE [Here are entered nonfiction works on the history and criticism of ghosts as portrayed in literature.]

GIANTS
- BT Legends

GIFTED CHILDREN
- UF Children, Gifted

Girl into woman
- USE Maturation (Psychology)

GIRLS [Here are entered works dealing with female children in general and up to and including 12 years of age in particular. The age of the girl may be added to this heading (for example, *Girls—Ten*\; *Girls—Eleven*\, etc.) although this is not a Library of Congress practice.]
- BT Women
- NT Maturation (Psychology)

Teenage girls [13 to 17 years of age, inclusive]

GLADIATORS [Gladiators are trained fighters who entertain. They are not necessarily soldiers.]
- RT Soldiers

GLASGOW (SCOTLAND)
- BT Scotland

GLOOMY FICTION [Here are entered works characterized by a *noire* treatment or outlook that do not fit under narrower headings.]
- UF Cheerless fiction
- BT Fiction
- RT Apocalyptic fiction\
   Cheerful fiction\
- NT Detective and mystery stories, Hardboiled\
   Dystopias
   Violent fiction\

GOLD MINES AND MINING

GOLF STORIES [Here are entered stories and novels dealing with golf.]
- BT Fiction

GOOD AND EVIL
- RT Allegories
   Literary Fiction\
   Philosophical fiction\

GOTHIC LITERATURE [Here are entered works of literature by Goths, a Germanic people of the early centuries of the Christian era. Use *Gothic revival fiction*\ for works of fiction produced from the late 18th century to the present that are characterized by remote settings, the supernatural, and a woman in danger.]
- RT Gothic revival fiction\

GOTHIC REVIVAL (LITERATURE) [Here are entered works about the literature of the Gothic revival.]

GOTHIC REVIVAL FICTION [Here are entered works of fiction characterized by supernatural horror, a heroine with threatened sanity, remote or isolated settings which are frequently ruined or haunted castles or large old houses; often contain elements of romantic love. Works that may also use the supernatural and often the occult but which generally lack romantic involvement and whose purpose is primarily to produce true fright are entered under *Horror tales*. Works of suspense dominated by romance are entered under *Romantic suspense fiction*\. Works dealing primarily with ghosts are entered under *Ghost stories*. Works that deal primarily with the supernatural, of which ghosts are only a small part, and whose prime purpose is not fright are entered under *Supernatural*.]
- UF Gothics
- BT Adventure stories
   Fiction
   Thrillers\
- RT Ghost stories
   Gothic literature [Literature written by Goths]
   Horror tales
   Romantic suspense fiction\
   Supernatural

Gothics
- USE Gothic revival fiction\

GOVERNESSES [Here are entered works dealing with women who are charged with the care of children in a private household and who usually also function as a teacher for the children. Works dealing with a girl or woman who takes care of children but does not teach are entered under *Child care workers*.]
- UF Nannies
   Nursemaids
- BT Child care workers
   Domestics

GOVERNESSES AS DETECTIVES
- BT Women detectives

GOVERNESSES IN LITERATURE [Here are entered nonfiction works on the history and criticism of governesses as portrayed in literature.]

Government employees
- USE Bureaucracy
   Diplomatic and consular service
   Postal service

GRADUATE STUDENTS
- BT Intellectual life
   Students
- RT Learning and scholarship
   Scholars

GRAIL
- BT Legends
- RT Quests\

GRAIN
- NT Corn

Grammar schools
- USE Elementary schools

BT Schools
Grandchildren
  USE Grandparent and child
GRANDFATHERS
  BT Domestic fiction
  NT Great-grandfathers \
GRANDMOTHERS
  BT Domestic fiction
GRANDPARENT AND CHILD
  UF Great-grandchildren
  BT Children
     Domestic fiction
Graphic fiction
  USE Comic books, strips, etc.
Graphic novels
  USE Comic books, strips, etc.
Grave robbing
  USE Body snatching
GREAT BRITAIN
  UF Britain
     United Kingdom
  RT Ireland
  SA headings beginning with the word *British*
  NT Channel Islands
     England
     Isle of Man
     Northern Ireland
     Scotland
     Wales
GREAT BRITAIN—FOREIGN RELATIONS—SOVIET UNION
  UF British-Russian relations
     Russian-British relations
GREAT BRITAIN—HISTORY—ANGLO SAXON PERIOD, 449-1066
  BT Anglo-Saxons
     Saxons
GREAT BRITAIN—HISTORY—WARS OF THE ROSES, 1455-1485
  UF War of the Roses, 1455-1485
GREAT BRITAIN—HISTORY—TUDORS, 1485-1603
  UF Tudor England
  BT Renaissance
GREAT BRITAIN—HISTORY—ELIZABETH, 1558-1603
  UF Elizabethan England
GREAT BRITAIN—HISTORY—EARLY STUARTS, 1603-1649
  BT Renaissance
GREAT BRITAIN—HISTORY—GEORGE I, 1714-1727
  NT Love stories, Georgian \

GREAT BRITAIN—HISTORY—1714-1837
  UF Georgian England
  NT Love stories, Georgian \
GREAT BRITAIN—HISTORY—GEORGE III, 1760-1820
  UF England, Regency
     Regency England
  NT Love stories, Regency \
GREAT BRITAIN—HISTORY—VICTORIA, 1837-1901
  UF Victorian England
GREAT BRITAIN—HISTORY—EDWARD VII, 1901-1910
  UF Edwardian England
GREAT BRITAIN—HISTORY—GEORGE V, 1910-1936
  UF Georgian England
GREAT BRITAIN—NOBILITY
  NT England—Nobility
Great Britain—Prime ministers
  USE Prime ministers—Great Britain
GREAT BRITAIN. ARMY. SPECIAL AIR SERVICE
  UF Special Air Service
Great Britain. Imperial Security Intelligence Service
  USE Great Britain. MI5
GREAT BRITAIN. MI5 [Here are entered works dealing with the British internal security and counterintelligence agency similar to the U.S. Federal Bureau of Investigation.]
  UF Great Britain. Imperial Security Intelligence Service
     M.I.5
  BT Spy stories
GREAT BRITAIN. MI6 [Here are entered works dealing with the British foreign intelligence agency similar to the U.S. Central Intelligence Agency.]
  UF Great Britain. Secret Intelligence Service
     M.I.6
  BT Spy stories
GREAT BRITAIN. PARLIAMENT. HOUSE OF COMMONS
  UF House of Commons
GREAT BRITAIN. PARLIAMENT. HOUSE OF LORDS
  UF House of Lords
GREAT BRITAIN. ROYAL AIR FORCE
  UF R.A.F.
     Royal Air Force
GREAT BRITAIN. ROYAL MARINES
  BT Marines

GREAT BRITAIN. ROYAL MILITARY COLLEGE
  USE Royal Military College, Sandhurst
GREAT BRITAIN. ROYAL NAVY
  UF Royal Navy
Great Britain. Secret Intelligence Service
  USE Great Britain. MI6
Great-Grandchildren
  USE Grandparent and child
GREAT-GRANDFATHERS \
  BT Grandfathers
GREAT SMOKY MOUNTAINS (N.C. AND TENN.)
  BT Appalachian Mountains
GREEK LETTER SOCIETIES [Here are entered works dealing with fraternities and sororities.]
  BT College stories
Green Berets
  USE United States. Army. Special Forces
GREENLAND
  RT Arctic regions
GREENWICH VILLAGE (NEW YORK, N.Y.)
  BT New York (N.Y.)
GRIEF [Here are entered works dealing with deep distress caused by, or seemingly caused by, bereavement. Works dealing with an utter loss of hope or confidence are entered under *Despair*. Works dealing with an often prolonged disordered psychological state of low spirits and unhappiness whose cause is often internal in origin are entered under *Depression, Mental*. Works dealing with a mood of dejection, discouragement, or pensiveness which is of a more transitory nature and with an external cause are entered under *Melancholy*. Works dealing with the atmosphere or effect produced by depression, melancholy, grief, or despair are entered under *Sadness*. *Sadness* can also be used as a general term for low spirits or unhappiness when there is no clear explanation of the cause or extent.]
  BT Bereavement
  RT Depression, Mental
    Despair
    Melancholy
    Sadness
GUARDIAN AND WARD [Here are entered works dealing with legal guardianship of a child. Works dealing with children receiving parental care although they are not legally or biologically related to the caregiver are entered under *Foster children*.]
  RT Adoption
    Domestic fiction
    Foster children
GUESTS \
  UF Houseguests
  RT House parties \
GUILT [Here are entered works dealing with being responsible for a crime or a sin and deserving severe punishment. Works dealing with humiliating disrepute or disgrace (the reaction to other people's criticism) are entered under *Shame*.]
  RT Atonement
    Shame
GULF STREAM
  BT Atlantic Ocean
GUNFIGHTERS \
  BT Criminals
  RT Western stories
GYNECOLOGISTS
  BT Physicians

HALF-BROTHERS \
  BT Brothers
HALF-SISTERS \
  BT Sisters
Halfbreeds
  USE Indians of North America—Mixed bloods
HALIFAX (N.S.)
  BT Nova Scotia
HALLOWEEN
  RT Masquerades
HALLUCINATIONS AND ILLUSIONS [Here are entered works dealing with the perception of visual and other sensory impressions that have no reality. Works dealing with deception either by oneself or by others are entered under *Delusions*.]
  RT Delusions
    Mental Illness
Hamptons
  USE Long Island (N.Y.)
HANDICAPPED DETECTIVES \
HANDYMEN \
  RT Hired men \
HANGING
  NT Lynching

Hard liquor
- USE Liquors

Hardboiled detectives
- USE Detective and mystery stories, Hardboiled\

HARLEM (NEW YORK, N.Y.)
- BT New York (N.Y.)

HARTFORD (CONN.)
- BT Connecticut

HARVARD UNIVERSITY
- RT Cambridge (Mass.)

HASIDIM
- UF Jews, Hasidic

HAUNTED HOUSES [Here are entered works dealing with the haunted house as a structure. Works dealing primarily with the ghosts that haunt a house are entered under *Ghost stories*.]
- RT Ghost stories

HEALTH RESORTS, WATERING PLACES, ETC.
- RT Hotels, taverns, etc.
  Vacations

HEART—DISEASES
- NT Heart—Infarction

HEART—INFARCTION
- UF Heart attack
- BT Heart—Diseases

Heart attack
- USE Heart—Infarction

HEBREW FICTION [Here is entered fiction originally written in the Hebrew language by non-Israelis. Fiction produced by Israelis in Hebrew or in several languages collectively is entered under *Israeli fiction*. Fiction originally produced in the Yiddish language is entered under *Yiddish fiction*. Collections of fiction produced by Jews of an unspecified nationality and in an unspecified language are entered under *Jewish fiction*. Individual works of fiction produced by Jews are entered only under the fiction of their nationality.]
- RT Israeli fiction
  Jewish fiction
  Yiddish fiction

HEDONISM [Here are entered works dealing with the belief that pleasure and happiness are the main purpose of life. Works dealing with having little or no religion coupled with uninhibited seeking after material goods and sensual pleasure are entered under *Paganism*. Works dealing with reckless extravagance or spendthrifts are entered under *Prodigals*.]
- UF Libertines
- RT Paganism
  Prodigals

Heiresses
- USE Inheritance and succession

HELDENSAGE [Here is entered German epic literature from the 13th century dealing with the struggles and conquests of the Germanic tribes during the epoch of migrations. Broad and lengthy works that recount the deeds of a legendary or historical hero are entered under *Epic literature*. Works that deal with shorter narratives passed on by word of mouth about common or illiterate people are entered under *Folk literature*.]
- BT Epic literature
- RT Folk literature

HELENA (MONT.)
- BT Montana

HELICOPTERS

Helvetia
- USE Switzerland

HERMITS [Here are entered works dealing with persons who are recluses for religious reasons.]
- BT Recluses

HEROID [Here are entered poetic narratives in epistolary form that express the sentiments between heroes or heroines and their wives or sweethearts.]
- BT Epistolary fiction
  Letters
- NT Imaginary letters

HEROIN HABIT
- RT Drug traffic

High school theater
- USE Amateur theater

HIGH SCHOOLS
- RT Junior high schools [Generally including but not necessarily confined to 7th, 8th, and 9th grades]

HIGHLANDS (SCOTLAND)
- BT Scotland

HIJACKING OF AIRCRAFT
- UF Airplane hijacking
  Airplanes, Hijacking of

HIJACKING OF SHIPS
- UF Ship hijacking

HIJACKING OF TRUCKS\
- UF Truck hijacking

HIRED MEN
  RT Domestics
     Handymen
HISTORIC SITES—CONSERVATION AND RESTORATION
  RT Conservation of natural resources
HISTORICAL FICTION [Here are entered works set in unspecified historical periods, collections of works of historical fiction, and nonfiction works on the history and criticism of historical fiction. For fiction, prefer the specific period, person, or incident, for example *United States—History—Civil War, 1861-1865*; *Burr, Aaron*; or *Jameson's Raid, 1895-1896*. Works dealing with history as a topic are entered under *History*.]
  BT Fiction
  RT History
  NT Love stories, Historical
HISTORICAL FICTION, ALBANIAN (American, etc.) [Here are entered collections of historical fiction by Albanian (American, etc.) authors and nonfiction works on the history and criticism of Albanian (American, etc.) historical fiction.]
Historical romance fiction
  USE Love stories, Historical
HISTORY [Here are entered works dealing with history as a topic.]
  RT Historical fiction
History, Alternate
  USE Imaginary histories
Hit men
  USE Assassins
HOARDING OF MONEY [Here are entered works dealing with the economic effects of the amassment of money or capital in an unreasonable fashion. Works dealing with an excessive desire for gain or wealth are entered under *Avarice*. Works dealing with persons who live wretched lives in order to hoard their wealth are entered under *Misers*.]
  RT Avarice
     Misers
     Prodigals
HOBART (TAS.)
  BT Tasmania
Holdups
  USE Mugging
     Robbery

HOLLYWOOD (LOS ANGELES, CALIF.)
  BT California
     Los Angeles (Calif.)
HOLOCAUST, JEWISH (1939-1945)
  BT Antisemitism
     Atrocities
     Jews
  RT Concentration camps
     World War, 1939-1945—Concentration camps
HOLOCAUST SURVIVORS
Homecoming
  USE Reunions
HOMELESSNESS [Here are entered works dealing with people who do not have a dwelling to live in. Works dealing with aimless persons who wander from place to place and job to job are entered under *Drifters*. Works dealing with traveling beggars who will not work are entered under *Tramps*. Works dealing with the legal charge of being a tramp are entered under *Vagrancy*. Works dealing with persons who travel as a way of life are entered under *Wayfaring life*. Works dealing with wandering, disorderly, or dissolute, but not necessarily displeasing persons are entered under *Rogues and vagabonds*.]
  RT Drifters
     Rogues and vagabonds
     Tramps
     Vagrancy
     Wayfaring life
HOMICIDE [Here are entered works dealing with the killing of a human being in a situation which is not necessarily a crime or in a neutral sense with no moral or legal quality. Works dealing with the unlawful killing of a human being with malice aforethought are entered under *Murder*. Works of generally lighter fiction that are concerned with the detection or solution of crimes are entered under *Detective and mystery stories*.]
  RT Detective and mystery stories
     Murder
Homosexual love affairs
  USE Gay male couples
     Lesbian couples
HONDURAS

HONEYMOON
- BT Newlyweds\
- RT Betrothal
  Weddings

HOODLUMS
- UF Mobsters
- RT Organized crime

HORROR TALES [Here are entered works of prose fiction whose primary purpose is to produce true fright, that employ the supernatural and occult, and that generally lack romantic involvement. Works characterized by supernatural horror, a heroine with threatened sanity, remote or isolated settings which are frequently ruined or haunted castles or large old houses, with elements of romantic love are entered under *Gothic revival fiction*\. Works dealing primarily with ghosts are entered under *Ghost stories*. Works that deal primarily with the supernatural, but of which ghosts are only a small part and whose prime purpose is not fright, are entered under *Supernatural.*]
- BT Adventure stories
  Fiction
  Light fiction\
  Thrillers\
- RT Demoniac possession
  Demonology
  Ghost stories
  Gothic revival fiction\
  Monsters
  Supernatural
  Suspense Fiction\
  Vampires
  Werewolves

HORROR TALES, AMERICAN (German, etc.) [Here are entered collections of horror tales by American (German, etc.) authors.]

HORSE-RACING

HORSE STEALING
- UF Horse thieves
- NT Thieves

Horse thieves
- USE Horse stealing

HORSES

Hospital stories
- USE Medical fiction\

HOSPITALS [Here are entered works dealing with institutions that give the sick and injured medical and surgical care. Works dealing with the medical world, including doctors, nurses, and hospitals, are entered under the genre heading *Medical fiction*\. Works dealing with planned residential developments for the aged that also provide meal service, medical care, etc., are entered under *Life care communities*. Works dealing with private institutions that provide long-term personal and nursing care to the aged or chronically ill are entered under *Nursing homes*. Works that deal with institutions that provide housing and general care for the convalescent are entered under *Rest homes*. Works that deal with institutions that provide housing and general care for the aged are entered under *Old age homes*. Works that deal with institutions that provide long term care and therapy together with a regimen such as diet or exercise are entered under *Sanatoriums.*]
- RT Life care communities
  Medical fiction\
  Nurses
  Nursing homes
  Old age homes
  Physicians
  Rest homes
  Sanatoriums
  Sick

HOSTAGES
- RT Kidnapping

Hostels
- USE Tourist camps, hostels, etc.
  Youth hostels

HOTELS, TAVERNS, ETC.
- UF Boarding houses
- RT Apartment houses
  Health resorts, watering places, etc.
  Lodging-houses [Includes rooming houses]
  Resorts
  Youth hostels

HOTLINES (COUNSELING)
- UF Telephone counseling

House of Commons
- USE Great Britain. Parliament. House of Commons

House of Lords
- USE Great Britain. Parliament. House of Lords

House of Representatives
  USE United States. Congress. House
HOUSE PAINTING
  UF Housepainting
  RT Painting
HOUSE PARTIES\ [Here are entered works dealing with parties where the guests stay overnight.]
  UF Houseguests
      Parties, House
  BT Entertaining
  RT Dinners and dining
Houseguests
  USE Guests
      House parties\
Housepainting
  USE House painting
HOUSTON (TEX.)
  BT Texas
HUMAN SACRIFICE
  UF Sacrifice, Human
  NT Blood accusation [Ritual murder]
      Suttee [Cremation of a Hindu widow on her husband's funeral pyre]
      Ver sacrum [Greek and Italian custom of animal sacrifice and the sending away of 20-year-old humans]
HUMOROUS STORIES [Here are entered novels and stories written in a comical and amusing manner.]
  UF Comic fiction
      Farcical fiction
  BT Fiction
      Light fiction\
      Wit and humor
  RT Cheerful fiction\
      Parodies
      Practical jokes
      Satirical fiction\
  NT Black humor fiction\
      Detective and mystery stories, Humorous\
      Fantastic fiction, Humorous\
      Science fiction, Humorous\
      Spy stories, Humorous\
HUMOROUS STORIES, AMERICAN (Brazilian, etc.) [Here are entered collections of humorous stories by American (Brazilian, etc.) authors.]
Hunchbacks
  USE Back—Abnormalities
HUNS
  UF Barbarians

HUNTING STORIES [Here are entered novels and stories dealing with hunting.]
  BT Fiction
  RT Outdoor life
      Shooting
HURRICANES [Here are entered works dealing with cyclonic storms in the West Indies. Works dealing with cyclonic storms of the China Seas and the Philippines are entered under *Typhoons*. Works dealing with an unusually large sea wave or tidal wave associated with high winds are entered under *Tsunamis*.]
  RT Tsunamis
      Typhoons
HUSBAND AND WIFE [Here are entered works dealing with the legal relations between husband and wife. Works of fiction that deal primarily with the relationship of husband and wife are entered under *Marriage*. Works dealing with the life of a nuclear or extended family in a single household or with several generations reacting together in the span of a single generation are entered under *Domestic fiction*.]
  BT Marriage
  RT Domestic fiction
HUSBAND AND WIFE DETECTIVES\
  BT Marriage
  RT Woman Detectives
HUSBANDS
  BT Men
  RT Wives
  NT Mariticide\ [Murder of a husband by his wife]
      Uxoricide [Murder of a wife by her husband]
HYPERSOMNIA
  UF Sleep, Prolonged
      Suspended animation
  RT Coma
      Dormancy (Biology)

I.R.A.
  USE Irish Republican Army
I.W.W.
  USE Industrial Workers of the World
IDAHO
  NT Boise (Idaho)

IDENTITY [Here are entered works dealing with who one is or is known as. Works dealing with someone who has two separate identities, each of his own invention, are entered under *Double identity*\. Works dealing with persons who are innocently mistaken for someone else are entered under *Mistaken identity*\. Works that deal with assuming the personality, behavior, or appearance of someone for other than deceitful intent are entered under *Impersonation*. Works that deal with assuming an identity with the intent to deceive are entered under *Impostors and imposture*.]
- UF Personal identity
- NT Double identity\
  Impersonation
  Impostors and imposture
  Mistaken identity\
  Victims, Unidentified\

Illegal immigrants
- USE Aliens, Illegal

ILLINOIS
- NT Chicago (Ill.)

Illusionists
- USE Magicians

ILLUSTRATED BOOKS [Here are entered nonfiction works on the history and criticism of books that are illustrated.]
- RT Comic books, strips, etc. [Use for graphic novels]

IMAGINARY BOOKS AND LIBRARIES [Here are entered nonfiction works on the history and criticism of imaginary books and libraries. Works dealing with books or libraries imagined by the author are entered under *Books*, or *Libraries*.]
- BT Books
  Libraries

IMAGINARY CONVERSATIONS [Here are entered nonfiction works on the history and criticism of imaginary conversations. Works that are centered about conversations or in which conversation is heavily relied upon as a literary device are entered under *Conversations*\. Works that contain collections of dialogues are entered under *Dialogues*.]
- BT Conversations\
  Dialogues

Imaginary countries
- USE Geographical myths

IMAGINARY HISTORIES [Here are entered works dealing with the world as it might have been if history had been different.]
- UF Alternate history
  Alternate worlds
  History, Alternate
  Other worlds
- RT Parallel worlds\
  Science fantasy\
  Science fiction

IMAGINARY LANGUAGES [Here are entered works dealing with imaginary languages or which make heavy use of an imaginary language in the narrative.]

IMAGINARY LANGUAGES IN LITERATURE [Here are entered nonfiction works on the history and criticism of imaginary languages as used or portrayed in literature.]

IMAGINARY LETTERS [Here are entered nonfiction works on the history and criticism of imaginary letters (epistles). Works in which the author narrates a significant part of the story in letter format are entered under *Epistolary fiction*. Works which are about letters (epistles) are entered under *Letters*. Poetic narratives in epistolary form that express the sentiments between heroes or heroines and their wives or sweethearts are entered under *Heroid*.]
- BT Letters
  Epistolary fiction
  Heroid

Imaginary planets
- USE Extraterrestrial bases
  Extraterrestrial beings\
  Life on other planets
  Science fiction
  Space colonies

IMAGINARY REVOLUTIONS [Here are entered nonfiction works on the history and criticism of imaginary revolutions.]
- BT Revolutions

IMAGINARY SOCIETIES [Here are entered nonfiction works on the history and criticism of imaginary clubs, associations, and similar groups.]
- BT Societies

IMAGINARY WARS AND BATTLES [Here are entered nonfiction works on the history

and criticism of imaginary wars and battles.]
- BT Battles
  War stories
- **IMMIGRANTS—UNITED STATES**
  - NT Americanization
- Immigrants, Illegal
  - USE Aliens, Illegal
- **IMPERSONATING AN OFFICER** [Here are entered works that deal with imposture of a public official as a legal charge. Works that deal with the trial of someone accused of this charge are entered under *Trials (Impostors and imposture)*.]
  - BT False personation [The legal charge of imposture]
    Impersonation
    Impostors and imposture
  - RT Double identity
    Mistaken identity
    Trials (Impostors and imposture)
- **IMPERSONATION** [Here are entered works that deal with assuming the personality, behavior, or appearance of someone for other than deceitful intent. Works that deal with assuming an identity with the intent to deceive are entered under *Impostors and imposture*. Works that deal with imposture as a legal charge are entered under *False personation*. Works that deal with imposture of a public official as a legal charge are entered under *Impersonating an officer*. Works dealing with who one is or is known as are entered under *Identity*. Works dealing with someone who has two separate identities, each of his own invention, are entered under *Double identity*. Works dealing with persons who are innocently mistaken for someone else are entered under *Mistaken identity*.]
  - UF Disguise
  - BT Identity
    Impostors and imposture
  - RT Double identity\
    Masquerades
    Mistaken identity\
  - NT False personation
    Impersonating an officer
- **IMPOSTORS AND IMPOSTURE** [Here are entered works that deal with assuming an identity with the intent to deceive. Works that deal with assuming the personality, behavior, or appearance of someone for other than deceitful intent are entered under *Impersonation*. Works that deal with imposture as a legal charge are entered under *False personation*. Works that deal with imposture of a public official as a legal charge are entered under *Impersonating an officer*. Works that deal with trials of someone accused of either false personation or impersonating an officer are entered under *Trials (Impostors and imposture)*. Works dealing with who one is or is known as are entered under *Identity*. Works dealing with someone who has two separate identities, each of his own invention, are entered under *Double identity*. Works dealing with persons who are innocently mistaken for someone else are entered under *Mistaken identity*.]
  - UF Disguise
  - BT Identity
  - RT Double identity\
    Masquerades
    Mistaken identity\
    Practical jokes
  - NT Changelings\
    False personation
    Impersonating an officer
    Impersonation
    Trials (Impostors and imposture)
- **IMPROBABLE FICTION** [Here are entered works that are essentially realistic, but incorporate some extremely unlikely events, yet fall outside the conventions of readily identifiable genres such as Fantastic fiction, Science fiction, etc. Works dealing with nonexistent, incredible, or unreal worlds, characters, and physical principles are entered under *Fantastic fiction*. Works of fantasy that are centered upon fairies are entered under *Fairy tales*. Works of fantasy that deal with possible although not necessarily probable events and are based upon scientific principles approximately as we know them are entered under *Science fiction*. Works that invent a new cosmology, new scientific principles, or new laws of nature and are a blending of science fiction and fantastic fiction are entered under *Science fantasy*. Works of

prose fiction characterized by bragging and exaggeration of the truth are entered under *Tall tales*.]
   UF Exaggeration
   BT Fiction
   RT Allegories
         Experimental fiction
         Fairy tales
         Fantastic fiction
         Science fantasy \
         Science fiction
         Tall tales
In-laws
   USE Brothers-in-law \
          Daughters-in-law
          Fathers-in-law
          Mothers-in-law
          Sisters-in-law \
          Sons-in-law \
INCEST
   RT Problem families
INDIA
   NT East Indians [Persons from India]
        Indic fiction [Fiction written by persons from India]
INDIA—HISTORY—BRITISH OCCUPATION, 1765-1947
   BT British—India
Indian fiction
   USE American fiction—Indian authors
          Canadian fiction—Indian authors \
          Indian literature
          Indic fiction [Written by authors from India]
INDIAN LITERATURE [Here are entered collections of works written by natives of the Western Hemisphere in Indian languages. Collections of fiction written by American Indians are entered under *American fiction—Indian authors*. Works written by persons from India are entered under *Indic fiction*.]
   UF Indian fiction
        North American Indian fiction
   RT American fiction—Indian authors
        Indic fiction
INDIANS OF CENTRAL AMERICA
   UF Central American Indians
INDIANS OF MEXICO
   UF Mexican Indians
        Mexico—Indians
INDIANS OF NORTH AMERICA—CAPTIVITIES
     [Here are entered works dealing with persons captured by Indians of North America.]
   RT Kidnapping
INDIANS OF NORTH AMERICA—MIXED BLOODS
   UF Halfbreeds
INDIANS OF NORTH AMERICA—RELATIONS WITH WHITES \
INDIANS OF NORTH AMERICA AS DETECTIVES \
   UF North American Indian detectives
INDIANS OF SOUTH AMERICA
   UF South American Indians
INDIC FICTION [Here are entered works of fiction written in Indic languages by persons from India.]
   UF Indian fiction
   BT India
   RT East Indians [Persons from India]
        Indian literature [Works of literature written by natives of the Western Hemisphere]
INDIC FICTION (ENGLISH) [Here are entered works of fiction written in English by persons from India.]
INDONESIA
   UF Netherlands East Indies
Industrial conditions
   USE Industrial relations
          Work environment
INDUSTRIAL RELATIONS
   UF Industrial conditions
   RT Work environment
INDUSTRIAL WORKERS OF THE WORLD
   UF I.W.W.
        Wobblies
   BT Trade-unions
INDUSTRIALISTS
   RT Capitalists and financiers
INDUSTRIALIZATION
   RT Working class
INFANTICIDE [Here are entered works dealing with the murder of a child.]
   BT Murder
INFANTICIDE IN LITERATURE [Here are entered nonfiction works on the history and criticism of infanticide as portrayed in literature.]
INFERTILITY, FEMALE
   RT Fertilization in vitro, Human
        Surrogate mothers
INFORMERS
   UF Traitors
   BT Betrayal \
INHERITANCE AND SUCCESSION
   UF Heiresses

INQUISITION
- **BT** Catholic Church

Insane asylums
- **USE** Psychiatric hospitals

INSANE, CRIMINAL AND DANGEROUS
- **UF** Criminally insane
  Mentally ill, Criminal and dangerous
  Psychopaths
- **BT** Mentally ill

Insect study
- **USE** Entomology

Instructors
- **USE** Teachers

INSURANCE INVESTIGATORS AS DETECTIVES \

INTELLECTUAL LIFE [Here are entered works dealing generally with learning and scholarship, the arts, literature, etc. Works dealing with the academic process of thorough study, investigation, and interpretation are entered under *Learning and scholarship*. Works dealing with persons who through long and systematic study have acquired mastery of an academic discipline together with investigative and interpretive skills are entered under *Scholars*. Works about men or women of literature and letters are entered under *Litterateurs*.]
- **RT** Books
- **NT** Authors
  College students
  College teachers
  Graduate students
  Learning and scholarship
  Scholars

INTERFAITH LOVE AFFAIRS \
- **UF** Love affairs, Interfaith

International intrigue
- **USE** Adventure stories
  Spy stories
  Terrorism
  Thrillers \
  World politics
- **SA** Names of particular countries, and headings such as *United States—Foreign relations—Soviet Union*; *Russians—United States* [for Russians in the United States], etc.

INTERPERSONAL RELATIONS [Here are entered works dealing with the broad concept of relations with others. Works dealing with what it means to be friends or with the concept of friendship are entered under *Friendship*. Works dealing specifically with relations between women or girls are entered under *Female-female relationships* \. Works dealing specifically with relations between men or boys are entered under *Male-male relationships* \. Works dealing specifically with relations between men and women or girls and boys are entered under *Female-male relationships* \.]
- **NT** Female-female relationships \
  Female-male relationships \
  Friendship
  Male-male relationships \

INTERPLANETARY VOYAGES [Here are entered general works and imaginary accounts dealing with travel to other planets. Works dealing with travel to the stars are entered under *Interstellar travel*. Works dealing with the physics and technical aspects of flight beyond the earth's atmosphere are entered under *Space flight*.]
- **BT** Science fiction
  Space flight
- **RT** Interstellar travel

INTERRACIAL MARRIAGE
- **UF** Marriage, Mixed race
  Mixed race marriage
  Racial intermarriage
- **BT** Blacks
  Race relations
- **RT** Miscegenation

INTERSTELLAR TRAVEL [Here are entered general works and imaginary accounts dealing with travel to the stars. Works dealing with travel to the planets are entered under *Interplanetary voyages*. Works dealing with the physics and technical aspects of flight beyond the earth's atmosphere are entered under *Space flight*.]
- **BT** Science fiction
  Space flight
- **RT** Interplanetary voyages

Intrigue
- **USE** Conspiracies
  Courts and courtiers
  Political fiction
  Sabotage
  Spy stories
  Terrorism
  Thrillers \
  World politics

INVALIDS
- RT Nursing homes
- Physically handicapped

INVECTIVE [Here are entered works about the use of abuse to expose or discredit human vice or folly. Works that use humor for these purposes with an eye toward improvement are entered under *Satirical fiction*. Works characterized by the use of obscene or foul language are entered under *Linguistically profane fiction*.]
- RT Linguistically profane fiction\
- Satirical fiction\
- Swearing

INVENTORS
- RT Scientists

IOWA
- NT Des Moines (Iowa)

IRAN
- UF Persia

IRANIAN FICTION [Here are entered works written by Iranians regardless of the language in which it was written. Works written in the Persian language are entered under *Persian fiction*.]
- RT Persian fiction

IRELAND [If a place is located in Ireland, add the identifier *(Ireland)*; see 23.4D2 in *AACR2R* for further information.
- RT Great Britain
- NT Clare (Ireland) [For County Clare]
- Dublin (Ireland)
- Kerry (Ireland) [For County Kerry]
- Northern Ireland
- Orangemen
- Scots-Irish
- Ulster (Northern Ireland and Ireland)

IRISH [Here are entered works dealing with persons from Ireland as well as persons from Northern Ireland.]
- BT British
- Northern Ireland
- Scots-Irish [Scottish settlers in Northern Ireland and their descendants]

IRISH—ENGLAND

IRISH—UNITED STATES [Here are entered works dealing with Irish visiting or living in the United States.]
- NT Irish Americans

IRISH AMERICANS [Here are entered works dealing with Americans of Irish ancestry.]
- BT Irish—United States

Irish dialect fiction
- USE Dialect fiction—Irish\

IRISH FICTION [Here are entered works written in the Irish or English languages by Irish authors. Works written in English by Irish authors or collections of works written exclusively in English by Irish authors are also entered under *English fiction—Irish authors*.]
- UF Northern Irish fiction
- RT English fiction—Irish authors

IRISH REPUBLICAN ARMY [An underground group formed about 1918; it is not the official army of the Republic of Ireland.]
- UF I.R.A.
- RT Fenians [A 19th-century group]
- Terrorism

ISLAM

ISLAMIC STORIES [Here are entered novels and stories on Islamic topics or themes.]
- BT Fiction
- Religious fiction

ISLAMIC STORIES, ARABIC (Indonesian, etc.) [Here are entered Islamic stories by Arabic (Indonesian, etc.) authors.]

ISLANDS [Here are entered works on islands in general or on unspecified islands. Works on specific islands or island groups are entered under those names, such as *New Zealand*; *Islands of the Pacific*, etc.]

ISLANDS OF THE CARIBBEAN
- BT Caribbean Sea

ISLANDS OF THE MEDITERRANEAN
- BT Mediterranean Sea

ISLANDS OF THE PACIFIC
- BT Pacific Ocean

ISLE OF MAN [If a place is located on the Isle of Man, use *(Isle of Man)* as an identifier, for example *Ramsey (Isle of Man)*. See 23.4D2 in *AACR2R* for further information.]
- UF Man, Isle of
- BT Great Britain
- RT England

ISLE OF WIGHT (ENGLAND)
- UF Wight, Isle of
- BT England

ISRAEL
- RT Jerusalem

ISRAEL-ARAB CONFLICTS
- RT Jewish-Arab relations

Israel—Collective settlements
- USE Kibbutzim

ISRAELI FICTION [Here is entered fiction produced by Israelis in Hebrew or in several languages collectively. Fiction originally written in the Hebrew language by non-Israelis is entered under *Hebrew fiction*. Fiction originally produced in the Yiddish language is entered under *Yiddish fiction*. Collections of fiction produced by Jews of an unspecified nationality and written in an unspecified language are entered under *Jewish fiction*. Individual works of fiction produced by Jews are entered under the fiction for their nationality.]
- RT Hebrew fiction
  Jewish fiction
  Yiddish fiction

ITALIAN AMERICANS [Here are entered works dealing with Americans of Italian ancestry.]
- BT Italians—United States

ITALIAN FICTION

ITALIANS
- NT Romans [Use only for Romans up to 476 A.D. Works dealing with Romans after that time are entered under *Italians*.]

ITALIANS—UNITED STATES [Here are entered works dealing with Italians visiting or living in the United States.]
- NT Italian Americans

ITALY [Here are entered works dealing with Italy, including the Roman empire. Works dealing with the Roman empire to 476 A.D. are entered under *Rome*. Works dealing with the city of Rome since 476 A.D. are entered under *Rome (Italy)*.]
- NT Florence (Italy)
  Rome
  Rome (Italy)
  Sicily (Italy)

ITALY—HISTORY—TO 476 [Here are entered works dealing with the historical events in Italy in Roman and pre-Roman times. Works dealing only with historical events of the Roman empire are entered under *Rome—History*.]
- NT Rome—History

ITALY—HISTORY—15TH CENTURY
- BT Renaissance

ITALY—HISTORY—16TH CENTURY
- BT Renaissance

ITALY—NOBILITY

Ivorian fiction
- USE Ivory Coast fiction

IVORY COAST FICTION
- UF Ivorian fiction

JACKSON (MISS.)
- BT Mississippi

JACOBITES [Here are entered works dealing with partisans of James II, King of Great Britain from 1685 to 1688, or of the Stuarts after the revolution of 1688.]

JADE
- RT Jewelry

JAMAICA

JAPAN
- NT Samurai [Warriors]
  Yakuza [Organized crime]

JAPANESE—UNITED STATES [Here are entered works dealing with Japanese visiting or living in the United States.]
- NT Japanese Americans

JAPANESE AMERICANS [Here are entered works dealing with Americans of Japanese ancestry.]
- BT Japanese—United States

JAPANESE AMERICANS—EVACUATION AND RELOCATION, 1942-1945
- UF World War, 1939-1945—Japanese internment
- BT World War, 1939-1945—Concentration camps

JAPANESE FICTION

JAPANESE TEA CEREMONY
- BT Rites and ceremonies—Japan

JAZZ MUSIC
- UF Music, Jazz
- BT Musical fiction

JEALOUSY [Here are entered works dealing with intolerance of a rival for what one regards as one's own. Works dealing with coveting something which belongs to another are entered under *Envy*.]
- RT Envy

JERUSALEM
- BT Palestine
- RT Israel

JESUITS
   BT Catholic Church
JESUITS IN LITERATURE [Here are entered nonfiction works on the history and criticism of the Jesuits as portrayed in literature.]
JESUS CHRIST
   BT Bible—History of Biblical events
JESUS CHRIST IN FICTION, DRAMA, POETRY, ETC. [Here are entered nonfiction works on the history and criticism of Jesus Christ as portrayed in literature.]
JEWELRY
   UF Lockets
   NT Diamonds
        Emeralds
        Jade
        Opals
        Pearls
Jewish Americans
   USE Jews, American
JEWISH-ARAB RELATIONS
   RT Israel-Arab conflicts
Jewish-Christian relations
   USE Christianity and other religions—Judaism *and* Judaism—Relations—Christianity
**JEWISH DETECTIVES **
   BT Jews
JEWISH FICTION [Here are entered collections of fiction produced by Jews of an unspecified nationality and in an unspecified language. Works that deal with Jewish religious topics and themes are entered under *Jewish religious fiction*. Fiction originally written in the Hebrew language by non-Israelis authors is entered under *Hebrew fiction*. Fiction originally produced in the Yiddish language is entered under *Yiddish fiction*. Fiction produced by Israelis in Hebrew or several languages collectively is entered under *Israeli fiction*. Individual works of fiction produced by Jews is entered under the fiction of their nationality.]
   RT Hebrew fiction
        Israeli fiction
        Yiddish fiction
   NT Jewish religious fiction
JEWISH RELIGIOUS EDUCATION
   UF Yeshiva

JEWISH RELIGIOUS FICTION [Here are entered works dealing with Jewish religious topics and themes.]
   BT Fiction
        Jewish fiction
        Jewish way of life
        Religious fiction
JEWISH WAY OF LIFE
   BT Jews
   NT Jewish religious fiction
JEWS
   NT Antisemitism
        Holocaust, Jewish (1939-1945)
        Jewish detectives \
        Jewish way of life
        Judaism
        Rabbis
        Synagogues
Jews—Ghettos
   USE Jews—Segregation
JEWS—SEGREGATION
   UF Jews—Ghettos
JEWS—UNITED STATES [Here are entered works dealing with Jews who are living or visiting in the United States. Works dealing with Jews who are citizens of the United States are entered under *Jews, American*. Works dealing with Jewish nationals of specific countries are entered under that nationality, for example, *Israelis—United States*.]
   NT Jews, American
JEWS, AMERICAN [Here are entered works dealing with Jews who are citizens of the United States. Works dealing with Jews who are living or visiting in the United States are entered under *Jews—United States*.]
   UF Jewish Americans
   BT Jews—United States
JEWS, GERMAN
Jews, Hasidic
   USE Hasidim
JEWS, POLISH
JEWS, RUSSIAN
JINN
   UF Djinn
        Genies
JOHOR
   BT Malaysia
JOURNALISTS
   BT Newspapers
   NT Critics
        Reporters and reporting

JOURNALISTS AS DETECTIVES \
  UF Reporters as detectives \
  RT Publishers as detectives \
  NT Television journalists as detectives \
JUDAISM
  BT Jews
  NT Antisemitism
       Rabbis
JUDAISM—RELATIONS—CHRISTIANITY [Note that if this heading is used, the parallel heading *Christianity and other religions—Judaism* must also be used.]
  UF Christian-Jewish relations
       Jewish-Christian relations
  BT Religions—Relations
  RT Christianity and other religions—Judaism
JUDGES
  USE Legal stories
JUDO
  BT Martial arts fiction
Juice loans
  USE Usury
JUNIOR HIGH SCHOOLS [Here are entered works dealing with schools teaching grades between elementary and high school, generally including, but not necessarily confined to the 7th, 8th, and 9th grades. Works dealing with schools teaching grades above third but below junior high school level, generally including but not necessarily confined to 4th, 5th, and 6th grades are entered under *Middle schools*.]
  BT Schools
  RT High schools
  NT Middle schools
JURY—CORRUPT PRACTICES
  UF Corruption of juries
       Jury tampering
Jury tampering
  USE Jury—Corrupt practices
JUVENILE DELINQUENTS
  BT Children
       Criminals
       Social problems
       Teenagers
  RT Problem children
       Reformatories
       Runaway children
       Runaway teenagers

K.G.B.
  USE Soviet Union. Komitet gosudarstvennoĭ bezopastnosti
KANSAS
  NT Topeka (Kan.)
KANSAS CITY (MO.)
  BT Missouri
KARATE
  BT Martial arts fiction
KAZAKH S.S.R.
  BT Soviet Union
  NT Alma-Ata (Kazakh S.S.R.)
KEDAH
  BT Malaysia
KELANTAN
  BT Malaysia
KENTUCKY
  NT Louisville (Ky.)
KERRY (IRELAND)
  UF County Kerry (Ireland)
  BT Ireland
KEY WEST (FLA.)
  BT Florida
KIBBUTZIM
  UF Israel—Collective settlements
KIDNAPPING [Here are entered works dealing with a person seized and detained against his or her will or that of his or her legal guardian. Works dealing with a female, usually below the age of consent, who is carried off with or without her permission for purposes of marriage, seduction, or rape are entered under *Abduction*.]
  BT Crime
       Missing persons
  RT Abduction
       Disappeared persons [for political kidnappings or killings]
       Hostages
       Indians of North America—Captivities
       Thrillers \
  NT Changelings \
KIEV (UKRAINE)
  BT Ukraine
King Arthur
  USE Arthurian romances
KINGS AND RULERS
  RT Nobility
       Princes
  SA subdivisions *Kings and rulers* and *Queens* under names of countries, cities, etc., and ethnic groups, for example, *Great Britain—Kings and*

rulers; Great Britain—Queens; Zulu (African people)—Kings and rulers

KIRGIZ S.S.R.
  BT Soviet Union
  NT Frunze (Kirgiz S.S.R.)

KISHINEV (MOLDAVIAN S.S.R.)
  BT Moldavian S.S.R.

KLEPTOMANIA
  RT Thieves

KLONDIKE RIVER VALLEY (YUKON)
  BT Yukon Territory

KNIGHTS AND KNIGHTHOOD [Here are entered works dealing with knights and knighthood. Works dealing with the elaborate medieval system of manners and morals and in which knights appear are entered under *Chivalry*. Works of adventure produced in the Middle Ages that deal with knights, kings, or ladies in distress acting under the impulse of love, religion, or the desire for adventure are entered under *Romances*.]
  RT Aristocracy
    Chivalry
    Crusades
    Gentry
    Nobility
    Romances
    Upper classes

KNIGHTS AS DETECTIVES \
  RT Aristocrats as detectives \
    Nobles as detectives \

KOREA [Here are entered works dealing with Korea before partition in 1948 or with North and South Korea together.]

KOREA (NORTH)

KOREA (SOUTH)

KOREAN WAR, 1950-1953

KOREAN WAR, 1950-1953—VETERANS

Kris Kringle
  USE Santa Claus

KUALA LUMPUR (MALAYSIA)
  UF Kuala Lumpur Federal Territory

Kuala Lumpur Federal Territory
  USE Kuala Lumpur (Malaysia)

Labor and laboring classes
  USE Working class

LABOR CAMPS [Here are entered works dealing with camps for the housing of noncompulsory workers.]
  RT Forced labor

LABOR DISPUTES
  RT Factories

LABRADOR (NFLD.)
  BT Newfoundland

Land speculation
  USE Real estate investment

LANDSLIDES
  BT Natural disasters

LAPLAND
  RT Finland
    Norway
    Soviet Union
    Sweden

LARCENY [Here are entered works dealing with stealing as a crime. Works dealing with the ethical and psychological aspects of theft are entered under *Stealing*. Works dealing with taking another's property using violence or the threat of violence are entered under *Robbery*. Works dealing with persons who commit robbery are entered under *Brigands and robbers*. Works dealing with robbery committed on the street and involving a beating or other physical assault are entered under *Mugging*. Works dealing with persons who commit theft or burglary are entered under *Thieves*. Works dealing with breaking and entering for the purpose of theft or robbery are entered under *Burglary*. Works dealing with persons who steal, profiteer, or kill, especially in a merciless manner, are entered under *Outlaws*.]
  UF Capers (Criminal)
  RT Brigands and robbers
    Burglary
    Mugging
    Outlaws
    Robbery
    Stealing
    Thieves
    Thrillers \

LAS VEGAS (NEV.)
  BT Nevada

LATIN AMERICA
  SA names of individual Latin American countries
  NT Central America

Mexico
South America
LATVIA
  BT Soviet Union
  NT Riga (Latvia)
LAW IN LITERATURE [Here are entered works of nonfiction on the history and criticism of law as portrayed in literature.]
LAWYERS AS DETECTIVES\
  RT District attorneys as detectives\
LEARNING AND SCHOLARSHIP [Here are entered works dealing with the academic process of thorough study, investigation, and interpretation. Works dealing generally with learning and scholarship, the arts, literature, etc., are entered under *Intellectual life*. Works dealing with persons who through long and systematic study have acquired mastery of an academic discipline together with investigative and interpretive skills are entered under *Scholars*.]
  BT Intellectual life
  RT College students
      College teachers
      Graduate students
  NT Scholars
LEGAL STORIES [Here are entered novels and stories that deal with the law, lawyers, judges, etc.]
  UF Attorneys general
      Courtroom fiction
      Judges
      Public prosecutors
  BT Fiction
  NT Trials
LEGENDS [Here are entered works of traditional narrative that are shorter than epics but still purport to have some basis in reality. Legends of American Indian groups are entered under the form *Aztecs—Legends*, etc. For further information, see H 1627 in LC's *Subject Cataloging Manual*. Works of traditional narrative that are shorter than epics but deal more with the supernatural and less with the historical are entered under *Mythology*. Works that deal with shorter narratives passed on by word of mouth about common or illiterate people are entered under *Folk literature*. Collections of traditional narratives that are for the most part fictitious and are told primarily for entertainment are entered under *Tales*. Broad and lengthy works that recount the deeds of a legendary or historical hero are entered under *Epic literature*.]
  BT Fiction
  RT Epic literature
      Folk literature
      Monsters
      Mythology
      Tales
  NT Arthurian romances
      Giants
      Grail
      Quests\
      Sagas
      Wandering Jew
LEGENDS, BUDDHIST (Christian, etc.) [Here are entered collections of Buddhist (Christian, etc.) legends. This form is only used with religions.]
LEGISLATORS—UNITED STATES
  UF United States congressmen
      United States senators
  BT United States. Congress. House
      United States. Congress. Senate
LEGISLATORS AS DETECTIVES—UNITED STATES\
  UF Congressmen as detectives
      Senators as detectives
LEISURE CLASS [Here are entered works dealing with persons who are so wealthy that they do not work.]
  BT Upper classes
  RT Millionaires
      Wealth
LESBIAN COUPLES
  UF Homosexual love affairs
      Love affairs, Homosexual
      Love affairs, Lesbian
  BT Female-female relationships\
LESBIAN DETECTIVES\
  BT Women detectives
LESBIAN FICTION\ [Here are entered works by lesbian authors dealing with lesbian topics and themes.]
  BT Fiction
      Gay fiction\
      Lesbians
LESBIANS
  BT Gays
  RT Bisexuality
  NT Lesbian fiction\
LETTERS [Here are entered works which are about letters (epistles). Works in

which the author narrates a significant part of the story in letter format are entered under *Epistolary fiction.* Works of nonfiction on the history and criticism of imaginary letters are entered under *Imaginary letters.* Poetic narratives in epistolary form that express the sentiments between heroes or heroines and their wives or sweethearts are entered under *Heroid.*]
- NT Epistolary fiction
  Heroid
  Imaginary letters

Letters—Stories told in letter form
- USE Epistolary fiction

LETTERS IN LITERATURE [Here are entered nonfiction works on the history and criticism of letters as represented in literature.]

Libertines
- USE Degeneration
  Hedonism
  Picaresque fiction\
  Prodigals

LIBRARIANS AS DETECTIVES\

LIBRARIES [Here are entered works dealing with either real libraries or libraries imagined by the author. Works of nonfiction on the history and criticism of imaginary books and libraries are entered under *Imaginary books and libraries.*]
- NT Imaginary books and libraries

Lies
- USE Mythomania
  Truthfulness and falsehood

LIFE CARE COMMUNITIES [Here are entered works dealing with planned residential developments for the aged that also provide meal service, medical care, etc. Works that deal with institutions that provide housing and general care for the convalescent are entered under *Rest homes.* Works that deal with institutions that provide housing and general care for the aged are entered under *Old age homes.* Works dealing with private institutions that provide long-term personal and nursing care to the aged or chronically ill are entered under *Nursing homes.* Works that deal with institutions that provide long-term care and therapy together with a regimen such as diet or exercise are entered under *Sanatoriums.* Works dealing with institutions that give the sick and injured medical and surgical care are entered under *Hospitals.*]
- RT Hospitals
  Nurses
  Nursing homes
  Old age homes
  Physicians
  Rest homes
  Sanatoriums

LIFE ON OTHER PLANETS [Here are entered works dealing with life forms on other planets that are not of earthly origin. Works dealing with beings on earth or in a predominantly human society that are from other planets are entered under *Extraterrestrial beings\.* Works dealing with communities established by man on planets other than Earth are entered under *Space colonies.* Works dealing with manned installations existing for specific functions, such as servicing space ships, etc., in orbit around natural extraterrestrial bodies or the earth are entered under *Space stations.* Works dealing with manned installations existing for specific functions, such as servicing space ships, etc., on natural extraterrestrial bodies are entered under *Extraterrestrial bases.*]
- UF Civilizations in space
  Galactic empires
  Imaginary planets
  Martians
  Other worlds
  Space civilizations
- BT Outer space
- RT Extraterrestrial bases
  Extraterrestrial beings\
  Parallel worlds\
  Science fiction
  Space colonies
  Space stations

Life, Philosophy of
- USE Philosophical fiction\

LIGHT FICTION\ [Here are entered works of fiction that have no serious intent and are written solely for purposes of amusement. Prefer a narrower term that implies a work written for entertainment value.]
- BT Fiction

Melodramatic fiction \
  NT Detective and mystery stories
       Fantastic fiction
       Horror tales
       Humorous stories
       Love stories
       Science fiction
       Thrillers \
       Western stories
Light houses
  USE Lighthouses
LIGHTHOUSES
  UF Light houses
Lines (Queues)
  USE Queues \
LINGUISTICALLY PROFANE FICTION \ [Here are entered works characterized by the use of foul or obscene language. Works about foul or obscene language are entered under *Swearing*.]
  UF Explicit language in fiction
       Profanity in fiction
  BT Fiction
  RT Invective
       Swearing
  NT Detective and mystery stories, Hardboiled \
Liquor traffic
  USE Distilling, Illicit
       Prohibition
LIQUORS
  UF Hard liquor
LISBON (PORTUGAL)
  BT Portugal
LITERACY
  RT Books
       Reading
LITERARY FICTION \ [Here are entered works of serious intent written in a literary style. Prefer a narrower term that implies literary treatment.]
  UF Serious fiction
  BT Fiction
  RT Experimental fiction
       Good and evil
       Philosophical fiction \
Literary life
  USE Authors
       Books
       Litterateurs
       Publishers and publishing
LITHUANIA
  BT Soviet Union
  NT Vilnius (Lithuania)

LITTERATEURS [Here are entered works on men and women of letters, literature, or general literary pursuits. Works dealing with writers are entered under *Authors*.]
  UF Literary life
  RT Authors
LITTLE ROCK (ARK.)
  BT Arkansas
LIVRES Á CLEF [Here are entered works in which real people and real events have been disguised for literary purposes. Works of factual representation having the objective quality and authority of the real event are listed under *Nonfiction novels* \. Works in which people who actually exist or existed appear in minor roles are entered under *Real people* \. Works dealing loosely with actual occurrences are entered under *Real events* \. Works dealing predominately with an actual person are entered under *Biographical fiction*. Works written by the author about his or her own life are entered under *Autobiographical fiction*, even if the main character is given another name.]
  UF Documentary fiction
  BT Fiction
  RT Autobiographical fiction
       Biographical fiction
       Nonfiction novels \
       Real events \
       Real people \
LJUBLJANA (SLOVENIA)
  BT Slovenia
Loan sharks
  USE Usury
LOBBYISTS
  BT Political fiction
Locked room mysteries
  USE Detective and mystery stories, Locked room \
Lockets
  USE Jewelry
LODGING-HOUSES
  UF Rooming houses
  RT Apartment houses
       Hotels, taverns, etc. [Includes boarding houses]
LONDON (ENGLAND)
  BT England
LONDON SUBURBAN AREA (ENGLAND)

LONELINESS [Here are entered works dealing with a lack of intimate association with others and the resultant sadness therefrom. Works dealing with a situation where there are no others of one's kind with whom to associate or to a mental state in which by wish or compulsion one is cut off from normal contacts with family, friends, colleagues, or neighbors are entered under *Solitude*. Works dealing with a state of society in which normative standards of conduct and belief have weakened or disappeared, or with a similar condition in an individual, commonly characterized by personal disorientation, anxiety, and isolation are entered under *Anomy*. Works dealing with detachment from others, either because of one's own wish or from causes beyond one's control, are entered under *Social isolation*. Works dealing with estrangement and loss or lack of adjustment between an individual and his or her social or intellectual environment are entered under *Alienation (Social psychology)*.]
   RT Alienation (Social psychology)
       Anomy
       Social isolation
       Solitude
LONG ISLAND (N.Y.)
   UF Hamptons
   BT New York Suburban Area
LONGEVITY
   RT Old age
       Rejuvenation
LOS ANGELES (CALIF.)
   BT California
   NT Hollywood (Los Angeles, Calif.)
LOS ANGELES SUBURBAN AREA (CALIF.)
   NT Beverly Hills (Calif.)
Loss of memory
   USE Amnesia
LOTTERIES [Here are entered works dealing with a drawing of lots in which prizes are distributed to the winners. Works dealing with contests in which the entire prize goes to a single winner are entered under *Sweepstakes*.]
   UF Numbers racket
   RT Sweepstakes
LOUISIANA
   RT Cajuns
   NT New Orleans (La.)
LOUISVILLE (KY.)
   BT Kentucky
LOVE [Here are entered works dealing with love in a general or abstract sense. Works dealing with love between two persons of the opposite sex that does not involve libidinal attraction or with the love of the beautiful or ideal are entered under *Platonic love*. Works dealing with love affairs as part of a larger work dealing equally or mainly with other themes or topics are entered under *Love affairs*. Works whose prime purpose for being is to detail the specifics of a love affair are entered under *Love stories*.]
   NT Love affairs\
       Love stories
       Platonic love
LOVE AFFAIRS [Here are entered works that deal with love affairs, but only as part of a larger work that deals equally or mainly with other themes or topics. Works that deal primarily with romantic love are entered under *Love stories*. Love affairs dealing with the period leading up to formal engagement for marriage are entered under *Courtship*. Works dealing with love affairs in which one or both parties are married to someone else are entered under *Adultery*. Works dealing with love affairs in which three or more people are romantically involved but for at least one person, the love is not returned are entered under *Love triangles*. Works dealing with love in a general or abstract sense are entered under *Love*.]
   UF Romantic love
   BT Love
   RT Adultery
       Courtship
       Love stories
   NT Love triangles\
Love affairs, Homosexual
   USE Gay male couples
        Lesbian couples
Love affairs, Interfaith
   USE Interfaith love affairs\
Love affairs, Lesbian
   USE Lesbian couples
LOVE AFFAIRS, MAY-DECEMBER [Here are entered works dealing with love affairs

in which one partner is much older than the other.]
LOVE STORIES [Here are entered novels and stories dealing primarily with romantic love. Works that deal with romantic love, but only as part of a larger work are entered under *Love affairs*\. Love affairs dealing with the period leading up to formal engagement for marriage are entered under *Courtship*. Works dealing with love affairs in which one or both parties are married to someone else are entered under *Adultery*. Works dealing with love in a general or abstract sense are entered under *Love*.]
- UF Romance
  Romantic love
- BT Female-male relationships\
  Fiction
  Light fiction\
  Love
- RT Adultery
  Betrothal
  Courtship
  Love affairs\
  Melodramatic fiction\
  Romantic suspense fiction\

LOVE STORIES, AMERICAN (Canadian, etc.) [Here are entered collections of love stories by American (Canadian, etc.) authors.]

LOVE STORIES, GEORGIAN\ [Here are entered works of love fiction set in Georgian Great Britain in the years 1714-1830. It does not apply to the reign of King George V, from 1919 to 1936.]
- UF England, Georgian
  Georgian England
- BT Great Britain—History—George I, 1714-1727 [and similar headings for the other King Georges]
  Great Britain—History, 1714-1837
  Love stories, Historical\
- NT Love stories, Regency\

LOVE STORIES, HISTORICAL\ [Here are entered works of love fiction set in historical times. Also use the historical period if known, for example, *Great Britain—History—Wars of the Roses, 1455-1485*.]
- UF Bodice rippers
  Historical romance fiction
- BT Historical fiction

- NT Love stories, Georgian\
  Love stories, Regency\

LOVE STORIES, REGENCY\ [Here are entered works of love fiction set in Great Britain in the regency period for King George III, 1811-1820.]
- UF England, Regency
  Regency England
  Regency romance
- BT Great Britain—History—George III, 1760-1820
  Love stories, Georgian\
  Love stories, Historical\
- RT Upper classes

LOVE TRIANGLES\ [Here are entered works dealing with love affairs in which three or more people are romantically involved but for at least one person, the love is not returned.]
- BT Love affairs\

Lower classes
  USE Working class
LOWLANDS (SCOTLAND)
  BT Scotland)
Luck
  USE Fortune
Luftwaffe
  USE Germany. Luftwaffe
LYNCHING [Here are entered works dealing with unlawful hanging.]
  BT Hanging
    Murder
  RT Execution and executioners
LYRICISTS
  BT Musical fiction
    Musicians

M.I. 5
  USE Great Britain. MI5
M.I. 6
  USE Great Britain. MI6
MACEDONIA (REPUBLIC)
  BT Yugoslavia
  NT Skopje (Macedonia)
MAFIA
  UF Cosa Nostra
    Mobsters
Mages
  USE Wizards
MAGIC [Here are entered works dealing with the use of charms and spells and what are believed to be supernatural powers.

68   MAGIC REALISM (LITERATURE)

   Works dealing with entertainment that uses tricks to simulate the supernatural are entered under *Conjuring*.]
 RT Conjuring
   Fantastic fiction, Sword and sorcery\
   Supernatural
   Voodooism
   Witchcraft
   Wizards
MAGIC REALISM (LITERATURE) [Here are entered nonfiction works of history and criticism on magic realism in literature.]
MAGIC REALISTIC FICTION\ [Here are entered works of fiction that use magic, dream, and fantasy combined with realistic elements and that have an emphasis on freshness of language and spontaneity. Works of conventional style and technique that juxtapose objects, characters, and actions usually considered incongruous are entered under *Surrealistic fiction*\.]
 BT Experimental fiction
   Fiction
 RT Absurdist fiction\
   Surrealistic fiction\
   Symbolic fiction\
MAGICIANS [Here are entered works dealing with people who use charms and spells and are believed to have supernatural powers as well as works dealing with conjurers who perform tricks. Works dealing with a man who practices witchcraft or who is exceptionally skilled in the occult arts or who can achieve the seemingly impossible are entered under *Wizards*.]
 UF Illusionists
 RT Fantastic fiction, Sword and sorcery\
   Wizards
MAGICIANS AS DETECTIVES\
MAINE
 NT Augusta (Me.)
   Portland (Me.)
MAJORCA (SPAIN)
 BT Spain
MALACCA (MALACCA) [Here are entered works dealing with the city of Malacca in the Malaysian state of Malacca.]
 BT Malacca (State)
MALACCA (STATE)
 BT Malaysia
 NT Malacca (Malacca)

Maladjusted children
 USE Problem children
MALAYSIA [Do not add any geographic identifier to the name of a Malaysian state or territory. For further information, see 23.4C in *AACR2R*. East Malaysia, located on the island of Borneo, consists of Sabah and Sarawak. West Malaysia is located on the Malay Peninsula and consists of Kuala Lumpur, Johor, Kedah, Kelantan, Malacca, Negeri Sembilan, Pahang, Pinang, Perak, Perlis, Selangor, and Terengganu.]
 RT Singapore
 NT Johor
   Kedah
   Kelantan
   Kuala Lumpur (Malaysia)
   Malacca (State)
   Negeri Sembilan
   Pahang
   Perak
   Perlis
   Pinang
   Sabah
   Sarawak
   Selangor
   Terengganu
Male-female relationships
 USE Female-male relationships\
MALE-MALE RELATIONSHIPS\ [Here are entered works dealing generally with relations between men or boys. Works dealing with what it means to be friends or with the concept of friendship are entered under *Friendship*. Works dealing with the broader concept of relations with others, whether male or female, are entered under *Interpersonal relations*.]
 UF Men, Relations between
 BT Interpersonal relations
 RT Friendship
 NT Brothers
   Fathers and sons
   Gay male couples
MALICIOUS ACCUSATION
 UF False accusation
   Frame-ups
   Unjust accusation
Man, Isle of
 USE Isle of Man
MAN, PREHISTORIC
 UF Prehistoric life

NT Cro-Magnon man
　　Neanderthals
MANCHESTER (N.H.)
　BT New Hampshire
MANHATTAN (NEW YORK, N.Y.)
　BT New York (N.Y.)
　RT Wall Street [For financial activities only]
　NT Central Park (New York, N.Y.)
Manhood
　USE Masculinity (Philosophy)
　　Masculinity (Psychology)
　　Maturation (Psychology)
Manhunts
　USE Escapes
　　Fugitives from justice
MANILA (PHILIPPINES)
　BT Philippines
MANITOBA
　BT Canada
　NT Winnipeg (Man.)
MANNED UNDERSEA RESEARCH STATIONS
　RT Underwater colonies
MARATHON RUNNING
　RT Track-athletics
MARINES
　RT Soldiers
　NT Great Britain. Royal Marines
　　United States. Marine Corps
**MARITICIDE ** [Here are entered works dealing with the murder of a husband by his wife. Works dealing with the murder of a wife by her husband are entered under *Uxoricide*.]
　BT Crime passionel [Killing for sexual motives]
　　Husbands
　　Murder [Killing with malice aforethought]
　　Wives
　RT Uxoricide
MARITIME PROVINCES
　BT Canada
MARRIAGE [Here are entered works that deal primarily with the relationship of husband and wife. Works on the legal relations between husband and wife are entered under *Husband and wife*. Works dealing with the life of a nuclear or extended family in a single household or with several generations reacting together in the span of a single generation are entered under *Domestic fiction*.]
　BT Female-male relationships \
　RT Domestic fiction
　　Family chronicles \
　NT Husband and wife
　　Husband and wife detectives \
　　Newlyweds \
　　Polygamy
　　Problem marriages \
Marriage, Mixed race
　USE Interracial marriage
MARRIAGE BROKERAGE
　UF Matchmakers (Marriage)
Marriage problems
　USE Problem marriages \
MARSHALS [Here are entered works dealing with air marshals or field marshals in the military. Works dealing with marshals serving in American federal courts are entered under *United States marshals*. Works dealing with peace officers are entered under *Peace officers*.]
　RT Peace officers
　　United States marshals
MARTIAL ARTS FICTION [Here are entered works of fiction dealing with martial arts.]
　BT Fiction
　　Sports stories
　NT Judo
　　Karate
MARTIAL ARTS FICTION, CHINESE (Korean, etc.) [Here are entered collections of martial arts fiction by Chinese (Korean, etc.) authors.]
Martians
　USE Extraterrestrial beings \
　　Life on other planets
MARY, BLESSED VIRGIN, SAINT
　BT Bible—History of Biblical events
MARYLAND
　NT Annapolis (Md.)
　　Baltimore (Md.)
MASCULINITY (PHILOSOPHY)
　UF Manhood
MASCULINITY (PSYCHOLOGY)
　UF Manhood
MASOCHISM [Here are entered works dealing with delight or sexual gratification from having cruelty inflicted upon oneself. Works dealing with delight or sexual gratification from inflicting cru-

elty on others are entered under *Sadism*.]
  BT Cruelty
  RT Sadism

MASOCHISM IN LITERATURE [Here are entered nonfiction works on the history and criticism of masochism as represented in literature.]

MASQUERADES
  UF Costume parties
       Disguise
       Parties, Costume
  BT Entertaining
  RT Carnival [Used for Mardi Gras]
       Halloween
       Impersonation
       Impostors and imposture

MASS MURDER [Here are entered works dealing with the slaying of several people at the same time, in the same general area, by the same person or group of persons. Works involving repetitive homicides over a period of time, usually involving one victim at a time, by the same person or group of persons are entered under *Serial murders*.]
  BT Murder
  RT Serial murders

MASSACHUSETTS
  NT Berkshire Hills (Mass.)
       Boston (Mass.)
       Cambridge (Mass.)

Matchmakers (Marriage)
  USE Marriage brokerage

MATURATION (PSYCHOLOGY) [Here are entered works of fiction dealing with the developing maturity of a protagonist. This may take place in middle or old age as well as in youth. Works of nonfiction on the history and criticism of literary works dealing with maturation are entered under *Bildungsroman*.]
  UF Boy into man
       Coming of age
       Girl into woman
       Manhood
       Womanhood
  BT Boys
       Children
       Fiction
       Girls
       Teenagers
  RT Bildungsroman

MAYORS
  BT Political fiction

MEDICAL FICTION [Here are entered genre works dealing with the medical world; including doctors, nurses, and hospitals.]
  UF Doctor stories
       Hospital stories
       Nurse stories
  BT Fiction
       Medicine
  RT Hospitals
       Nurses
       Physicians

MEDICAL LITERATURE [Here are entered nonfiction works on medical writings.]

MEDICINE [Here are entered works dealing with the medical profession in general; this is primarily a nonfiction heading. Works of genre fiction dealing with the medical world are entered under *Medical fiction*. Works dealing with medicines are entered under *Drugs*.]
  RT Drugs
  NT Medical fiction\

MEDICINE IN LITERATURE [Here are entered nonfiction works on the history and criticism of the medical profession as portrayed in literature.]

Medicines
  USE Drugs

Medieval life
  USE Middle Ages—History

MEDITERRANEAN SEA
  NT Islands of the Mediterranean

MEDIUMS [Here are entered works dealing with persons who claim to have the ability to communicate with the dead. Works on persons who believe in communication with the dead are entered under *Spiritualists*.]
  BT Spiritualists

MELANCHOLY [Here are entered works dealing with a mood of dejection, discouragement, or pensiveness which is of a transitory nature and which was an external cause. Works dealing with an often prolonged disordered psychological state of low spirits and unhappiness whose cause is often internal in origin are entered under *Depression, Mental*. Works dealing with deep distress caused by or seemingly caused by bereavement are entered under *Grief*.

Works dealing with an utter loss of hope or confidence are entered under *Despair*. Works dealing with the atmosphere or effect produced by depression, melancholy, grief, or despair are entered under *Sadness*. *Sadness* can also be used as a general term for low spirits or unhappiness when there is no clear explanation indication of the cause or extent.]
- RT Depression, Mental
  Despair
  Grief
  Sadness

MELBOURNE (VIC.)
- BT Victoria

MELODRAMATIC FICTION \ [Here are entered works characterized by sensationalism, extravagant emotional appeal, and the subordination of characterization to plot. Works dealing with the production or performance of soap operas on radio or television, or the use of either as a setting are entered under *Soap operas*.]
- UF Bodice rippers
  Romance
- BT Fiction
- RT Light fiction \
  Love stories
  Soap operas

Memory loss
- USE Amnesia

MEN
- RT Boys
  Sons
- NT Fathers
  Husbands
  Teenage boys [13 to 17 years old]
  Widowers
  Young men [18 to 25 years old]

Men, Relations between
- USE Male-male relationships \

Men, Relations with women
- USE Female-male relationships \

MENTAL ILLNESS
- RT Hallucinations and illusions
  Multiple personality
  Neuroses
  Paranoia
  Personality disorders
  Psychiatrists
  Psychoanalysts
  Psychologists
- NT Mentally ill

MENTALLY HANDICAPPED
- UF Retarded people
- RT Abnormalities, Human
  Down's syndrome

MENTALLY HANDICAPPED CHILDREN
- UF Children, Mentally handicapped

MENTALLY HANDICAPPED TEENAGERS
- UF Teenagers, Mentally handicapped

MENTALLY ILL
- UF Psychopaths
  Psychotics
- BT Mental illness
- NT Insane, Criminal and dangerous

MENTALLY ILL—CARE
- NT Psychiatric hospitals

Mentally ill—Institutional care
- USE Psychiatric hospitals

Mentally ill, Criminal and dangerous
- USE Insane, Criminal and dangerous

MENTALLY ILL CHILDREN
- UF Children, Mentally ill

MENTALLY ILL IN LITERATURE [Here are entered nonfiction works on the history and criticism of the mentally ill as portrayed in literature.]

MERCENARY TROOPS [Here are entered works dealing with troops that serve a country other than their own, primarily or strictly on a wage basis. Works dealing with professional European mercenary troops in the 14th, 15th, and 16th centuries are entered under *Condottieri*. Works dealing with the mercenary troops maintained in former times by Irish chieftains are entered under *Galloglasses*. Works dealing with persons who follow a military career wherever there is the promise of adventure, profit, or pleasure are entered under *Soldiers of fortune*.]
- NT Condottieri
  Galloglasses
  Soldiers of fortune

MERCHANTS [Here are entered works dealing with persons who own or operate a retail business. Works dealing with retail stores are entered under *Stores, Retail*. Works dealing with the general business of retailing are entered under *Retail trade*.]
- UF Shopkeepers
  Traders
- BT Retail trade

    RT Stores, Retail
METEOROLOGISTS
    RT Weather
METROPOLITAN AREAS [Here are entered works dealing with a city and its surrounding suburbs generally. Works on a specific metropolitan are entered under a specific heading, for example, *New York Metropolitan Area*; *Los Angeles Metropolitan area (Calif.)*. Works dealing with a city's suburbs only are entered under a specific heading, such as *Chicago Surburban Area (Ill.)*.]
    RT Cities and towns
Mexican American fiction (English)
    USE American fiction—Mexican American authors
MEXICAN AMERICANS [Here are entered works dealing with Americans of Mexican ancestry.]
    BT Mexicans—United States
MEXICAN FICTION
Mexican Indians
    USE Indians of Mexico
Mexican Revolution
    USE Mexico—History—Revolution, 1910-1920
          Mexico—History—Revolution, 1923-1924
MEXICANS—UNITED STATES [Here are entered works dealing with Mexicans visiting or living in the United States.]
    NT Mexican Americans
MEXICO
    BT Latin America
    NT Baja California (Mexico)
MEXICO—HISTORY—REVOLUTION, 1910-1920
    UF Mexican Revolution
MEXICO—HISTORY—REVOLUTION, 1923-1924
    UF Mexican Revolution
Mexico—Indians
    USE Indians of Mexico
MIAMI (FLA.)
    BT Florida
MICHIGAN
    NT Detroit (Mich.)
MIDDLE AGE
    NT Midlife crisis
MIDDLE AGED MEN
MIDDLE AGED WOMEN

MIDDLE AGES—HISTORY
    UF Medieval life
MIDDLE AGES IN LITERATURE [Here are entered nonfiction works on the history and criticism of the Middle Ages as portrayed in literature.]
MIDDLE ATLANTIC STATES
    UF United States—East
          United States—Northeast
    BT United States
MIDDLE CLASSES
    NT Yuppies \
MIDDLE CLASSES IN LITERATURE [Here are entered nonfiction works on the history and criticism of the middle classes as portrayed in literature.]
MIDDLE EAST
MIDDLE SCHOOLS [Here are entered works dealing with schools teaching grades above 3rd but below junior high school level, generally including but not necessarily confined to 4th, 5th, and 6th grades. Works dealing with schools teaching grades between elementary and high school, generally including, but not necessarily confined to 7th, 8th, and 9th grades are entered under *Junior high schools*.]
    BT Junior high schools
          Schools
MIDDLE WEST [Here are entered works dealing with the region that includes Illinois, Indiana, Iowa, Kansas, Michigan, Minnesota, Missouri, Nebraska, North Dakota, Ohio, South Dakota, and Wisconsin.]
    UF United States—Middle West
    BT United States
MIDLIFE CRISIS [Here are entered works dealing with a period of emotional turmoil occurring in middle age characterized by a desire for change. Works dealing with the physical changes that occur as one passes from middle to old age are entered under *Climacteric*.]
    BT Middle age
    RT Climacteric
MIGRANT LABOR
    RT Farm life
Military life
    USE subdivision *Military life* under names of individual military services, such as *United States. Army—Military life*. This subdivision is also used

with navies in the case of military life on land-based installations. For naval military life at sea, use the subdivision *Sea life*, for example, *Great Britain. Royal Navy—Sea life.*

MILLIONAIRES
  UF Billionaires
        Rich people
        Tycoons
  RT Leisure class
        Upper classes

MILWAUKEE (WIS.)
  BT Wisconsin

MINNEAPOLIS (MINN.)
  BT Minnesota

MINNESOTA
  NT Minneapolis (Minn.)
        St. Paul (Minn.)

MINSK (BYELORUSSIAN S.S.R.)
  BT Byelorussian S.S.R.

MISCEGENATION
  UF Mixed bloods
  BT Interracial marriage

MISERS [Here are entered works dealing with persons who live wretched lives in order to hoard their wealth. Works dealing with an excessive desire for gain or wealth are entered under *Avarice*. Works dealing with the economic effects of the amassment of money or capital in an unreasonable fashion are entered under *Hoarding of money*.]
  RT Avarice
        Hoarding of money
        Prodigals

MISSING CHILDREN

MISSING PERSONS
  UF Disappearances
  NT Disappeared persons [Political kidnappings and murder]
        Kidnapping

MISSIONARY STORIES [Here are entered novels and stories for children which deal with missionaries. This heading is not used with adult fiction.]
  BT Fiction

MISSISSIPPI
  NT Jackson (Miss.)

MISSOURI
  NT Kansas City (Mo.)

MISTAKEN IDENTITY [Here are entered works dealing with persons who are innocently mistaken for someone else. Works dealing with someone who has two separate identities, each of his own invention, are entered under *Double identity*. Works that deal with assuming the personality, behavior, or appearance of someone for other than deceitful intent are entered under *Impersonation*. Works that deal with assuming an identity with the intent to deceive are entered under *Impostors and imposture*. Works that deal with imposture as a legal charge are entered under *False personation*. Works that deal with imposture of a public official as a legal charge are entered under *Impersonating an officer*. Works that deal with trials of someone accused of either false personation or impersonating an officer are entered under *Trials (Impostors and imposture)*. Works dealing with who one is or is known as are entered under *Identity*.]
  UF Disguise
  BT Identity
  RT Double identity\
        False personation
        Impersonating an officer
        Impersonation
        Impostors and imposture
        Trials (Impostors and imposture)

MISTRESSES [Here are entered works dealing with women who habitually fornicate with a particular man but do not sell themselves. Works dealing with the state of being a mistress or the keeping of a mistress are entered under *Concubinage*. Works dealing with couples living together as man and wife are entered under *Cohabitation*. Works dealing with women who sell themselves for fornication are entered under *Prostitutes*. Works dealing with women who prostitute themselves to men of high rank or wealth are entered under *Courtesans*. Works dealing with Japanese women trained in lighthearted entertainment primarily for men are entered under *Geishas*. Geishas are not, per se, Japanese prostitutes or courtesans.]
  BT Unmarried couples
        Women
  RT Cohabitation
        Concubinage

Courtesans
Geishas
Prostitutes
Mixed bloods
  USE Eurasians
    Miscegenation
    Mulattoes
Mixed race marriage
  USE Interracial marriage
MOBILE (ALA.)
  BT Alabama
Mobsters
  USE Hoodlums
    Mafia
    Organized crime
    Yakuza [Japanese organized crime]
MOCK-HEROIC LITERATURE [Here are entered works that use the epic formula to overstate something and thus make it ridiculous and which are generally shorter than epic works. Broad and lengthy works that recount the deeds of a legendary or historical hero are entered under *Epic literature*.]
  BT Epic literature
MODELS, FASHION
  RT Costume designers
MOLDAVIAN S.S.R.
  BT Soviet Union
  NT Kishinev (Moldavian S.S.R.)
MONASTIC AND RELIGIOUS LIFE
  UF Religious orders
  BT Catholic Church
    Monks
    Religious fiction
MONASTIC AND RELIGIOUS LIFE OF WOMEN
  UF Convent life
    Religious orders
  BT Nuns
  RT Convents
MONEY
  RT Capitalists and financiers
MONKS
  RT Catholic Church—Clergy
  NT Monastic and religious life
MONKS AS DETECTIVES \
  RT Catholic Church—Clergy as detectives \
    Clergy as detectives \
MONOLOGUE [Here are entered nonfiction works on the technique of the monologue as a literary form.]
MONOLOGUES IN LITERATURE [Here are entered nonfiction works on the history and criticism of monologues in literature]
MONOMANIA
  UF Obsession
MONSTERS
  BT Demonology
  RT Animals, Mythical
    Horror tales
    Legends
    Vampires
    Werewolves
MONTANA
  NT Helena (Mont.)
MONTENEGRO
  BT Yugoslavia
  NT Titograd (Montenegro)
MONTREAL (QUEBEC)
  BT Quebec (Province)
MORMON CHURCH
  RT Polygamy
  NT Church of Jesus Christ of Latter Day Saints
MOROCCO
MOSCOW (R.S.F.S.R.)
  BT Russian S.F.S.R.
    Soviet Union
MOSES
  BT Bible—History of Biblical events
MOTHER AND DAUGHTER DETECTIVES \
  BT Daughters as detectives \
MOTHER AND SON DETECTIVES \
  BT Sons as detectives \
MOTHERS
  BT Domestic fiction
  RT Fertilization in vitro, Human
    Foster parents
    Single-parent family
  NT Filicide [Murder of a son or daughter by mother or father]
    Parricide [Murder of a mother or father by a son or daughter]
    Unmarried mothers
MOTHERS AND DAUGHTERS
  BT Female-female relationships \
  RT Parent and child
MOTHERS AND SONS
  BT Female-male relationships \
  RT Parent and child
MOTHERS AS DETECTIVES \
  BT Women detectives
Mother's helpers
  USE Child care workers
MOTHERS-IN-LAW
  UF In-laws

MOTHERS IN LITERATURE [Here are entered nonfiction works on the history and criticism of mothers as portrayed in literature.]
MOTION PICTURE ACTORS AND ACTRESSES
 RT Motion pictures
 NT Actors as detectives\
  Actresses as detectives\
MOTION PICTURE FICTION\ [Here are entered works of fiction-based stories originally written for motion picture scripts or works of fiction made into motion pictures.]
 UF Movie novels
  Movie tie-in fiction
 BT Fiction
MOTION PICTURE PRODUCERS AND DIRECTORS
MOTION PICTURES
 RT Motion picture actors and actresses
  Screenwriters
MOTORCYCLE GANGS
MOUNTAIN LIFE
 BT Mountains
MOUNTAINS
 NT Mountain life
Mounties
 USE Royal Canadian Mounted Police
Movie novels
 USE Motion picture fiction\
Movie tie-in fiction
 USE Motion picture fiction\
MUGGING [Here are entered works dealing with robbery committed on the street and involving a beating or other physical assault. Works dealing with taking another's property using violence or the threat of violence are entered under *Robbery*. Works dealing with persons who commit robbery are entered under *Brigands and robbers*. Works dealing with the ethical and psychological aspects of theft are entered under *Stealing*. Works dealing with stealing as a crime are entered under *Larceny*. Works dealing with persons who commit theft or burglary are entered under *Thieves*. Works dealing with breaking and entering for the purpose of theft or robbery are entered under *Burglary*. Works dealing with persons who steal, profiteer, or kill, especially in a merciless manner, are entered under *Outlaws*.]
 UF Holdups
 BT Brigands and robbers
  Crime
 RT Larceny
  Robbery
  Stealing
  Thieves
 RT Burglary
MULATTOES
 UF Mixed bloods
MULTIPLE PERSONALITY
 UF Dual personality
  Split personality
 RT Mental illness
  Schizophrenics
  Split self in literature [Nonfiction history and criticism]
MUMMIES
 BT Antiquities
MUNITIONS
MURDER [Here are entered works dealing with the unlawful killing of a human being with malice aforethought. Works dealing with the killing of a human being in a situation which is not necessarily a crime or in a neutral sense with no moral or legal quality is entered under *Homicide*. Works of generally lighter fiction that are concerned with the detection or solution of murder or homicide are entered under *Detective and mystery stories*.]
 UF Murderers
 BT Crime
 RT Detective and mystery stories
  Homicide
  Victims, Unidentified\
 NT Crime passionel [Killing for sexual motives]
  Dismemberment, Bodily\
  Filicide [Son or daughter slain by a parent]
  Fratricide [Brother slain by a sibling]
  Infanticide [Child slaying]
  Lynching
  Mariticide\ [Husband slain by wife]
  Mass murder [Several slain at one time]
  Parricide [Parent slain by a son or daughter]
  Serial murders [Repetitive slayings by the same assailant]
  Sororicide [Sister slain by a sibling]
  Suicide
  Uxoricide [Wife slain by her husband]

Murderers
  USE Murder
Music, Folk
  USE Folk music
Music, Jazz
  USE Jazz music
Music, Opera
  USE Opera
Music, Rock
  USE Rock music
MUSICAL FICTION [Here are entered works dealing with musical topics and themes.]
  BT Fiction
  NT Folk music
     Jazz music
     Lyricists
     Musicians
     Opera
     Orchestra
     Rock music
MUSICIANS
  BT Musical fiction
  NT Lyricists
     Orchestra
Mutes
  USE Mutism
MUTISM
  UF Mutes
MYTHOLOGY [Here are entered works of traditional narrative that are shorter than epics but deal more with the supernatural and less with historical fact. Works of traditional narrative that are shorter than epics but which still purport to have some basis in reality are entered under *Legends*. Works that deal with shorter narratives passed on by word of mouth about common or illiterate people are entered under *Folk literature*. Collections of traditional narratives that are for the most part fictitious and are told primarily for entertainment are entered under *Tales*. Broad and lengthy works that recount the deeds of a legendary or historical hero are entered under *Epic literature*.]
  RT Epic literature
     Folk literature
     Legends
     Tales
  NT Sagas

MYTHOMANIA [Here are entered works dealing with an abnormal propensity for exaggeration and lying.]
  UF Exaggeration
     Lies

N.A.S.A.
  USE United States. National Aeronautics and Space Administration
N.A.T.O.
  USE North Atlantic Treaty Organization
Nannies
  USE Child care workers
     Governesses
NARCISSISM [Here are entered works dealing with self-love and the overvaluation of oneself. Works dealing with self-absorption and concentration on oneself and one's interests are entered under *Egoism*. Works dealing with a concern for oneself at the expense of others are entered under *Self-interest*.]
  BT Egoism
  RT Self-interest
NASA
  USE United States. National Aeronautics and Space Administration
NASHVILLE (TENN.)
  BT Tennessee
NATIONAL PARKS AND RESERVES
  RT Wildlife refuges
NATIONAL SOCIALISM
  RT Antisemitism
NATIONAL SOCIALISTS
  UF Ex-Nazis
     Neo-Nazis
NATO
  USE North Atlantic Treaty Organization
NATURAL DISASTERS
  BT Thrillers \
  NT Avalanches
     Disaster relief
     Disaster victims
     Landslides
Nature
  USE Nature stories
NATURE AND NURTURE [Here are entered works dealing with heredity and environment.]
  UF Environment

NATURE STORIES [Here are entered novels and stories dealing with nature.]
- UF Environment
- Nature
- BT Fiction
- RT Outdoor life
- NT Conservation of natural resources
- Ecology
- Pollution
- Wildlife conservation

NATURE STORIES, AMERICAN (Danish, etc.) [Here are entered collections of nature stories by American (Danish, etc.) authors.]

Naval life
- USE Seafaring life [Civilians and merchant marine]
- subdivision *Sea life* under navies, for example, *United States. Navy—Sea life*; for fiction about naval life on shore installations, use the subdivision *Military life* under navies, for example, *Great Britain. Royal Navy—Military life*

Naval warfare
- USE names of wars with the subdivision *Naval operations*, for example, *United States—History—Civil War, 1861-1865—Naval operations*; *World War, 1939-1945—Naval operations*

Navy life
- USE Seafaring life [Civilians and merchant marine]
- subdivision *Sea life* under navies, for example, *United States. Navy—Sea life*; for fiction about naval life on shore installations, use the subdivision *Military life* under navies, for example *Great Britain. Royal Navy—Military life*

NEANDERTHALS
- BT Man, Prehistoric

NEBRASKA
- NT Omaha (Neb.)

NEGERI SEMBILAN
- BT Malaysia

Negro dialect fiction
- USE Dialect fiction, Afro-Americans \

NEIGHBORHOOD
- UF Neighbors

Neighbors
- USE Neighborhood

Neo-Nazis
- USE National Socialists

NEPAL

NEPALI FICTION

NEPHEWS \
- BT Domestic fiction
- RT Aunts
- Uncles

Netherlands East Indies
- USE Indonesia

NEUROSES [Here are entered works dealing with functional nervous disorders that lack any obvious physical cause. Works dealing with an individual's life pattern that is deviant or maladaptive even though he shows no psychotic disorganization or neurotic symptoms are entered under *Personality disorders*.]
- RT Mental illness
- Personality disorders

NEUTRON BOMB
- RT Nuclear weapons

NEVADA
- NT Las Vegas (Nev.)

NEW BRUNSWICK
- BT Canada
- NT St. John (N.B.)

NEW ENGLAND [Here are entered works dealing with the region that includes Connecticut, Maine, Massachusetts, New Hampshire, Rhode Island, and Vermont.]
- UF United States—East
- United States—New England
- United States—Northeast

New England dialect fiction
- USE Dialect fiction, New Englanders \

NEW FRANCE [Here are entered works dealing with the French in North America; from 1534 to 1627 this was confined to exploration; from 1627 to 1763 there were settlements in Canada. The last U.S. settlements were handed over in 1803.]

NEW HAMPSHIRE
- NT Manchester (N.H.)

NEW JERSEY
- NT Atlantic City (N.J.)
- Newark (N.J.)
- Paterson (N.J.)

NEW MEXICO
- NT Albuquerque (N.M.)
- Santa Fe (N.M.)

NEW ORLEANS (LA.)
  BT Louisiana
NEW SOUTH WALES
  BT Australia
  NT Sydney (N.S.W.)
New Southwest
  USE Southwest, New
NEW YEAR
  UF New Year's Eve
New Year's Eve
  USE New Year
NEW YORK (N.Y.)
  UF New York City
  RT Wall Street [For financial activities only]
  NT Bronx (New York, N.Y.)
     Brooklyn (New York, N.Y.)
     Central Park (New York, N.Y.)
     Greenwich Village (New York, N.Y.)
     Harlem (New York, N.Y.)
     Manhattan (New York, N.Y.)
     Queens (New York, N.Y.)
NEW YORK (STATE)
NEW YORK SUBURBAN AREA
  NT Long Island (N.Y.)
New York City
  USE New York (N.Y.)
NEW ZEALAND
  NT Auckland (N.Z.)
     Christchurch (N.Z.)
NEWARK (N.J.)
  BT New Jersey
NEWFOUNDLAND
  BT Canada
  NT Labrador (Nfld.)
     St. John's (Nfld.)
NEWLYWEDS\
  BT Marriage
  RT Weddings
  NT Honeymoon
NEWSPAPERS
  NT Editors
     Journalists
NICARAGUA
NIECES
  BT Domestic fiction
  RT Aunts
     Uncles
NIHILISM IN LITERATURE [Here are entered nonfiction works on the history and criticism of nihilism in literature.]
NIHILISTIC FICTION\ [Here are entered works that represent life as senseless and useless and which deny the objectivity of moral truth and/or represent social organization as so poor that destruction is desirable for its own sake even if there is no possibility of reform. Works that represent life as essentially meaningless, absurd, not explainable by reason or scientific means, but only through concrete experience or as man acts upon it to create meaning, even though such actions only lead to a greater awareness of loneliness or despair are entered under *Existential fiction*\. Works that represent the absurdity of man's existence by bizarre or fantastic means are entered under *Absurdist fiction*\.]
  BT Experimental fiction
     Fiction
     Philosophical fiction\
  RT Absurdist fiction\
     Existential fiction\
NOBILITY [Here are entered works dealing with persons whose rank is inferior to royalty but superior to all others and whose rank is either directly granted by a ruler or is inherited. Note that *Nobility* includes baronets, even though they would be excluded in British popular usage. Works dealing with persons of an ideally superior caste, not invariably a fixed or definite group, are entered under *Aristocracy*. Works dealing with persons who are not nobility but who are entitled to bear a coat of arms, and hence, are considered gentlemen or ladies in the technical sense, and are landed proprietors are entered under *Gentry*. Works dealing with persons considered of the highest class of people either because of wealth or prestige are entered under *Upper classes*.]
  UF Baronets
     Barons
     Dukes
     Earls
  RT Aristocracy
     Courts and courtiers
     Gentry
     Kings and rulers
     Knights and knighthood
     Princes
     Princesses

Queens
Upper classes
NOBILITY—ENGLAND
NOBILITY—GREAT BRITAIN
NOBLES AS DETECTIVES \
   RT Aristocrats as detectives \
       Knights as detectives \
Noncommissioned officers [Used only as a subdivision with headings for armies, air forces, and marines, for example, *United States. Army—Noncommissioned officers*. For navies, use the subdivision *Petty officers*.]
NONFICTION NOVEL [Here are entered works of nonfiction dealing with the history and criticism of nonfiction novels.]
   BT Fiction
NONFICTION NOVELS \ [Here are entered works of factual representation having the objective quality and authority of the real event. Works in which real people and real events have been disguised for literary purposes are entered under *Livres á clef*. Works in which people who actually exist or who existed appear in minor roles are entered under *Real people* \ . Works dealing loosely with actual occurrences are entered under *Real events* \ . Works dealing predominately with an actual person are entered under *Biographical fiction*. Works written by the author about his or her own life are entered under *Autobiographical fiction*, even if the main character is given another name.]
   UF Documentary fiction
   BT Fiction
   RT Livres á clef
       Real events \
       Real people \
   NT Autobiographical fiction
       Biographical fiction
NORMANDY (FRANCE)
   BT France
North American Indian detectives
   USE Indians of North America as detectives \
North American Indian fiction
   USE American fiction—Indian authors
        Canadian fiction—Indian authors \
        Indian literature

NORTH ATLANTIC TREATY ORGANIZATION
   UF N.A.T.O
       NATO
NORTH CAROLINA
   NT Charlotte (N.C.)
NORTH DAKOTA
   NT Fargo (N.D)
NORTH SEA
   BT Atlantic Ocean
NORTHEASTERN STATES [Here are entered works dealing with the region that includes Connecticut, Delaware, Illinois, Indiana, Maine, Maryland, Massachusetts, Michigan, New Hampshire, New Jersey, New York, Ohio, Pennsylvania, Rhode Island, Vermont, and Wisconsin.]
   UF United States—East
       United States—Northeast
   BT United States
NORTHERN IRELAND [Here are entered works dealing with or set in the country of Northern Ireland. If a place is located in Northern Ireland, add the identifier *(Northern Ireland)*, for example *Londonderry (Northern Ireland)*. For further information see 23.4D2 in *AACR2R*.]
   BT Great Britain
       Ireland
   RT Ulster (Northern Ireland and Ireland) [Although sometimes popularly used as a synonym for Northern Ireland, Ulster a subject heading applies only to the former province of Ulster in the north of Ireland. In 1920, the counties of Antrim, Armagh, Down, Fermanagh, Londonderry, and Tryone were joined to form the new state of Northern Ireland. The remaining counties of Cavan, Donegal, and Monaghan became the province of Ulster in Eire, the Republic of Ireland.]
   NT Belfast (Northern Ireland)
       Irish
       Orangemen
       Scots-Irish
Northern Irish fiction
   USE English fiction—Irish authors [Written in English]
        Irish fiction [Written in the Irish language by Irish authors]

NORTHERN TERRITORY [Here are entered works dealing with the Northern Territory, an Australian province.]
   BT Australia
   NT Darwin (N.T.)
NORTHMEN
   NT Danes
NORTHWEST, OLD
   UF Old Northwest
       United States—Old Northwest
NORTHWEST, PACIFIC
   RT Northwestern states
NORTHWEST TERRITORIES
   BT Canada
   NT Yellowknife (N.W.T.)
NORTHWESTERN STATES [Here are entered works dealing with the region that includes Idaho, Montana, Oregon, Washington, and Wyoming.]
   UF United States—Northwest
       United States—Pacific Northwest
   BT United States
       West (U.S.)
   RT Northwest, Pacific
NORWAY
   RT Lapland
NORWEGIAN FICTION
NOVA SCOTIA
   BT Canada
   NT Halifax (N.S.)
Novelettes
   USE Novellas (Short novels)
NOVELLAS (SHORT NOVELS)\ [Here are entered novels of less than usual length, usually having the compact structure of a short story together with the fuller development of character, plot, and/or theme of a novel.]
   UF Novelettes
       Short novels
   BT Fiction
NOVELLE [Here are entered nonfiction works on the brief fictional yet realistic narrative form, moral or satiric, in prose or poetry, which were popular in medieval and Renaissance times.]
   BT Fiction
Novels, Unfinished
   USE Unfinished books
Novels in verse
   USE Fiction in verse\
Novels with short stories
   USE Frame-stories

Nuclear bombs
   USE Nuclear weapons
NUCLEAR ENERGY
   NT Radioactive wastes
NUCLEAR WARFARE
   NT Radioactive fallout
       Survival after nuclear warfare\
NUCLEAR WEAPONS
   UF Nuclear bombs
   RT Neutron bomb
   NT Radioactive fallout
Numbers racket
   USE Lotteries
NUNS
   BT Catholic Church
   RT Abbesses, Christian
       Catholic Church—Clergy
       Women clergy
   NT Convents
       Monastic and religious life of women
NUNS AS DETECTIVES\
   BT Women detectives
   RT Catholic Church—Clergy as detectives\
       Clergy as detectives\
Nurse stories
   USE Medical fiction\
Nursemaids
   USE Childcare workers
       Governesses
NURSES [Here are entered works dealing with nurses. Works dealing with nurses in a general way in a medical environment are entered under the genre heading *Medical fiction*\.]
   RT Hospitals
       Life care communities
       Medical fiction\
       Nursing homes
       Old age homes
       Physicians
NURSES AS DETECTIVES\
   BT Women detectives
NURSING HOMES [Here are entered works dealing with private institutions that provide long-term personal and nursing care to the aged or chronically ill. Works dealing with planned residential developments for the aged that also provide meal service, medical care, etc., are entered under *Life care communities*. Works that deal with institutions that provide housing and general care for the convalescent are entered under *Rest homes*. Works that deal

with institutions that provide housing and general care for the aged are entered under *Old age homes*. Works that deal with institutions that provide long-term care and therapy together with a regimen such as diet or exercise are entered under *Sanatoriums*. Works dealing with institutions that give the sick and injured medical and surgical care are entered under *Hospitals*.]
- RT Hospitals
  Invalids
  Life care communities
  Nurses
  Physicians
  Rest homes
  Sanatoriums
  Sick

OBESITY
- RT Appetite disorders
  Eating disorders

Obsession
- USE Monomania

OBSTETRICIANS
- BT Physicians

OCCULTISM [Here are entered works dealing with mysterious or secret knowledge supposedly attainable only through magical or supernatural means and not through ordinary human reason. Works dealing in a more general way with phenomena that appear to transcend the laws of nature or that are related to an order of existence beyond the observable universe are entered under *Supernatural*. Works dealing with a man who practices witchcraft or who is exceptionally skilled in the occult arts or who can achieve the seemingly impossible are entered under *Wizards*.]
- BT Supernatural
- NT Wizards

OCEAN
- NT Ocean travel

OCEAN TRAVEL
- BT Ocean
- RT Sea stories
  Seafaring life
- NT Sailing ships
  Yachts and yachting

OCEAN TRAVEL IN LITERATURE [Here are entered nonfiction works on the history and criticism of ocean travel as portrayed in literature.]

Odd people
- USE Eccentrics and eccentricities

OFFICE PARTIES \
- UF Parties, Office
- BT Entertaining

Officers
- USE headings such as *Great Britain, Army—Officers*; *United States, Navy—Officers*, etc,

OHIO
- NT Cincinnati (Ohio)
  Cleveland (Ohio)

OLD AGE
- RT Longevity
  Rejuvenation
  Senile dementia

OLD AGE HOMES [Here are entered works that deal with institutions that provide housing and general care for the aged. Works dealing with private institutions that provide long-term personal and nursing care to the aged or chronically ill are entered under *Nursing homes*. Works dealing with planned residential developments for the aged that also provide meal service, medical care, etc. are entered under *Life care communities*. Works that deal with institutions that provide housing and general care for the convalescent are entered under *Rest homes*. Works that deal with institutions that provide long-term care and therapy together with a regimen such as diet or exercise are entered under *Sanatoriums*. Works dealing with institutions that give the sick and injured medical and surgical care are entered under *Hospitals*.]
- UF Old people's homes
  Retirement homes
- RT Hospitals
  Life care communities
  Nurses
  Physicians
  Rest homes
  Retirement, Places of [Areas or communities popular for retirement living]

Retirement communities [Planned residential developments for the aged]
Sanatoriums

OLD AGE IN LITERATURE [Here are entered nonfiction works on the history and criticism of old age as portrayed in literature.]

Old maids
  USE Single women

Old Northwest
  USE Northwest, Old

Old people
  USE Aged

Old people's homes
  USE Old age homes

Old Southwest
  USE Southwest, Old

OMAHA (NEB.)
  BT Nebraska

ONTARIO
  BT Canada
  NT Ottawa (Ont.)
      Toronto (Ont.)

OPALS
  RT Jewelry

OPERA
  UF Music, Opera
  BT Musical fiction

ORANGEMEN [Here are entered works dealing with the secret society organized in 1795 to support the Protestant religion in Northern Ireland. Works dealing with Scottish people who settled in Northern Ireland and their descendants are entered under *Scots-Irish*.]
  BT British
      Ireland
      Northern Ireland
  RT Scots-Irish

ORCHESTRA
  UF Orchestras
  BT Musical fiction
      Musicians

Orchestras
  USE Orchestra

OREGON
  NT Portland (Or.)

ORGANIZED CRIME
  UF Mobsters
      Underworld, Criminal
  BT Gangs
  RT Hoodlums

ORPHANS
  RT Adoption
      Foster children

Other worlds
  USE Extraterrestrial bases
      Extraterrestrial beings \
      Fantastic fiction
      Imaginary histories [The world if history were different]
      Life on other planets
      Parallel worlds [Worlds existing simultaneously in the same location]
      Science fantasy \
      Science fiction

OTTAWA (ONT.)
  BT Ontario

Outback
  USE Country life—Australia [If a specific province or territory is given, that name may be used as well.]

OUTDOOR LIFE
  RT Fishing stories
      Hunting stories
      Nature stories

OUTER SPACE
  RT Science fiction
  NT Life on other planets
      Space flight

OUTER SPACE—EXPLORATION
  NT Space probes

OUTLAWS [Here are entered works dealing with persons who steal, profiteer, or kill, especially in a merciless manner. Works dealing with taking another's property using violence or the threat of violence are entered under *Robbery*. Works dealing with persons who commit robbery are entered under *Brigands and robbers*. Works dealing with robbery committed on the street and involving a beating or other physical assault are entered under *Robbery*. Works dealing with the ethical and psychological aspects of theft are entered under *Stealing*. Works dealing with stealing as a crime are entered under *Larceny*. Works dealing with persons who commit theft or burglary are entered under *Thieves*. Works dealing with breaking and entering for the purpose of theft or robbery are entered under *Burglary*.]
  RT Brigands and robbers

Burglary
Larceny
Robbery
Stealing
Thieves
Western stories
OVERLAND JOURNEYS TO THE PACIFIC
  RT Caravans [Used for wagon trains]
Overpopulation
  USE Population
OXFORD (ENGLAND)
  BT England
  RT University of Oxford
Oxford University
  USE University of Oxford

PACIFIC OCEAN
  NT Islands of the Pacific
PAGANISM [Here are entered works dealing with having little or no religion coupled with uninhibited seeking after material goods and sensual pleasure. Works dealing with the belief that pleasure and happiness are the main purpose of life are entered under *Hedonism*. Works dealing with very early religions that are now extinct or have evolved are entered under *Religion, Primitive*.]
  UF Barbarians
  RT Hedonism
    Religion
    Religion, Primitive
PAHANG
  BT Malaysia
PAINTERS
PAINTING
  BT Art
  NT House painting
PAKISTANI FICTION
PALESTINE
  NT Jerusalem
PARABLES [Here are entered works in which the allegory is short and simple and which deals with a familiar occurrence in life or nature that by analogy conveys a spiritual truth. Works in which the allegory is short and simple, using animals acting as humans and illustrating the follies and weaknesses of people, are entered under *Fables*. Works in which the persons and objects represented have a meaning that lies outside the narrative itself are entered under *Allegories*. Allegories attempt to evoke an interest both in their characters, settings, and events, and in the ideas that they represent. Works that suggest other levels of meaning without making the structure of ideas a formative influence on the narrative are entered under *Symbolic fiction*\.]
  BT Allegories
  RT Fables
    Symbolic fiction\
PARALLEL WORLDS\ [Here are entered works about worlds that exist simultaneously in the same place. Works dealing with history as it might have been if history had been different are entered under *Imaginary histories*.]
  UF Other worlds
  RT Extraterrestrial beings\
    Fourth dimension
    Imaginary histories
    Life on other planets
PARANOIA
  RT Mental illness
PARAPLEGICS
  RT Quadriplegics
PARENT AND CHILD
  BT Domestic fiction
  RT Conflict of generations
    Daughters
    Domestic fiction
    Fathers and daughters
    Fathers and sons
    Filicide [Murder of a son or daughter by his or her mother or father]
    Mothers and daughters
    Mothers and sons
    Parricide [Murder of a mother or father by his or her son or daughter]
    Sons
PARIS (FRANCE)
  BT France
PARODIES [Here are entered works that imitate the language or style of a particular author or work to achieve comic effect. Note that the Library of Congress only authorizes collections of parodies here.]
  RT Burlesques
    Humorous stories
PARRICIDE [Here are entered works dealing with the murder of a mother or father

by his or her son or daughter. Works dealing with the murder of a son or daughter by a mother or father are entered under *Filicide*.]
  BT Daughters
        Fathers
        Mothers
        Murder
        Parent and child
        Sons
  RT Filicide

Parties, Birthday
  USE Birthdays

Parties, Costume
  USE Masquerades

Parties, Dinner
  USE Dinners and dining

Parties, House
  USE House parties \

Parties, Office
  USE Office parties \

PASQUINADES [Here are entered nonfiction works on squibs, libels, lampoons, or pieces of satire.]

PASTORAL FICTION [Here are entered works dealing with generally idealized rustic life and expressing complex ideas through supposedly simple characters, such as shepherds who speak in courtly language.]
  BT Country life
        Fiction
  RT Shepherds
        Villages

PASTORAL FICTION, ENGLISH (French, etc.) [Here are entered collections of pastoral fiction by English (French, etc.) authors.]

PATAGONIA (ARGENTINA AND CHILE)
  BT Argentina
        Chile

PATERNITY
  BT Fathers

PATERSON (N.J.)
  BT New Jersey

PEACE OFFICERS [Here are entered works that deal with various kinds of law enforcement officers or law enforcement officers generally. Works dealing with marshals serving in American federal courts are entered under *United States marshals*. Note that the heading *Marshals* is used for works dealing with air marshals or field marshals in the military. Works dealing with municipal peace officers are entered under *Police*. Works dealing with peace officers charged with both keeping the public peace and certain petty judicial matters are entered under *Constables*. Works dealing with peace officers who are elected county officials or who work as police in a department headed by such an official are entered under *Sheriffs*. Westerns that deal with law enforcement officers are entered under *Peace officers* if it cannot be readily determined if the officer is a marshal or sheriff. The heading *Police* is not used with westerns unless specifically so used in the text. It would usually be superfluous to use any of the peace officer headings with detective and mystery fiction.]
  RT Marshals
  NT Constables
        Police
        Sheriffs
        United States marshals

PEARLS
  RT Jewelry

PEASANTRY [Here are entered works dealing with agricultural laborers or owners of very small plots of farm land, especially in Europe, Asia, or South America. Works dealing with agricultural laborers bound to the land in service to its owner are entered under *Serfdom*. Works dealing with peasants who are slaves to their feudal lord but who are free in other respects are entered under *Villeinage*. Works dealing with laborers bound in servitude by prison sentence or indebtedness are entered under *Peonage*. Works dealing with the laboring classes are entered under *Working class*.]
  BT Farm life
        Working class
  RT Peonage
        Serfdom
  NT Villeinage

Peeping Toms
  USE Scopophilia

Penang
  USE Pinang

PENNSYLVANIA
  NT Philadelphia (Pa.)

Pittsburgh (Pa.)
Pocono Mountains (Pa.)
PEONAGE [Here are entered works dealing with laborers bound in servitude by prison sentence or indebtedness. Works dealing with agricultural laborers or owners of very small plots of farm land, especially in Europe, Asia, or South America, are entered under *Peasantry*. Works dealing with agricultural laborers bound to the land in service to its owner are entered under *Serfdom*. Works dealing with peasants who are slaves to their feudal lord but free in other respects are entered under *Villeinage*. Works dealing with the laboring classes are entered under *Working class*.]
  BT Farm life
       Serfdom
       Working class
  RT Peasantry
       Villeinage
PERAK
  BT Malaysia
PERIODICALS
  RT Editors
PERLIS
  BT Malaysia
Persia
  USE Iran
PERSIAN FICTION [Here are entered works written in the Persian language. Works written by Iranians are entered under *Iranian fiction*.]
  BT Iranian fiction
Personal identity
  USE Identity
        Personality
PERSONALITY
  UF Personal identity
PERSONALITY DISORDERS [Here are entered works dealing with an individual's life pattern that is deviant or maladaptive even though he or she shows no psychotic disorganization or neurotic symptoms. Works dealing with functional nervous disorders that lack any obvious physical cause are entered under *Neuroses*.]
  RT Mental illness
       Neuroses
PERTH (W.A.)
  BT Western Australia

Petty officers [Used only as a subdivision with navies, for example, *United States. Navy—Petty officers*. For armies, use the subdivision *Non-commissioned officers*.]
Pharaohs
  USE Egypt—Kings and rulers
PHILADELPHIA (PA.)
  BT Pennsylvania
PHILIPPINES
  NT Manila (Philippines)
PHILOSOPHICAL FICTION [Here are entered works that deal with philosophical questions and works that apply philosophy or philosophical viewpoints to the story. Works dealing with standards or behavior and works containing moral guidance and advice to the individual are entered under *Conduct of life*.]
  UF Life, Philosophy of
  BT Fiction
  RT Good and evil
       Literary fiction
  NT Conduct of life\
       Existential fiction\
       Nihilistic fiction\
PHILOSOPHICAL LITERATURE [Here are entered nonfiction works on the history and criticism of philosophical writings.]
PHILOSOPHY IN LITERATURE [Here are entered nonfiction works on the history and criticism of philosophy as portrayed in literature.]
PHYSICALLY HANDICAPPED
  RT Abnormalities, Human
       Invalids
PHYSICALLY HANDICAPPED CHILDREN
PHYSICALLY HANDICAPPED TEENAGERS
PHYSICALLY HANDICAPPED WOMEN
PHYSICIANS [Here are entered works dealing with physicians. Works dealing with physicians in a general way in a medical environment are entered under the genre heading *Medical fiction*.]
  RT Chiropractors
       Hospitals
       Life care communities
       Medical fiction\
       Nurses
       Nursing homes
       Old age homes
       Quacks and quackery

**PHYSICIANS AS DETECTIVES **

    NT Gynecologists
           Obstetricians
           Psychiatrists

**PHYSICIANS AS DETECTIVES **

**PICARESQUE FICTION ** [Here are entered works that are episodic in the detailing of the adventures of a rascal, rogue, or vagabond getting by on his or her wits. Examples include Miguel de Cervantes' *Don Quixote* and J.P. Donleavy's *The Ginger Man*. Works dealing with a rascal, rogue, or vagabond but lacking the episodic structure are entered under *Rogues and vagabonds*. Works of a more general nature that have little or no central plot and/or detail events that have little or no causal relationship to one another are entered under *Episodic novels *. Collections of a series of stories with a common narrative framework or stories that are contained within a novel or another story are entered under *Frame-stories*. Works dealing with aimless persons who wander from place to place and job to job are entered under *Drifters*. Works dealing with traveling beggars who will not work are entered under *Tramps*. Works dealing with the legal charge of being a tramp are entered under *Vagrancy*. Works dealing with persons who travel as a way of life are entered under *Wayfaring life*. Works in which a journey is a central part of the action are entered under *Road fiction *.]

    UF Dissipation
           Libertines
           Rascals
           Wastrels
    BT Fiction
    RT Degeneration
           Drifters
           Episodic novels \
           Frame-stories
           Rogues and vagabonds
           Tramps
           Vagrancy
           Wayfaring life
    NT Road fiction \

PICARESQUE LITERATURE [Here are entered nonfiction works on picaresque literature.]

    BT Fiction \

PIMPS

    RT Prostitutes

PINANG

    BT Malaysia
    NT George Town (Pinang)

Pinang (Pinang)

    USE George Town (Pinang)

PITTSBURGH (PA.)

    BT Pennsylvania

PLAGIARISM

    RT Authors

PLAGUE

    BT Epidemics

PLANTATION LIFE

    RT Slavery
           Southern states

PLATONIC LOVE [Here are entered works dealing with love between two persons of opposite sex that does not involve libidinal attraction or with love of the beautiful or ideal. Works dealing with love in a general or abstract sense are entered under *Love*.]

    RT Love

PLOT-YOUR-OWN STORIES [Here are entered novels and stories in which the reader chooses from a number of possible options for developing the story.]

    UF Choose your own adventure fiction
    BT Fiction

POCONO MOUNTAINS (PA.)

    BT Pennsylvania

POISONING

POLAND

    NT Polish fiction
           Warsaw (Poland)

POLES

    UF Polish

POLES—UNITED STATES [Here are entered works dealing with Poles visiting or living in the United States.]

    BT Polish Americans

POLICE [Here are entered works dealing with municipal peace officers. Works that deal with various kinds of law enforcement officers or law enforcement officers generally are entered under *Peace officers*. Works dealing with marshals serving in American federal courts are entered under *United States marshals*. Note that the heading *Marshals* is used for works dealing with air marshals or field marshals in the military. Works dealing with peace of-

ficers charged with both keeping the public peace and certain petty judicial matters are entered under *Constables*. Works dealing with peace officers who are elected county officials or work as police in a department headed by such an official are entered under *Sheriffs*. Westerns that deal with law enforcement officers are entered under *Peace officers* if it cannot be readily determined if the officer is a marshal or sheriff. The heading *Police* is not used with westerns unless specifically so used in the text. It would usually be superfluous to use any of the peace officer headings with detective and mystery fiction.]
- BT Peace officers
  Sheriffs
- RT United States marshals
- NT Constables
  Policewomen

POLICE CORRUPTION
- UF Abuse of power

Police procedurals
- USE Detective and mystery stories, Police procedural\

POLICEWOMEN [See note under *Police*.]
- BT Police
- NT Women detectives

Polish
- USE Poles

POLISH AMERICANS [Here are entered works dealing with Americans of Polish ancestry.]
- RT Poles—United States

POLISH FICTION
- BT Poland
- RT Yiddish fiction

POLITICAL FICTION [Here are entered works dealing with politics.]
- UF Intrigue
  Politics
- BT Fiction
- RT Conspiracies
- SA subdivision *Politics and government*
- NT Anarchism
  Diplomatic and consular service
  Elections
  Lobbyists
  Mayors
  Presidents
  Prime ministers
  Radicalism
  Women in politics
  World politics

POLITICAL FICTION, AMERICAN (Arabic, etc.) [Here are entered collections of political fiction written by American (Arabic, etc.) authors.]

POLITICIANS [Here are entered works dealing with persons engaged in politics. Works dealing with persons who exercise wise leadership in the best interest of the general public without petty partisanship are entered under *Statesmen*. Works dealing with persons engaged in conducting relations between nations are entered under *Diplomats*.]
- BT Statesmen
- RT Diplomats

Politics
- USE Political fiction
  subdivision *Politics and government*

Politics, International
- USE World politics

Politics and government [Used only as a subdivision under names of countries, states, cities, etc.]

POLITICS AND LITERATURE [Here are entered works dealing with the relationship between politics and literature.]

POLITICS IN LITERATURE [Here are entered nonfiction works on the history and criticism of politics as portrayed in literature.]

POLLUTION
- UF Environment
- BT Nature stories
- RT Conservation of natural resources
  Ecology

POLYGAMY
- BT Marriage
  Problem marriages\
- RT Mormon Church

POOR
- NT Welfare recipients

POPES
- BT Catholic Church
- RT Vatican City

POPULATION
- UF Overpopulation

PORCELAIN
- BT Art objects

PORNOGRAPHY [Here are entered works that deal with the production, distribution, or social effects of erotica. Works whose primary purpose is erotic stimu-

lation are entered under *Erotic stories*. Works of general fiction that have explicit portrayals of sexuality as a subsidiary part of a larger story are entered under *Sexually explicit fiction*. Works of nonfiction that deal with the history and criticism of sex as portrayed in literature are entered under *Sex in literature*.]
   RT Erotic stories
       Sex in literature
       Sexually explicit fiction\

PORTLAND (ME.)
   BT Maine

PORTLAND (OR.)
   BT Oregon

PORTUGAL
   NT Lisbon (Portugal)

POST-TRAUMATIC STRESS DISORDER
   RT Vietnamese Conflict, 1961-1975—Veterans

POSTAL SERVICE
   UF Government employees
   RT Civil service

Postapocalyptic fiction
   USE Apocalyptic fiction\

POVERTY
   BT Social problems
   RT Public welfare
       Slums

POWER (SOCIAL SCIENCES)
   UF Abuse of power

PRACTICAL JOKES
   RT Humorous stories
       Impostors and imposture

Prairie life
   USE Frontier and pioneer life

PRAIRIE PROVINCES [Here are entered works dealing with the region that includes Alberta, Manitoba, and Saskatchewan.]
   BT Canada

PRECOGNITION [Here are entered works dealing with the ability to foresee the future with the mind. Works dealing with persons who have or claim to have the ability to foresee the future because of precognition are entered under *Psychics*. Works dealing with the ability to see the future by supernatural or occult means are entered under *Fortune-telling*. Works dealing with the ability to foresee the future because of divine inspiration are entered under *Prophecy*.]
   UF Premonitions
   BT Extrasensory perception
   RT Fortune-telling
       Prophecy
   NT Psychics

PREGNANCY
   RT Childbirth
       Fertilization in vitro, Human
   NT Abortion
       Fetus

Prehistoric life
   USE Man, Prehistoric

PREJUDICES

Premonitions
   USE Precognition
       Prophecy

Prequels (literature)
   USE Sequels (Literature)

PRESENILE DEMENTIA
   RT Senile dementia

Preservation of natural resources
   USE Conservation of natural resources

PRESIDENTS [For works dealing with women presidents who are also heads of state, as in the United States, the heading *Women heads of state* may also be used.]
   UF Women presidents
   BT Political fiction
   NT Women heads of state

PRESIDENTS—UNITED STATES

PRESS AGENTS
   UF Publicists
   RT Public relations consultants

PRIME MINISTERS
   BT Political fiction

PRIME MINISTERS—GREAT BRITAIN
   UF Great Britain—Prime ministers

PRINCE EDWARD ISLAND [Do not confuse with the Prince Edward Islands in the Indian Ocean.]
   BT Canada
   NT Charlottetown (P.E.I.)

PRINCES
   RT Kings and rulers
       Nobility
   SA subdivision princes and princesses under names of countries, etc., and ethnic groups, for example, *Great Britain—Princes and princesses*; *Zulu (African people)—princes and princesses*

PRINCESSES
  RT Nobility
  SA subdivision princes and princesses under names of countries, etc., and ethnic groups, for example, *Great Britain—Princes and princesses*; *Zulu (African people)—princes and princesses*

PRISONERS
  UF Prisoners, Condemned
  NT False imprisonment

Prisoners, Condemned
  USE Executions and executioners
         Prisoners

Prisoners, Escaped
  USE Escapes
         Fugitives from justices

PRISONS
  NT Reformatories

Private detectives
  USE Detective and mystery stories
         Detectives

PRIVATE SCHOOLS

PROBLEM CHILDREN
  UF Emotionally maladjusted children
       Maladjusted children
  BT Teenagers
  RT Juvenile delinquents
       Runaway children
       Runaway teenagers

PROBLEM FAMILIES
  BT Domestic fiction
  RT Family chronicles \
       Family curses \
       Problem marriages \
  NT Incest

PROBLEM MARRIAGES \
  UF Marriage problems
  BT Domestic fiction
  RT Problem families
  NT Adultery
       Bigamy
       Desertion and nonsupport
       Divorce
       Polygamy
       Sex in marriage
       Sexual disorders
       Wife abuse

PRODIGALS \ [Here are entered works dealing with spendthrifts or with reckless extravagance. Works dealing with the belief that pleasure and happiness are the main purpose of life are entered under *Hedonism*.]
  UF Dissipation
       Extravagance
       Libertines
       Profligates
       Spendthrifts
       Wastrels
  RT Avarice
       Degeneration
       Hedonism
       Hoarding of money
       Misers

Profanity in fiction
  USE Linguistically profane fiction \

Profligates
  USE Degeneration
        Prodigals

PROHIBITION
  UF Bootlegging of alcoholic beverages
       Liquor traffic
  RT Distilling, Illicit

PROLETARIAN FICTION \ [Here are entered works that give a sympathetic portrayal of the working class and expose social injustice and inequality. Examples include Richard Wright's *Native Son* and James T. Farrell's *Studs Lonigan*.]
  BT Fiction
       Social problems
       Working class

PROLETARIAT [Here are entered works dealing with the working class from an economic point of view.]
  BT Working class

PROLETARIAT IN LITERATURE [Here are entered nonfiction works dealing with the proletariat as portrayed in literature.]

PROPHECIES

PROPHECY [Here are entered works dealing with the ability to foresee the future because of divine inspiration. Works dealing with the ability to foresee the future with the mind are entered under *Precognition*. Works dealing with the ability to see the future by supernatural or occult means are entered under *Fortune-telling*.]
  UF Premonitions
  RT Fortune-telling
       Precognition

PROPHETS

PROSTITUTES [Here are entered works dealing with women who sell themselves for fornication. Works dealing with women who prostitute themselves to men of high rank or wealth are entered under *Courtesans*. Works dealing with women who habitually fornicate with a particular man but do not sell themselves are entered under *Mistresses*. Works dealing with Japanese women trained in lighthearted entertainment primarily for men are entered under *Geishas*. Geishas are not, per se, Japanese prostitutes or courtesans.]
  BT Social problems
     Women
  RT Geishas
     Mistresses
     Pimps
  NT Courtesans

PROSTITUTES IN LITERATURE [Here are entered nonfiction works of history and criticism of prostitutes as portrayed in literature.]

PROVIDENCE (R.I.)
  BT Rhode Island

Provincial and rural life
  USE Country life
      Farm life
      Suburban life
      Villages

PSYCHIATRIC HOSPITALS
  UF Insane asylums
     Mentally ill—Institutional care
  BT Mentally ill—Care
  RT Psychiatrists
     Psychoanalysts
     Psychologists

PSYCHIATRISTS
  BT Physicians
  RT Mental illness
     Psychiatric hospitals

**PSYCHIC DETECTIVES **
  RT Fortune tellers as detectives \

PSYCHICS [Here are entered works dealing with persons who have extrasensory perception, including precognition or the ability to foresee the future by the power of the mind. Works dealing with persons who have the ability to perceive objects hidden from sight are entered under *Clairvoyants*. Works dealing with persons who have or claim to have the ability to foresee the future by occult or supernatural means are entered under *Fortune-tellers*.]
  BT Extrasensory perception
     Precognition
     Telepathy
  RT Fortune-tellers
  NT Clairvoyants

PSYCHOANALYSTS
  UF Analysts
  RT Mental illness
     Psychiatric hospitals
     Psychologists

PSYCHOLOGICAL FICTION [Here are entered works that deal with the thoughts and psychological motivation of the characters. Works that portray the uninterrupted and uneven flow of the consciousness of characters are entered under *Stream of consciousness fiction*.]
  BT Fiction
  RT Suspense fiction \
  NT Stream of consciousness fiction

PSYCHOLOGICAL FICTION, GERMAN (Russian, etc.) [Here are entered collections of psychological fiction by German (Russian, etc.) authors.]

PSYCHOLOGISTS
  RT Mental illness
     Psychiatric hospitals
     Psychoanalysts

PSYCHOLOGY AND LITERATURE [Here are entered works dealing with the relationship between psychology and literature.]

PSYCHOLOGY IN LITERATURE [Here are entered nonfiction works on psychology as portrayed in literature.]

Psychopaths
  USE Insane, Criminal and dangerous
      Mentally Ill

Psychotics
  USE Mentally ill

PUBLIC HOUSING
  RT Apartment houses
     Public welfare

Public prosecutors
  USE Legal stories

**PUBLIC PROSECUTORS AS DETECTIVES **
  UF State's attorneys as detectives
  RT Lawyers as detectives \

PUBLIC RELATIONS CONSULTANTS
  RT Press agents

PUBLIC RELATIONS CONSULTANTS AS DETECTIVES \
PUBLIC WELFARE
- RT Poverty
  - Public housing

Publicists
- USE Press agents

PUBLISHERS AND PUBLISHING
- UF Literary life
- RT Editors

PUBLISHERS AS DETECTIVES \
- RT Journalists as detectives \

PUNISHMENT
- BT Crime

PYROMANIA [Here are entered works dealing with the irresistible urge to start fires.]
- BT Fires

QUACKS AND QUACKERY
- BT Criminals
- RT Physicians

QUADRIPLEGICS
- UF Tetraplegics
- RT Paraplegics

QUARRELING
- UF Arguments
  - Family feuds
- RT Vendetta

Quebec City
- USE Quebec (Quebec)

QUEBEC (PROVINCE)
- BT Canada
- NT Montreal (Quebec)

QUEBEC (QUEBEC)
- UF Quebec City

QUEENS
- RT Nobility
- SA subdivision *Queens* under the names of countries, cities, etc., and ethnic groups, for example, *Great Britain—Queens*; *Zulu (African people)—Queens*.

QUEENS (NEW YORK, N.Y.)
- BT New York (N.Y.)

QUEENSLAND
- BT Australia
- NT Brisbane (Qld.)

QUESTS \
- UF Searches
- BT Legends
- RT Grail

QUESTS IN LITERATURE [Here are entered non-fiction works on the history and criticism of quests as portrayed in literature.]

QUEUES \
- UF Lines (Queues)

R.A.F.
- USE Great Britain. Royal Air Force

RABBIS
- BT Jews
  - Judaism
- RT Synagogues

RABBIS AS DETECTIVES \
- BT Clergy as detectives \

RACE RELATIONS
- UF Racial integration
- BT Blacks
  - Social problems
- SA subdivision *Race Relations* under names of regions, countries, cities, etc., for example, *South Africa—Race Relations*
- NT Interracial marriage

Racial integration
- USE Race relations

Racial intermarriage
- USE Interracial marriage

RADICALISM
- BT Political fiction
- RT Anarchism

RADIO BROADCASTING

RADIO STORIES [Here are entered works of fiction based on programs originally written for radio broadcasting.]
- UF Radio tie-in fiction
- BT Fiction
- RT Television stories \

Radio tie-in fiction
- USE Radio stories

RADIOACTIVE FALLOUT
- BT Nuclear warfare
  - Nuclear weapons
  - Survival after nuclear warfare \

RADIOACTIVE WASTES
- BT Nuclear energy

RAILROAD STORIES [Here are entered novels or short stories dealing with railroads or railroad travel.]
- UF Railroad travel
  - Railroads
  - Railroads—Trains

92 RAILROAD TRAVEL

 BT Fiction
Railroad travel
 USE Railroad stories
Railroads
 USE Railroad stories
Railroads—Trains
 USE Railroad stories
RAIN AND RAINFALL
 RT Droughts
  Floods
RAINSTORMS
 RT Floods
RANCH LIFE
 RT Farm life
  Western stories
Rangers, Texas
 USE Texas Rangers
RAPE
RARE BOOKS
 RT Book collectors
  Booksellers and bookselling
Rascals
 USE Picaresque fiction\
  Rogues and vagabonds
READING
 RT Literacy
REAL ESTATE INVESTMENT
 UF Land speculation
REAL EVENTS\ [Here are entered works loosely based on actual events. Works of factual representation having the objective quality and authority of the real event are entered under *Nonfiction novels*\. Works in which real people and real events have been disguised for literary purposes are entered under *Livres á clef*. Works in which people who actually exist or who existed appear in minor roles are entered under *Real people*\. Works dealing predominately with an actual person are entered under *Biographical fiction*. Works written by the author about his or her own life are entered under *Autobiographical fiction*, even if the main character is given another name.]
 UF Documentary fiction
 RT Autobiographical fiction
  Biographical fiction
  Livres á clef
  Nonfiction novels\
  Real people\
 SA names of real events, such as *World War, 1939-1945*, etc.

REAL PEOPLE\ [Here are entered works in which people who actually exist or who existed appear in minor roles. Works loosely based on actual events are entered under *Real events*\. Works of factual representation having the objective quality and authority of the real event are entered under *Nonfiction novels*\. Works in which real people and real events have been disguised for literary purposes are entered under *Livres á clef*. Works dealing loosely with actual occurrences are entered under *Real events*\. Works dealing predominately with an actual person are entered under *Biographical fiction*. Works written by the author about his or her own life are entered under *Autobiographical fiction*, even if the main character is given another name.]
 UF Documentary fiction
 RT Autobiographical fiction
  Biographical fiction
  Livres á clef
  Nonfiction novels\
  Real events\
 SA names of real people, such as *Washington, George*, etc.
RECLUSES
 NT Hermits [Religious recluses]
RECONCILIATION
 RT Atonement
REFORMATORIES
 BT Prisons
 RT Juvenile delinquents
REFUGEES [Here are entered works dealing with persons who have had to flee their homes for personal safety. Works dealing with persons who have been banished from their home country are entered under *Exiles*. Works dealing with persons who live in another country for other reasons are entered under their nationality with their country of residence as a subdivision, for example, *Polish—United States*, *Americans—France*, etc.]
 UF Emigres
  Expatriates
 RT Exiles
REFUGEES, JEWISH
REFUGEES, POLISH

Regency England
  USE Great Britain—History—George III, 1760-1820
    Love stories, Regency\
Regency romance
  USE Love stories, Regency\
REGINA (SASK.)
  BT Saskatchewan
Regulators (Vigilantes)
  USE Vigilantes
REJUVENATION
  RT Longevity
    Old age
Relatives
  USE Domestic fiction
RELIGION
  RT Agnosticism
    Bible—History of Biblical events
    Churches [Buildings used for worship]
    Clergy
    Cults
    Paganism
    Saints
    Spiritual healing [For faith healing]
    Theologians
  NT Religious fiction
RELIGION, PRIMITIVE [Here are entered works dealing with very early religions that are now extinct or that have evolved. Works dealing with having little or no religion coupled with uninhibited seeking after material goods and sensual pleasure are entered under *Paganism.*]
  RT Paganism
RELIGIONS
  NT Churches [Buildings used for worship]
    Religious fiction
RELIGIONS—RELATIONS
  UF Conflict of religions
    Religious conflict
  NT Christianity and other religions
    Judaism—Relations—Christianity
Religious conflict
  USE Religions—Relations
Religious conversion
  USE Conversion
RELIGIOUS EDUCATION [Here are entered works dealing with religious instruction given in schools, churches, and private life. Works dealing with general education in schools run under the auspices of a religion are entered under *Church schools.*]
  RT Church schools

RELIGIOUS FICTION [Here are entered works dealing with religion or with religious topics or themes.]
  UF Religious life
  BT Fiction
    Religion
    Religions
  NT Bible—History of Biblical events
    Bible—History of contemporary events
    Christian fiction
    Islamic stories
    Jewish religious fiction [Fiction on Jewish religious topics and themes]
    Monastic and religious life
Religious life
  USE Religious fiction
Religious orders
  USE Monastic and religious life
    Monastic and religious life of women
  SA names of individual religious orders such as *Dominicans, Jesuits,* etc.
RENAISSANCE [Here are entered works dealing with the break from the medieval period, the change in society, and the rebirth of arts and letters in the 14th to 16th centuries. In Italy, the fullest flowering was from approximately 1300 to 1599; in England, it was from approximately 1500 to 1649.]
  NT Great Britain—History—Early Stuarts, 1603-1649
    Great Britain—History—Tudors, 1485-1603
    Italy—History—15th Century
    Italy—History—16th Century
REPORTERS AND REPORTING [Here are entered works dealing with reporters working within print media only. Works dealing with television reporters are entered under *Television journalists.*]
  BT Journalists
  RT Television journalists
Reporters as Detectives
  USE Journalists as detectives\
    Television journalists as detectives\
RESEARCH
  NT Science—Experiments
RESORTS
  RT Camps
    Hotels, taverns, etc.
    Tourist camps, hostels, etc.
    Vacations

REST HOMES [Here are entered works that deal with institutions that provide housing and general care for the convalescent. Works that deal with institutions that provide housing and general care for the aged are entered under *Old age homes*. Works dealing with private institutions that provide long-term personal and nursing care to the aged or chronically ill are entered under *Nursing homes*. Works dealing with planned residential developments for the aged that also provide meal service, medical care, etc., are entered under *Life care communities*. Works that deal with institutions that provide long-term care and therapy together with a regimen such as diet or exercise are entered under *Sanatoriums*. Works dealing with institutions that give the sick and injured medical and surgical care are entered under *Hospitals*.]
   RT Hospitals
       Life care communities
       Nursing homes
       Old age homes
       Sanatoriums
       Sick

RESTAURANTS, LUNCH ROOMS, ETC.
   RT Caterers and catering
       Cooks

RETAIL TRADE [Here are entered works dealing with the general business of retailing. Works dealing with retail stores are entered under *Stores, Retail*. Works dealing with persons who own or operate a retail business are entered under *Merchants*.]
   BT Business
   NT Merchants
       Stores, Retail

Retarded people
   USE Mentally handicapped

RETIREMENT, PLACES OF [Here are entered works dealing with areas popular for retirement.]
   RT Old age homes

RETIREMENT COMMUNITIES
   RT Old age homes

Retirement homes
   USE Old age homes

REUNIONS
   UF Homecoming
   NT Family reunions

REVENGE
   NT Vendetta [Taking revenge for the killing of kin on the murderer, or the kin of the murderer]

Reviewers
   USE Critics

REVOLUTIONS [Prefer the name of a specific revolution, for example, *United States—History—Revolution, 1775-1783*.]
   NT Imaginary revolutions [Works of nonfiction on the history and criticism of imaginary revolutions]

RHODE ISLAND
   NT Providence (R.I.)

Rich people
   USE Capitalists and financiers
        Millionaires

RICHMOND (VA.)
   BT Virginia

RIGA (LATVIA)
   BT Latvia

RITES AND CEREMONIES

RITES AND CEREMONIES—JAPAN
   NT Japanese tea ceremony

RIVER LIFE
   SA names of rivers such as Mississippi River; Nile River; Thames River (England), etc., as listed in the subdivisions under *Rivers* in *The Library of Congress Subject Headings*.

RIVIERA (FRANCE)
   BT France

ROAD FICTION [Here are entered works in which a journey is a central part of the action. An example is Jack Kerouac's *On the Road*.]
   BT Automobile travel
       Fiction
       Picaresque fiction\
       Voyages and travels

ROAD TOWN (V.I.)
   BT British Virgin Islands

Robber barons
   USE Capitalists and financiers

ROBBERY [Here are entered works dealing with taking another's property using violence or the threat of violence. Works dealing with persons who commit robbery are entered under *Brigands and robbers*. Works dealing with the ethical and psychological aspects of theft are entered under *Stealing*. Works dealing with stealing as a crime

are entered under *Larceny*. Works dealing with persons who commit theft or burglary are entered under *Thieves*. Works dealing with breaking and entering for the purpose of theft or robbery are entered under *Burglary*. Works dealing with persons who steal, profiteer, or kill, especially in a merciless manner, are entered under *Outlaws*. Works dealing with robbery committed on the street and involving a beating or other physical assault are entered under *Mugging*.]
- UF Holdups
- BT Crime
  Thieves
- RT Burglary
  Larceny
  Mugging
  Outlaws
  Stealing
- NT Brigands and robbers

ROBINSONADES [Here are entered nonfiction works on literature that deal with an individual's survival without the aid of civilization, especially when marooned on a desert island.]
- RT Survival (After airplane accidents, shipwrecks, etc.)
  Survival after nuclear warfare \
  Wilderness survival

ROBOTS [Here are entered works dealing with machines that perform tasks normally associated with human beings or that seem to possess qualities similar to that of a human. Works dealing with robots that are in the shape of a human being are entered under *Androids*. Works dealing with humans altered with artificial parts are entered under *Cyborgs*\.]
- RT Androids
  Cyborgs \
  Science fiction

ROBOTS IN LITERATURE [Here are entered nonfiction works on the history and criticism of robots as portrayed in literature.]

ROCK MUSIC
- UF Music, Rock
- BT Musical fiction

ROGUES AND VAGABONDS [Here are entered works dealing with wandering, disorderly, or dissolute but not necessarily displeasing persons. Works that are episodic in the detailing of the adventures of a rascal, rogue, or vagabond getting by on his or her wits are entered under *Picaresque fiction*\. Works dealing with traveling beggars who will not work are entered under *Tramps*. Works dealing with the legal charge of being a tramp are entered under *Vagrancy*. Works dealing with aimless persons who wander from place to place and job to job are entered under *Drifters*. Works dealing with persons who travel as a way of life are entered under *Wayfaring life*.]
- UF Rascals
- RT Drifters
  Homelessness
  Picaresque fiction \
  Tramps
  Vagrancy
  Wayfaring life

ROGUES AND VAGABONDS IN LITERATURE [Here are entered nonfiction works on the history and criticism of rogues and vagabonds as portrayed in literature.]

Roman Republic
- USE Rome—History—Republic, 510-30 B.C.

Romance
- USE Betrothal
  Courtship
  Love stories
  Melodramatic fiction \
  Romantic suspense fiction \

ROMANCE FICTION [Here are entered nonfiction works about fiction written in the Romance languages (French, Spanish, Portuguese, Italian, Romanian).]

ROMANCES [Here are entered works of adventure produced in the Middle Ages that deal with knights, kings, or ladies in distress acting under the impulse of love, religion, or the desire for adventure. Works that are a collection of romances centering around some outstanding event or character and which are commonly traditional stories given form by a succession of authors are entered under *Cycles (Literature)*. Works dealing with the elaborate medieval system of manners and morals are entered under *Chivalry*.]
- BT Fiction

RT Chivalry
Crusades
Knights and knighthood
NT Arthurian romances [Romances involving King Arthur and/or his court]
Cycles (Literature)
ROMANS [Here are entered works dealing with Romans up to 476 A.D. Works dealing with Romans after that time are entered under *Italians*.]
BT Italians
Rome
ROMANS—ENGLAND
Romantic love
USE Love affairs\
Love stories
ROMANTIC SUSPENSE FICTION\ [Here are entered works of suspense in which romantic love plays a central part.]
UF Romance
Suspense fiction, Romantic
BT Fiction
Love stories
Suspense fiction\
Thrillers\
RT Gothic revival fiction\
ROMANTICISM [Here are entered nonfiction works dealing with the movement that began in the 18th century that emphasized feeling and imagination over intellect and reason.]
BT Fiction
ROME [Here are entered works dealing with the Roman empire up to 476 A.D. Works dealing with Italy are entered under *Italy*. Works confined to the city of Rome are entered under *Rome (Italy)*.]
BT Italy
RT Rome (Italy)
NT Romans
ROME—HISTORY [Here are entered works dealing with historical events in the Roman empire. Works dealing with or including pre-Roman times are entered under *Italy— History—To 476*.]
BT Italy—History—To 476
ROME—HISTORY—REPUBLIC, 510-30 B.C.
UF Roman Republic
Rome (Republic)
ROME—HISTORY—GERMANIC INVASIONS, 3D-6TH CENTURIES
UF Barbarians

ROME (ITALY) [Here are entered works confined to the city of Rome. Works dealing with the Roman Empire to 476 A.D. are entered under *Rome*. Works dealing with Italy are entered under *Italy*.]
BT Italy
RT Rome
Rome (Republic)
USE Rome—History—Republic, 510-30 B.C.
Rooming houses
USE Lodging-houses
Royal Air Force
USE Great Britain. Royal Air Force
ROYAL CANADIAN MOUNTED POLICE
UF Canada. Royal Canadian Mounted Police
Mounties
ROYAL MILITARY COLLEGE, SANDHURST
UF Great Britain. Royal Military College, Sandhurst
Sandhurst Royal Military College
Royal Navy
USE Great Britain. Royal Navy
RUNAWAY CHILDREN
RT Juvenile delinquents
Problem children
RUNAWAY TEENAGERS
UF Teenage runaways
RT Juvenile delinquents
Problem children
RUNAWAY WIVES
Russian-American relations
USE Soviet Union—Foreign relations—United States
United States—Foreign relations—Soviet Union
Russian-British relations
USE Great Britain—Foreign relations—Soviet Union
Soviet Union—Foreign relations—Great Britain
RUSSIAN FICTION
RUSSIAN S.F.S.R. [The Russian S.F.S.R. is one of the fifteen constituent republics of the Soviet Union. It is abbreviated R.S.F.S.R.]
BT Soviet Union
NT Moscow (R.S.F.S.R.)
Siberia (R.S.F.S.R.)
RUSSIANS [Here are entered works dealing with persons who are citizens of the Soviet Union or who are of Russian

heritage. Works dealing with local governing councils in the Soviet Union are entered under *Soviets (Councils)*.]
   RT Soviets (Councils)
RUSSIANS—ENGLAND
RUSSIANS—GREAT BRITAIN
RUSSIANS—UNITED STATES

S.I.D.S.
   USE Sudden infant death syndrome
SABAH
   BT Malaysia
SABOTAGE
   UF Intrigue
   RT Spy stories
   SA subdivisions *Secret service; Underground movements* under names of wars, for example, *World War, 1914-1918—Secret service*; *World War, 1939-1945—Underground movements*
Sacrifice, Human
   USE Human sacrifice
SADISM [Here are entered works dealing with delight or sexual gratification gained from inflicting cruelty on others. Works dealing with delight or sexual gratification from having cruelty inflicted upon oneself are entered under *Masochism*.]
   BT Cruelty
   RT Masochism
SADNESS [Here are entered works dealing with the atmosphere or effect produced by depression, melancholy, grief, or despair. *Sadness* can also be used as a general term for low spirits or unhappiness when there is no clear explanation or indication of the cause or extent. Works dealing with an often prolonged disordered psychological state of low spirits and unhappiness whose cause is often internal in origin are entered under *Depression, Mental*. Works dealing with a mood of dejection, discouragement, or pensiveness which is of a more transitory nature and which has an external cause are entered under *Melancholy*. Works dealing with deep distress caused by or seemingly caused by bereavement are entered under *Grief*. Works dealing with an utter loss of hope or confidence are entered under *Despair*.]
   RT Depression, Mental
       Despair
       Grief
       Melancholy
SAGAS [Here is entered medieval Scandinavian heroic adventure literature detailing historical and legendary occurrences, generally dealing with important families. Broad and lengthy works that recount the deeds of a legendary or historical hero are entered under *Epic literature*. Works of traditional narrative that are shorter than sagas but still purport to have some basis in reality are entered under *Legends*. Works of traditional narrative that are shorter than sagas but deal more with the supernatural and less with the historical are entered under *Mythology*. Works that deal with shorter narratives passed on by word of mouth about common or illiterate people are entered under *Folk literature*. Collections of traditional narratives that are for the most part fictitious and are told primarily for entertainment are entered under *Tales*.]
   BT Epic literature
       Folk literature
       Legends
       Mythology
       Tales
SAIGON (VIETNAM)
   BT Vietnam
SAILBOATS [Here are entered works dealing with smaller boats using sail power and operated on inland waterways or near the shore on oceans. Smaller boats usually powered by oars, paddles, poles, or outboard motors are entered under *Boats and boating*. Works dealing with large sailboats or powerboats with closed cabins and which are built for pleasure or private cruising are entered under *Yachts and yachting*. Works dealing with large seagoing sailing vessels used for other purposes are entered under *Sailing ships*. Large seagoing power vessels are entered under *Ships*.]
   BT Boats and boating
   RT Sailing ships

Ships
Yachts and yachting
SAILING SHIPS [Here are entered works dealing with large seagoing sailing vessels. Works dealing with smaller craft using sail power and operated on inland waterways or near the shore on oceans are entered under *Sailboats*. Works dealing with large sailboats or powerboats with closed cabins and which are built for pleasure or private cruising are entered under *Yachts and yachting*. Large seagoing power vessels are entered under *Ships*.]
- BT Ocean travel
Sea stories
Ships
- RT Sailboats
Yachts and yachting
- NT Clipper ships

SAINTS
- RT Religion

SAINTS IN LITERATURE [Here are entered nonfiction works on the history and criticism of saints as portrayed in literature.]

SALT LAKE CITY (UTAH)
- BT Utah

SALVADORAN FICTION
- UF Salvadorian fiction
- BT El Salvador

Salvadorian fiction
- USE Salvadoran fiction

SALVAGE [Here are entered works dealing with marine salvage only. Works dealing with derelict and abandoned marine craft are entered under *Derelicts*.]
- BT Ships
- RT Derelicts

SAMURAI
- BT Japan
- RT Soldiers

SAN FRANCISCO (CALIF.)
- BT California

SANATORIUMS [Here are entered works dealing with institutions that provide long-term care and therapy together with a regimen such as diet or exercise. Works dealing with institutions that give the sick and injured medical and surgical care are entered under *Hospitals*. Works that deal with institutions that provide housing and general care for the convalescent are entered under *Rest homes*. Works dealing with private institutions that provide long-term personal and nursing care to the aged or chronically ill are entered under *Nursing homes*. Works dealing with planned residential developments for the aged that also provide meal service, medical care, etc. are entered under *Life care communities*. Works that deal with institutions that provide housing and general care for the aged are entered under *Old age homes*.]
- RT Hospitals
Life care communities
Nursing homes
Old age homes
Rest homes
Sick

Sandhurst Royal Military College
- USE Royal Military College, Sandhurst

SANTA CLAUS
- UF Kris Kringle

SANTA FE (N.M.)
- BT New Mexico

SARAJEVO (BOSNIA AND HERCEGOVINA)
- BT Bosnia and Hercegovina

SARAWAK
- BT Malaysia

SASKATCHEWAN
- BT Canada
- NT Regina (Sask.)

SATANISM
- BT Devil
- RT Demoniac possession
Demonology
Exorcism
Voodooism
Witchcraft
- NT Yezidis [A Middle Eastern sect that worships an angel believed to have formerly been the author of evil, but now believed to be the chief angel of good]

SATIRE [Here are entered nonfiction works dealing with satire.]

SATIRICAL FICTION\ [Here are entered works of fiction that use humor to expose human vice or folly. Works that use the device of desperate, sardonic humor to induce laughter as the appropriate response to the apparent meaninglessness and absurdity of existence are entered under *Black humor fiction*\. Works that satirically portray the be-

havior and manners of a particular class or group (generally a sophisticated, artificial society) are entered under *Comedies of manners*\.]
- UF Comic fiction
  Farcical fiction
- BT Fiction
- RT Black humor fiction\
  Humorous stories
  Invective
- NT Comedies of manners\

SAXONS
- NT Great Britain—History—Anglo Saxon period, 449-1066

SCANDINAVIANS
- NT Finns

SCHIZOPHRENICS
- RT Multiple personality

SCHOLARS [Here are entered works dealing with persons who through long and systematic study have acquired mastery of an academic discipline together with investigative and interpretive skills. Works dealing with the academic process of thorough study, investigation, and interpretation are entered under *Learning and scholarship*. Works dealing generally with learning and scholarship, the arts, literature, etc., are entered under *Intellectual life*.]
- BT Intellectual life
  Learning and scholarship
- RT College students
  College teachers
  Graduate students

School alumni
- USE subdivision *Alumni* under types of schools, for example, *Public schools—Alumni*, or under names of schools, for example, *University of Oxford—Alumni*

School life
- USE Schools
  Students

School stories
- USE Schools

School teachers
- USE Teachers

School theater
- USE Amateur theater

SCHOOLS
- UF Campus life
  School life
  School stories
- BT Education
- RT College stories
- NT Elementary schools [Typically including but not necessarily confined to kindergarten through 6th grade or kindergarten through 8th grade]
  Junior high schools [Generally including but not necessarily confined to 7th, 8th, and 9th grades]
  Middle schools [Generally including but not necessarily confined to 4th, 5th, and 6th grades]
  Students
  Teachers

Schools, Vocational
- USE Trade schools

SCIENCE—EXPERIMENTS
- UF Scientific experiments
- BT Research

SCIENCE FANTASY\ [Here are entered works that invent a new cosmology, new scientific principles, or new laws of nature and are a blending of science fiction and fantastic fiction. Works that deal with non-existent, incredible, or unreal worlds, characters, and physical principles are entered under *Fantastic fiction*. Works of fantasy that deal with possible although not necessarily probable events and are based approximately on scientific principles as we know them are entered under *Science fiction*. Works that are essentially realistic, but which incorporate some extremely unlikely events, yet fall outside the conventions of readily identifiable genres such as *Fantastic fiction, Science fiction*, etc., are entered under *Improbable fiction*\.]
- UF Fantasy, Science
  Other worlds
- BT Fantastic fiction
  Fiction
- RT Allegories
  Imaginary histories
  Improbable fiction\
  Science fiction

SCIENCE FICTION [Here are entered works of fantasy that deal with possible though not necessarily probable events and are based approximately on scientific principles as we know them. Works that deal with non-existent, incredible, or

unreal worlds, characters, and physical principles are entered under *Fantastic fiction*. Works that invent a new cosmology, new scientific principles, or new laws of nature and are a blending of science fiction and fantastic fiction are entered under *Science fantasy*. Works that are essentially realistic but which incorporate some extremely unlikely events, yet fall outside the conventions of readily identifiable genres such as *Fantastic fiction, Science fiction*, etc., are entered under *Improbable fiction*.]
- UF Galactic empires
  Imaginary planets
  Other worlds
  Space adventure
  Space civilizations
  Space operas
- BT Fantastic fiction
  Fiction
  Light fiction\
  Thrillers\
- RT Allegories
  Apocalyptic fiction\
  Clones\
  Dystopias [The opposite of utopias]
  Extraterrestrial bases
  Extraterrestrial beings\
  Future\
  Imaginary histories [The world if history had been different]
  Improbable fiction\
  Interplanetary voyages [Travel to planets]
  Interstellar travel [Travel to stars]
  Life on other planets [Life that exists naturally on other planets]
  Outer space
  Robots
  Science fantasy\
  Space colonies [Communities established in space or on natural extraterrestrial bodies]
  Space stations [Manned installations in orbit around natural extraterrestrial bodies or the earth]
  Space warfare
  Time travel
  Utopias

SCIENCE FICTION, CYBERPUNK [Here are entered works of science fiction that combine a high tech ambience with a countercultural viewpoint. These works are often literary in style and can be humanistic.]
- RT Science fiction, Literary\

SCIENCE FICTION, HARD SCIENCE [Here are entered works of science fiction with a heavy scientific interest and an imaginative projection of scientific possibility for the future.]

SCIENCE FICTION, HUMOROUS
- BT Humorous stories
- RT Fantastic fiction, Humorous\

SCIENCE FICTION, LITERARY [Here are entered works of science fiction that seek to transcend the lighter aspects of the genre and use a literary style to deal with the philosophy and universal themes of human existence.]
- RT Science fiction, Cyberpunk\

Science fiction, Messianic
- USE Science fiction, Religious\

SCIENCE FICTION, MILITARY [Here are entered works of science fiction that emphasize military dictatorships, military life, and warfare.]

Science fiction, New Wave
- USE Science fiction, Social science\

SCIENCE FICTION, RELIGIOUS [Here are entered works of science fiction dealing with issues of theology and metaphysics posed by a universe expanded by science.]
- UF Science fiction, Messianic

SCIENCE FICTION, SOCIAL SCIENCE [Here are entered works of science fiction written from the viewpoint of the social sciences; emphasis is placed on the sociological structure of civilizations and the relations of members to their society.]
- UF Science fiction, New Wave

Scientific experiments
- USE Science—Experiments

SCIENTISTS
- RT Inventors

SCOPOPHILIA
- UF Peeping Toms

Scotch-Irish
- USE Scots-Irish

SCOTLAND [If a place is located in Scotland, add the identifier *(Scotland)*, for example, *Aberdeen (Scotland)*. For further information, see 23.4D2 in *AACR2R*.]
- BT Great Britain

- RT Clans—Scotland
- NT Edinburgh (Scotland)
  Glasgow (Scotland)
  Highlands (Scotland)
  Lowlands (Scotland)
  Shetland (Scotland)

SCOTS
- BT British

SCOTS—UNITED STATES [Here are entered works dealing with Scots visiting or living in the United States.]
- NT Scottish Americans

SCOTS-IRISH [Here are entered works dealing with Scottish people who settled in Northern Ireland and their descendants. Works dealing with the secret society organized in 1795 to support the Protestant religion in Northern Ireland are entered under *Orangemen*.]
- UF Scotch-Irish
- BT British
  Ireland
  Irish
  Northern Ireland
  Ulster (Northern Ireland and Ireland)
- RT Orangemen

SCOTTISH AMERICANS [Here are entered works dealing with Americans of Scottish ancestry.]
- BT Scots—United States

Scottish dialect fiction
- USE Dialect fiction—Scots \

SCOTTISH FICTION [Here are entered works written in the Scottish dialect or in English by Scottish authors. Works written in English by Scottish authors or collections of works written exclusively in English by Scottish authors are also entered under *English fiction—Scottish authors*.]
- RT English fiction—Scottish authors

SCREENWRITERS
- RT Motion pictures

SCULPTURE [Here are entered works dealing generally with the art of sculpting as well as with pieces of art that have been sculpted. Works dealing specifically with a sculpted, cast, or modeled image of an entire figure are entered under *Statues*. Works dealing with an image of a person engraved on a coin or sculpted for a sepulchral monument or with a crude representation of a particular person, such as a stuffed dummy, are entered under *Effigies*. Works dealing with a sculpted image of the upper part of the body are entered under *Busts*.]
- RT Statues
- NT Busts
  Effigies

Sea life
- USE Seafaring life [For non-military life at sea or for naval sea life where the navy is not identified]
  subdivision *Sea life* under navies, for example, *United States. Navy—Sea life*; for fiction about naval life on shore installations, use the subdivision *Military life* under navies, for example, *Great Britain. Royal Navy—Military life*

SEA STORIES [Here are entered novels and stories using the sea as a setting or dealing generally with the sea and its environment. Works dealing with civilian travel on a specific cruise are entered under *Ocean travel*. Works dealing with a specific ship as the center of the story are entered under *Ships*. Works dealing with professional life at sea and with navy life when no specific navy is involved are entered under *Seafaring life*.]
- BT Fiction
- RT Ocean travel
- NT Sailing ships
  Seafaring life
  Ship captains
  Ships
  Yachts and yachting

SEAFARING LIFE [Here are entered works dealing with professional life at sea and with navy life when no specific navy is involved. Works dealing with life at sea in a specific navy are entered under the navy with the subdivision *Sea life*, for example, *United States. Navy—Sea life*. Works using the sea as a setting or dealing generally with the sea and its environment are entered under *Sea stories*. Works dealing with civilian travel on a specific cruise are entered under *Ocean travel*. Works dealing with a specific ship as the center of the story are entered under *Ships*.]
- UF Naval life
- BT Sea stories

RT Ocean travel
Ships
SEALS
USE United States. Navy. Sea Air Land Team
Seamstresses
USE Dressmakers
Seances
USE Spiritualism
Searches
USE Quests \
SEATTLE (WASH.)
BT Washington (State)
Secret agents
USE Spy stories
Secret codes
USE Code and cipher stories
Secret service
USE Spy stories
Unites States. Secret Service
SEDITION [Here are entered works dealing with conduct leading to resistance to a government. Works dealing with overt acts of betrayal or acts of resistance to a government are entered under *Treason*.]
RT Treason
SELANGOR
BT Malaysia
Self-government (in education)
USE Student government
SELF-INTEREST [Here are entered works dealing with selfishness or a concern for oneself at the expense of others. Works dealing with self-absorption and concentration on oneself and one's interests are entered under *Egoism*. Works dealing with self-love and the overvaluation of oneself are entered under *Narcissism*.]
RT Egoism
Narcissism
Self-made men
USE Ambition
Capitalists and financiers
Success
SELF-RESPECT
Senate
USE United States. Congress. Senate
Senators as detectives
USE Legislators as detectives \
Women legislators as detectives \
SENILE DEMENTIA
RT Alzheimer's disease
Old age
Presenile dementia
SEQUELS (LITERATURE) [Here are entered works that are complete in themselves but which continue the narrative course of a previous book. A sequel usually involves the same characters but at a different time or in a different situation; a sequel does not necessarily have to be written by the same author. Works that have a collective title in addition to an individual title are entered under *Series (Publications)*. Series works are usually issued separately and successively, have the same physical appearance and format, bear a close relationship in topic or theme, and have a volume number. Works such as Agatha Christie's Miss Marple detective stories would thus be entered only under *Sequels (Literature)*, since the works do not have a separate series title and are not numbered. Works such as *Best American Short Stories, 1988* would be entered only under *Series (Publications)*, since the work does not continue the story of the previous volume nor share the same characters or settings. Works such as Charles Nordhoff and James Norman Hall's *Pitcairn Island*, which is the third volume of the Bounty trilogy, would be entered under both *Sequels (Literature)* and *Series (Publications)*. Works that are a collection of romances (medieval stories about knights and their deeds) centering around some outstanding event or character and which are commonly traditional stories given form by a succession of authors are entered under *Cycles (Literature)*. Single works of fiction that appear in serialized installments are entered under *Serialized fiction*.]
UF Prequels (Literature)
Tetralogies
Trilogies
BT Fiction
RT Cycles (Literature)
Serialized fiction
Series (Publications)
SERBIA
BT Yugoslavia

   NT Belgrade (Serbia)
SERFDOM [Here are entered works dealing with agricultural laborers bound to the land in service to its owner. Works dealing with laborers bound in servitude by prison sentence or indebtedness are entered under *Peonage*. Works dealing with agricultural laborers or owners of very small plots of farm land, especially in Europe, Asia, or South America, are entered under *Peasantry*. Works dealing with peasants who are slaves to their feudal lord but free in other respects are entered under *Villeinage*. Works dealing with the working classes are entered under *Working class*.]
   BT Farm life
         Working class
   RT Peasantry
         Villeinage
   NT Peonage
Sergeants
   USE subdivision *Noncommissioned officers* under armies, for example, *United States. Army—Noncommissioned officers*
SERIAL MURDERS [Here are entered works involving repetitive homicides over a period of time, usually involving one victim at a time and carried out by the same person or group of persons. Works dealing with the slaying of several people at the same time, in the same general area, and by the same person or group of persons are entered under *Mass murder*.]
   BT Murder
   RT Mass murder
SERIALIZED FICTION [Here are entered single works of fiction that appear in serialized installments. Works of fiction that appear in serialized installments in a newspaper are entered under *Feuilletons*.]
   BT Fiction
   RT Sequels (Literature)
         Series (Publications)
   NT Feuilletons
Series, Books in
   USE Series (Publications)
SERIES (PUBLICATIONS) [Here are entered works that have a collective title in addition to an individual title. Series works are usually issued separately and successively, have the same physical appearance and format, bear a close relationship in topic or theme and have a volume number. Works that are complete in themselves but which continue the narrative course of a previous book are entered under *Sequels (Literature)*. A sequel usually involves the same characters but at a different time or in a different situation; a sequel does not necessarily have to be written by the same author. Works such as Agatha Christie's Miss Marple detective stories would thus be entered only under *Sequels (Literature)*, since the works do not have a separate series title and are not numbered. Works such as *Best American Short Stories, 1988* would be entered only under *Series (Publications)*, since the work does not continue the story of the previous volume nor share the same characters or settings. Works such as Charles Nordhoff and James Norman Hall's *Pitcairn Island*, which is the third volume of the Bounty trilogy, would be entered under both *Sequels (Literature)* and *Series (Publications)*. Works that are part of a collection of romances (medieval stories about knights and their deeds) centering around some outstanding event or character and which are commonly traditional stories given form by a succession of authors are entered under *Cycles (Literature)*. Single works of fiction that appear in serialized installments are entered under *Serialized fiction*. Single novels that are published in three separate books are entered under *Three-decker novels*.]
   UF Books in series
         Series, Books in
         Tetralogies
         Trilogies
   BT Fiction
   RT Cycles (Literature)
         Sequels (Literature)
         Serialized fiction
         Three-decker novels
Serious fiction
   USE Literary fiction\

SERVANTS IN LITERATURE [Here are entered nonfiction works dealing with the history and criticism of servants as portrayed in literature. Works of fiction dealing with servants are entered under *Domestics*.]
  BT Domestics
SEX
  RT Sexually explicit fiction\
  NT Free love
SEX CRIMES
  UF Sex problems
SEX IN LITERATURE [Here are entered nonfiction works that deal with the history and criticism of sex as portrayed in literature. Works of general fiction that have explicit portrayals of sexuality as a subsidiary part of a larger story are entered under *Sexually explicit fiction*\. Works whose primary purpose is erotic stimulation are entered under *Erotic stories*. Works that deal with the production, distribution, or social effects of erotica are entered under *Pornography*.]
  RT Erotic stories
       Pornography
       Sexually explicit fiction\
SEX IN MARRIAGE
  RT Problem marriages\
Sex problems
  USE Sex crimes
        Sexual deviation
        Sexual disorders
SEX ROLE
SEXUAL DEVIATION
  UF Sex problems
  RT Degeneration
SEXUAL DISORDERS
  UF Sex problems
  RT Problem marriages\
SEXUAL HARASSMENT OF WOMEN
  BT Women
SEXUALLY EXPLICIT FICTION\ [Here are entered works of general fiction that have explicit portrayals of sexuality as part of a larger story. Works whose primary purpose is erotic stimulation are entered under *Erotic stories*. Works that deal with the production, distribution, or social effects of erotica are entered under *Pornography*. Nonfiction works that deal with the history and criticism of sex as portrayed in literature are entered under *Sex in literature*.]
  UF Explicit sex in fiction
  BT Fiction
  RT Detective and mystery stories, Hard-boiled\
       Erotic stories
       Pornography
       Sex
       Sex in literature
SHAME [Here are entered works dealing with humiliating disrepute or disgrace as a reaction to other people's criticism. Works dealing with being responsible for a crime or a sin and with deserving severe punishment are entered under *Guilt*.]
  RT Atonement
       Guilt
SHAME IN LITERATURE [Here are entered nonfiction works on the history and criticism of shame as portrayed in literature.]
SHEPHERDS
  RT Pastoral fiction [Deals with an idealized rustic life]
SHERIFFS [Here are entered works dealing with peace officers who are elected county officials or who work as police in a department headed by such an official. Works dealing with municipal peace officers are entered under *Police*. Works that deal with various kinds of law enforcement officers or with law enforcement officers generally are entered under *Peace officers*. Works dealing with marshals serving in American federal courts are entered under *United States marshals*. Note that the heading *Marshals* is used for works dealing with air marshals or field marshals in the military. Works dealing with peace officers charged with both keeping the public peace and certain petty judicial matters are entered under *Constables*. Westerns that deal with law enforcement officers are entered under *Peace officers* if it cannot be readily determined if the officer is a marshal or sheriff. The heading *Police* is not used with westerns unless specifically so used in the text. It would usually be superfluous to use

any of the peace officer headings with detective and mystery fiction.]
- BT Peace officers
- RT Constables
  Police
  United States marshals

SHETLAND (SCOTLAND) [Here are entered works dealing with the Shetland Islands.]
- BT Scotland

SHIP CAPTAINS
- BT Sea stories

Ship hijacking
- USE Hijacking of ships

SHIPPING
- RT Stevedores

SHIPS [Here are entered works dealing with large seagoing vessels. Works dealing with large seagoing sailing vessels are entered under *Sailing ships*. Works dealing with smaller craft operated on inland bodies of water or near the shore on oceans and usually powered by oars, paddles, poles, or outboard motors are entered under *Boats and boating*. Works dealing with boats using sail power are entered under *Sailboats*. Works dealing with large sailboats or powerboats with closed cabins and built for pleasure or private cruising are entered under *Yachts and yachting*.]
- BT Sea stories
- RT Boats and boating
  Sailboats
  Seafaring life
  Yachts and yachting
- NT Cargo ships
  Derelicts
  Sailing ships
  Salvage
  Tramp shipping

Ships, Abandoned
- USE Derelicts

SHIPWRECKS
- RT Derelicts

SHOOTING
- RT Hunting stories

Shopkeepers
- USE Merchants

SHOPLIFTING
- BT Crime
- BT Thieves

Short novels
- USE Novellas (Short novels)\

SHORT-SHORT STORIES\ [Here are entered collections of very brief short stories, of approximately 500 words.]
- BT Fiction
  Short stories

SHORT STORIES [Here are entered general collections of relatively short works of fiction with a definite formal development and unity, the intent of which is to reveal characters or situations using only a few actions or events. Collections of very brief short stories of approximately 500 words or less, are entered under *Short-short stories*\. Short stories contained within a novel or collections of short stories with a common character or setting are entered under *Frame-stories*. Collections of traditional narratives that are for the most part fictitious and are told primarily for entertainment are entered under *Tales*.]
- UF Stories
- BT Fiction
  Tales
- NT Frame-stories
  Short-short stories\

SHORT STORIES—HISPANIC AUTHORS [Here are entered collections of short stories by more than one Hispanic author.]

SHORT STORIES—WOMEN AUTHORS [Here are entered collections of short stories by more than one woman author.]

SHORT STORIES, AMERICAN (English, etc.) [Here are entered collections of short stories by more than one American (English, etc.) author.]

SHORT STORIES, AMERICAN—AFRO-AMERICAN AUTHORS [Here are entered collections of short stories by more than one Afro-American author.]

SHORT STORIES, AMERICAN—MEXICAN AMERICAN AUTHORS [Here are entered collections of short stories by more than one Mexican-American author.]

SHORT STORIES, AMERICAN—MINORITY AUTHORS [Here are entered collections of short stories by more than one American author who is a member of a minority group. Prefer a more specific heading, such as *Short stories, American—Afro-American authors*.]

SHORT STORIES, AMERICAN—WOMEN AUTHORS [Here are entered collections of

short stories by more than one American woman author.]
Short stories within a novel
   USE Frame-stories
SIBERIA (R.S.F.S.R.)
   BT Russian S.F.S.R.
      Soviet Union
SICILY (ITALY)
   BT Italy
SICK
   RT Hospitals
      Nursing homes
      Rest homes
      Sanatoriums
   NT Terminally ill
SICK IN LITERATURE [Here are entered nonfiction works on the history and criticism of the sick as portrayed in literature.]
SILVER MINES AND MINING
SINGAPORE [Singapore was a state of Malaysia from 1963 to 1965 but was independent before and has been independent since.]
   RT Malaysia
SINGERS
   BT Entertainers
SINGLE MEN
   NT Widowers
SINGLE-PARENT FAMILY [Here are entered works dealing with family units that have only one parent, whether unwed, divorced, or widowed.]
   BT Domestic fiction
   RT Fathers
      Mothers
      Unmarried mothers
SINGLE WOMEN
   UF Old maids
SINGLE WOMEN IN LITERATURE [Here are entered nonfiction works on the history and criticism of single women as portrayed in literature.]
SIOUX FALLS (S.D.)
   BT South Dakota
SISTERS
   BT Domestic fiction
      Female-female relationships \
   RT Triplets
      Twins
   NT Half-sisters \
      Sororicide [Murder of a sister by a sibling]
      Stepchildren

SISTERS AS DETECTIVES \
   BT Women detectives
SISTERS-IN-LAW \
   UF In-laws
SKI RESORTS
   BT Skis and skiing
SKIS AND SKIING
   NT Ski resorts
SKOPJE (MACEDONIA)
   BT Macedonia
SLAVERY
   RT Afro-Americans
      Blacks
      Plantation life
      Underground railroad
SLAVERY AND SLAVES IN LITERATURE [Here are entered nonfiction works on the history and criticism of slavery and slaves as portrayed in literature.]
Sleep, Prolonged
   USE Hypersomnia
SLOVENIA
   BT Yugoslavia
   NT Ljubljana (Slovenia)
SLUMS
   BT Social problems
   RT Poverty
Small town life
   USE City and town life
      Country life
      Suburban life
      Villages
SNOBS AND SNOBBISHNESS [Here are entered works dealing with persons who refuse to associate with persons they feel are beneath their class or attainment. Works dealing with conflict that arises because of social classes are entered under *Social conflict*. Works dealing with the awareness of the social class to which a person belongs are entered under *Class consciousness*.]
   RT Class consciousness
      Social conflict
SNOWSTORMS \
   BT Storms
   RT Avalanches
   NT Blizzards
SOAP OPERAS [Here are entered works dealing with the production or performance of soap operas on radio or television. Works characterized by sensationalism, extravagant emotional appeal, and the subordination of character to

plot, are entered under *Melodramatic fiction\.*]
- RT Melodramatic fiction\

Social alienation
- USE Alienation (Social psychology)

Social conditions [Used only as a subdivision under names of countries, cities, etc., such as *France—Social conditions*, and under classes of persons and ethnic groups, such as *Women—Social conditions*; *Hispanic Americans—Social conditions*, etc.]

SOCIAL CONFLICT [Here are entered works dealing with conflict that arises because of social classes. Works dealing with the awareness of the social class to which a person belongs are entered under *Class consciousness*. Works dealing with persons who refuse to associate with persons they feel are beneath their class or attainment are listed under *Snobs and snobbishness*.]
- UF Conflict of classes
  Conflict of social classes
- RT Class consciousness
  Snobs and snobbishness

SOCIAL HISTORY
- BT Civilization

SOCIAL ISOLATION [Here are entered works dealing with detachment from others either because of one's own wish or from causes beyond one's control. Works that deal with a state of society in which normative standards of conduct and belief have weakened or disappeared or with a similar condition in an individual, commonly characterized by personal disorientation, anxiety, and isolation, are entered under *Anomy*. Works dealing with a situation where there are no others of one's kind with whom to associate or with a mental state in which by wish or compulsion one is cut off from normal contacts with family, friends, colleagues, or neighbors are entered under *Solitude*. Works dealing with a lack of intimate association with others and the resultant sadness are entered under *Loneliness*. Works dealing with estrangement and loss or lack of adjustment between an individual and his social or intellectual environment are entered under *Alienation (Social psychology)*.]
- RT Alienation (Social psychology)
  Anomy
  Loneliness
  Solitude

SOCIAL PROBLEMS
- BT Civilization
- NT Antisemitism
  Crime
  Juvenile delinquents
  Poverty
  Proletarian fiction\
  Prostitutes
  Race relations
  Slums

SOCIETIES [Here are entered works dealing with clubs, associations, and similar groups. Works of nonfiction on the history and criticism of imaginary clubs, associations, and similar groups are entered under *imaginary societies*.]
- NT Imaginary societies

Society life
- USE Upper classes

SOLDIERS [Here are entered works dealing with soldiers generally or with soldiers in an unspecified army. Works dealing with soldiers in a particular army are entered under the name of the army with the subdivision *Military life*, for example, *United States. Army—Military life*.]
- RT Gladiators
  Marines
  Samurai
- NT Cossacks

SOLDIERS OF FORTUNE [Here are entered works dealing with persons who follow a military career wherever there is the promise of adventure, profit, or pleasure. Works dealing with the mercenary troops maintained in former times by Irish chieftains are entered under *Galloglasses*. Works dealing with professional European mercenary troops in the 14th, 15th, and 16th centuries are entered under *Condottieri*. Works dealing with troops that serve a country other than their own primarily or strictly on a wage basis are entered under *Mercenary troops*.]
- BT Mercenary troops

NT Condottieri
   Galloglasses
SOLITUDE [Here are entered works dealing with a situation where there are no others of one's kind with whom to associate or with a mental state in which by wish or compulsion one is cut off from normal contacts with family, friends, colleagues, or neighbors. Works dealing with a lack of intimate association with others and the resultant sadness therefrom are entered under *Loneliness*. Works dealing with detachment from others either because of one's own wish or from causes beyond one's control are entered under *Social isolation*. Works that deal with a state of society in which normative standards of conduct and belief have weakened or disappeared or with a similar condition in an individual, commonly characterized by personal disorientation, anxiety, and isolation are entered under *Anomy*. Works dealing with estrangement and loss or lack of adjustment between an individual and his social or intellectual environment are entered under *Alienation (Social psychology)*.]
   RT Alienation (Social psychology)
      Anomy
      Loneliness
      Social isolation
SONS \
   RT Men
      Parent and child
   NT Filicide [Murder of a son or daughter by a mother or father]
      Parricide [Murder of a mother or father by his or her son or daughter]
      Stepchildren
SONS AS DETECTIVES \
   RT Father and son detectives \
      Mother and son detectives \
SONS-IN-LAW \
   UF In-laws
Sorcery
   USE Fantastic fiction, Sword and sorcery \
SORORICIDE \ [Here are entered works dealing with the murder of a sister by one of her siblings.]
   BT Murder
      Sisters
SOUL MUSIC

SOUTH AFRICA
   UF Union of South Africa
SOUTH AFRICA—RACE RELATIONS
   NT Apartheid
SOUTH AFRICAN FICTION
SOUTH AFRICAN WAR, 1899-1902
   UF Boer War
SOUTH AMERICA
   BT Latin America
   RT Central America
South American Indians
   USE Indians of South America
SOUTH ATLANTIC STATES
   UF United States—East
      United States—Southeast
   BT United States
SOUTH AUSTRALIA [Here are entered works dealing with the Australian province of South Australia.]
   BT Australia
   NT Adelaide (S. Aust.)
SOUTH CAROLINA
   NT Charleston (S.C.)
SOUTH DAKOTA
   NT Sioux Falls (S.D.)
SOUTH PACIFIC OCEAN
   UF South Seas
South Seas
   USE South Pacific Ocean
Southern dialect fiction
   USE Dialect fiction—Southerners \
SOUTHERN STATES [Here are entered works dealing with the region that includes Arkansas, Florida, Georgia, Kentucky, Louisiana, Mississippi, North Carolina, South Carolina, Tennessee, Virginia, and West Virginia.]
   UF United States—South
      United States—Southeast
   BT United States
   RT Plantation life
SOUTHWEST, NEW
   UF New Southwest
      United States—Southwest, New
   BT United States
SOUTHWEST, OLD
   UF Old Southwest
      United States—Southwest, Old
   BT United States
SOUTHWESTERN STATES
   UF United States—Southwest
      United States—Southwest, Old
   BT United States
      West (U.S.)

SOVIET UNION [There are fifteen constituent republics in the Soviet Union: Armenian S.S.R.; Azerbaijan S.S.R., Byelorussian S.S.R.; Estonia, Georgian S.S.R.; Kazakh S.S.R.; Kirgiz S.S.R.; Latvia; Lithuania; Moldavian S.S.R.; Russian S.F.S.R.; Tajik S.S.R.; Turkmen S.S.R.; Ukraine; Uzbek S.S.R. Note that Siberia is part of the Russian S.F.S.R. and not a separate republic. Do not add any geographic identifier to the name of a republic of the Soviet Union. For further information, see 23.4C in *AACR2R*.]
- UF U.S.S.R.
  Union of Soviet Socialist Republics
- SA headings beginning with either *Russia* or *Russians*
- RT Lapland
- NT Armenian S.S.R.
  Azerbaijan S.S.R.
  Byelorussian S.S.R.
  Estonia
  Georgian S.S.R.
  Kazakh S.S.R.
  Kirgiz S.S.R.
  Latvia
  Lithuania
  Moldavian S.S.R.
  Moscow (R.S.F.S.R.)
  Russian S.F.S.R.
  Siberia (R.S.F.S.R.)
  Tajik S.S.R.
  Turkmen S.S.R.
  Ukraine
  Uzbek S.S.R.

SOVIET UNION—FOREIGN RELATIONS—GREAT BRITAIN
- UF British-Russian relations
  Russian-British relations

SOVIET UNION—FOREIGN RELATIONS—UNITED STATES
- UF American-Russian relations
  Russian-American relations

SOVIET UNION—KINGS AND RULERS
- UF Czars
  Tsars

Soviet Union. Air Force
- USE Soviet Union. Voenno-Vozdushnye Sily

Soviet Union. Army
- USE Soviet Union. Rabosche-Krest'iânskaia Krasnaia Armiia

Soviet Union. K.G.B.
- USE Soviet Union. Komitet gosudarstvennoĭ bezopastnosti

SOVIET UNION. KOMITET GOSUDARSTVENNOI BEZOPASTNOSTI
- UF K.G.B.
  Soviet Union. K.G.B.
- RT Spy stories

Soviet Union. Navy
- USE Soviet Union. Voenno-Morskoĭ Flot

SOVIET UNION. RABOSCHE-KREST'IÂNSKAIA KRASNAIA ARMIIA
- UF Soviet Union. Army
- NT Cossacks

SOVIET UNION. VOENNO-MORSKOI FLOT
- UF Soviet Union. Navy

SOVIET UNION. VOENNO VOZDUSHNYE SILY
- UF Soviet Union. Air Force

SOVIETS (COUNCILS) [Here are entered works dealing with local governing councils in the Soviet Union. Works dealing with persons who are citizens of the Soviet Union or who are of Russian heritage are entered under *Russians*.]
- RT Russians

Space adventure
- USE Science fiction

Space civilizations
- USE Extraterrestrial bases
  Extraterrestrial beings \
  Life on other planets
  Science fiction
  Space colonies

SPACE COLONIES [Here are entered works dealing with communities established by man on planets other than earth. Works dealing with life forms on other planets and not native to Earth are entered under *Life on other planets*. Works dealing with manned installations existing for specific functions such as servicing space ships, etc., on natural extraterrestrial bodies are entered under *Extraterrestrial bases*. Works dealing with manned installations existing for specific functions, such as servicing space ships, etc., in orbit around natural extraterrestrial bodies or the earth are entered under *Space stations*.]
- UF Civilizations in space
  Imaginary planets
  Space civilizations
- BT Science fiction

RT Extraterrestrial bases
Life on other planets
Space stations

SPACE FLIGHT [Here are entered works dealing with the physics and technical aspects of flight beyond the earth's atmosphere. Works dealing generally with travel to the planets are entered under *Interplanetary voyages*. Works dealing generally with travel to the stars are entered under *Interstellar travel*.]
BT Outer space
NT Interplanetary voyages
Interstellar travel

SPACE FLIGHT IN LITERATURE [Here are entered nonfiction works on the history and criticism of space flight as portrayed in literature.]

Space operas
USE Science fiction

SPACE PROBES
BT Outer space—Exploration

SPACE STATIONS [Here are entered works dealing with manned installations existing for specific functions, such as servicing space ships, etc., in orbit around natural extraterrestrial bodies or the earth. Works dealing with manned installations existing for specific purposes, such as servicing space ships, etc., on natural extraterrestrial bodies are entered under *Extraterrestrial bases*. Works dealing with communities established by man on planets other than Earth are entered under *Space colonies*. Works dealing with life forms on other planets and not native to Earth are entered under *Life on other planets*.]
RT Extraterrestrial bases
Life on other planets
Science fiction
Space colonies

SPACE WARFARE
BT War stories
RT Science fiction

SPAIN
NT Canary Islands
Majorca (Spain)

SPANISH FICTION

Special Air Service
USE Great Britain. Army. Special Air Service

Special Forces
USE United States. Army. Special Forces

Spendthrifts
USE Prodigals \

SPERM BANKS
RT Artificial insemination

SPIES [Here are entered non-genre works dealing with spies. Prefer *Spy stories*. Genre works about female spies, however, would also be given the heading *Women spies*.]
NT Spy stories
Women spies

SPIRITUAL HEALING
RT Evangelists
Religion

SPIRITUALISM [Here are entered works dealing with communication with the dead. Works dealing with the communication between one mind and another without the use of ordinary senses are entered under *Telepathy*.]
UF Seances
RT Extrasensory perception
Telepathy

SPIRITUALISTS [Here are entered works dealing with persons who believe in communication with the dead. Works on persons who claim to have the ability to communicate with the dead are entered under *Mediums*.]
NT Mediums

Split personality
USE Multiple personality

SPLIT SELF IN LITERATURE [Here are entered works dealing with the history and criticism of multiple personality as portrayed in literature.]
RT Multiple personality

SPORTS STORIES [Here are entered novels and stories dealing with sports. Prefer a narrower heading designating the specific sport.]
BT Fiction
NT Martial arts fiction

SPY STORIES [Here are entered genre novels and stories dealing with espionage and spies. Spy stories featuring female spies are also given the heading *Women spies*. Works dealing with industrial spying are entered under *Business intelligence*. Nonfiction works

dealing with the art and science of spying are entered under *Espionage*.]
- UF Counter espionage
  Double agents
  International intrigue
  Intrigue
  Secret agents
  Secret service
  Traitors
- BT Adventure stories
  Espionage
  Fiction
  Spies
  Thrillers\
- RT Business intelligence
  Defectors
  Great Britain. M.I.5 [Responsible for internal security, like the American F.B.I.]
  Great Britain. MI6 [Responsible for external intelligence, like the American C.I.A.]
  Soviet Union. Komitet gosudarstvennoĭ bezopastnosti [Used for the K.G.B.]
  Suspense fiction\
  Treason
  United States. Central Intelligence Agency
  United States. Federal Bureau of Investigation
  Wiretapping
  World War, 1914-1918—Secret service
  World War, 1939-1945—Secret service
- NT Women spies

SPY STORIES, HUMOROUS\
- BT Humorous stories

ST. JOHN (N.B.)
- BT New Brunswick

ST. JOHN'S (NFLD.)
- BT Newfoundland

ST. LOUIS (MO.)
- BT Missouri

ST. PAUL (MINN.)
- BT Minnesota

Stage coaches
- USE Coaching

State's attorneys as detectives
- USE Public prosecutors as detectives\

STATESMEN [Here are entered works dealing with persons who exercise wise leadership without petty partisanship in the best interest of the general public. Works dealing with persons engaged in politics are entered under *Politicians*. Works dealing with persons engaged in conducting relations between nations are entered under *Diplomats*.]
- NT Diplomats
  Politicians

STATUES [Here are entered works dealing specifically with a sculpted, cast, or modeled image of an entire figure. Works dealing with an image of a person engraved on a coin or sculpted for a sepulchral monument or with a crude representation of a particular person, such as a stuffed dummy, are entered under *Effigies*. Works dealing with a sculpted image of the upper part of the body are entered under *Busts*. Works dealing generally with the art of sculpting as well as with pieces of art that have been sculpted are entered under *Sculpture*.]
- RT Sculpture
- NT Busts
  Effigies

Statuettes
- USE Art objects

STEALING [Here are entered works dealing with the ethical and psychological aspects of theft. Works dealing with stealing as a crime are entered under *Larceny*. Works dealing with taking another's property using violence or the threat of violence are entered under *Robbery*. Works dealing with persons who commit robbery are entered under *Brigands and robbers*. Works dealing with breaking and entering for the purpose of theft or robbery are entered under *Burglary*. Works dealing with persons who commit theft or burglary are entered under *Thieves*. Works dealing with persons who steal, profiteer, or kill, especially in a merciless manner, are entered under *Outlaws*. Works dealing with robbery committed on the street and involving a beating or other physical assault are entered under *Mugging*.]
- RT Brigands and robbers
  Larceny
  Mugging
  Outlaws

       Robbery
       Thieves
  NT Burglary
Stepbrothers
  USE Stepchildren
STEPCHILDREN
  UF Stepbrothers
       Stepdaughters
       Stepsisters
       Stepsons
  BT Brothers
       Brothers and sisters
       Daughters
       Domestic fiction
       Sisters
       Sons
Stepdaughters
  USE Stepchildren
STEPFATHERS
  BT Domestic fiction
STEPMOTHERS
  BT Domestic fiction
Stepsisters
  USE Stepchildren
Stepsons
  USE Stepchildren
STEVEDORES
  RT Shipping
STEWARDS
  BT Domestics
STORES, RETAIL [Here are entered works dealing with retail stores. Works dealing with persons who own or operate a retail business are entered under *Merchants*. Works dealing with the general business of retailing are entered under *Retail trade*.]
  BT Business enterprises
       Retail trade
  RT Merchants
Stories [Generally, when this term is used as part of a compound term, such as *Adventure stories* or *War stories*, it is meant to include all types of prose fiction, including short stories, novels, and novellas (short novels). Collections of short fiction should also be entered under *Short stories* or *Tales*, depending on form.]
  USE Short stories
       Tales
Stories in verse
  USE Fiction in verse \

Stories within a novel
  USE Frame-stories
STORMS
  RT Floods
       Tsunamis
  NT Disaster relief
       Disaster victims
       Snowstorms \
Story poems
  USE Fiction in verse \
STRASBOURG (FRANCE)
  BT France
Stratford-on-Avon (England)
  USE Stratford-upon-Avon (England)
STRATFORD-UPON-AVON (ENGLAND)
  UF Stratford-on-Avon (England)
STREAM OF CONSCIOUSNESS FICTION [Here are entered works that portray the uninterrupted and uneven flow of the consciousness of characters. Works that deal with the thoughts and psychological motivation of characters are entered under *Psychological fiction*.]
  BT Experimental fiction
       Fiction
       Psychological fiction
STRIKES AND LOCKOUTS
  BT Trade-unions
       Working class
STRIPTEASERS
  BT Dancers
STUDENT GOVERNMENTS
  UF Self-government (in education)
Student theater
  USE Amateur theater
       College theater
       Theater
STUDENTS
  UF Campus life
       School life
  BT Children
       Schools
  RT College stories
       Teachers
  NT Graduate students
SUBMARINE BOATS
  UF U-Boats
SUBURBAN AREAS [Here are entered works dealing with suburban areas generally, or an unspecified suburban area. Works dealing with a city's suburbs only are entered under a specific heading such as *Chicago Suburban Area (Ill.)*. Works dealing with cities and

their suburbs generally or an unspecified city and its suburbs are entered under *Metropolitan Areas.* Works on a specific metropolitan area are entered under a specific heading, for example, *Washington Metropolitan Area.* Note that only Washington, D.C., New York City, and Jerusalem do not have parenthetical geographic qualifiers when used in a metropolitan or suburban area heading. See H362 in LC's *Subject Heading Manual* for further information.]

SUBURBAN LIFE [Here are entered works dealing with life in the suburbs generally. Works dealing with villages and small towns in specific suburban areas are entered under the name of the area, for example, *New York Suburban Area,* unless the name of the specific suburb is known. Works dealing with life in rural areas, including rural villages, are entered under *Country life.* Works dealing predominately with rural villages are entered under *Villages.*]
- UF Provincial and rural life
  Small town life
- RT City and town life
  Country life
  Villages

SUCCESS
- UF Rich
  Self-made men
- RT Ambition
  Capitalists and financiers

SUCCESS—WOMEN
- UF Women—Success

SUCCESS IN BUSINESS

SUCCESS IN BUSINESS—WOMEN
- UF Women—Success

SUCCESS IN LITERATURE [Here are entered nonfiction works on the history and criticism of success as portrayed in fiction.]

SUDDEN INFANT DEATH SYNDROME
- UF S.I.D.S.

SUICIDE
- BT Murder

SUMMER RESORTS
- RT Camps

Summer vacations
- USE Camps
  Vacations

SUPERNATURAL [Here are entered works that deal primarily with the supernatural, but of which ghosts play only a small part and whose primary purpose is not fright. Works whose primary purpose is to produce true fright, which employ the supernatural and occult, and which generally lack romantic involvement are entered under *Horror tales.* Works characterized by supernatural horror, a heroine with threatened sanity, remote or isolated settings which are frequently ruined or haunted castles or large old houses, and which contain elements of romantic love are entered under *Gothic revival fiction\.* Works dealing primarily with ghosts are entered under *Ghost stories.* Works dealing with mysterious or secret knowledge supposedly attainable only through magical or supernatural means and not through ordinary human reason are entered under *Occultism.*]
- RT Ghost stories
  Gothic revival fiction\
  Horror tales
  Magic
  Voodooism
- NT Occultism
  Witchcraft

SUPERNATURAL IN LITERATURE [Here are entered nonfiction works on the history and criticism of the supernatural as portrayed in literature.]

SUPERSTITION
- RT Taboo

SURPRISE
- UF Surprise endings

Surprise endings
- USE Surprise

SURREALISM (LITERATURE) [Here are entered nonfiction works on the history and criticism of surrealism in fiction.]

SURREALISTIC FICTION [Here are entered works of conventional style and technique that juxtapose objects, characters, and actions usually considered incongruous. Works that use magic, dream, and fantasy combined with realistic elements and which emphasize freshness of language and spontaneity are entered under *Magic realistic fiction\.*]
- BT Experimental fiction
  Fiction

RT Magic realistic fiction\
SURROGATE MOTHERS
   RT Infertility, Female
SURVIVAL (AFTER AIRPLANE ACCIDENTS, SHIP-WRECKS, ETC.)
   BT Accidents
   RT Robinsonades [Nonfiction works on the literature of survival]
Survival after disasters
   USE Disaster relief
       Disaster victims
SURVIVAL AFTER NUCLEAR WARFARE [Here are entered works dealing with surviving specific effects of nuclear war. Works dealing with life in a society that has collapsed because of a great disaster such as ecological breakdown or nuclear war are entered under *Apocalyptic fiction*.]
   BT Apocalyptic fiction\
       Nuclear warfare
   RT Robinsonades [Nonfiction works on the literature of survival]
   NT Radioactive fallout
Survival in the wilderness
   USE Wilderness survival
Suspended animation
   USE Dormancy (Biology)
       Hypersomnia
SUSPENSE FICTION [Here are entered works whose prime purpose is to produce a feeling of frightened anticipation. These works may contain secondary elements involving crime, espionage, romance, or psychology and are usually narrated by a potential victim, someone suspiciously involved, or someone who is mentally disturbed. Works of suspense dominated by romance are entered under *Romantic suspense fiction*.]
   BT Fiction
       Thrillers\
   RT Detective and mystery stories
       Horror tales
       Psychological fiction
       Spy stories
   NT Romantic suspense fiction\
Suspense fiction, Romantic
   USE Romantic suspense fiction\
SUTTEE [Here are entered works dealing with the cremation of a Hindu widow on her husband's funeral pyre.]
   BT Human sacrifice

SWEARING [Here are entered works dealing with profane language. Works characterized by the frequent use of foul or obscene language are entered under *Linguistically profane fiction*. Works about the use of abuse to expose or discredit human vice or folly are entered under *Invective*.]
   RT Invective
       Linguistically profane fiction\
SWEDEN
   RT Lapland
SWEDES
SWEDES—UNITED STATES [Here are entered works dealing with Swedes visiting or living in the United States.]
   NT Swedish Americans
SWEDISH AMERICANS [Here are entered works dealing with Americans of Swedish ancestry.]
   BT Swedes—United States
Swedish dialect fiction
   USE Dialect fiction—Swedes\
SWEDISH FICTION
SWEEPSTAKES [Here are entered works dealing with contests in which the entire prize goes to a single winner. Works dealing with a drawing of lots in which prizes are distributed to multiple winners are entered under *Lotteries*.]
   BT Gambling
   RT Lotteries
SWINDLERS AND SWINDLING
SWISS—UNITED STATES
SWITZERLAND
   UF Helvetia
   SA headings beginning with *Swiss*
   NT Geneva (Switzerland)
Sword and sorcery fantastic fiction
   USE Fantastic fiction, Sword and sorcery\
SYDNEY (N.S.W.)
   BT New South Wales
SYMBOLIC FICTION [Here are entered works that suggest other levels of meaning without making the structure of ideas a formative influence on the narrative. Works in which the meaning of the persons and objects represented lies outside the narrative itself are entered under *Allegories*. (Allegories attempt to evoke an interest both in its characters, setting, and events, and in the ideas that they represent.) Works in which the allegory is short and simple

and deals with a familiar occurrence in life or nature that by analogy conveys a spiritual truth are entered under *Parables*. Works in which the allegory is short and simple, using animals acting as humans and illustrating the follies and weaknesses of people are entered under *Fables*.]
- BT Experimental fiction
  Fiction
- RT Allegories
  Fables
  Magic realistic fiction\
  Parables

SYMBOLISM IN LITERATURE [Here are entered nonfiction works dealing with the history and criticism of symbolism in literature.]

SYNAGOGUES
- RT Churches
  Jews
  Rabbis

TABOO
- RT Superstition

Tadzhik S.S.R.
- USE Tajik S.S.R.

TAILORS
- RT Dressmakers

TAIWAN
- RT China

TAJIK S.S.R.
- UF Tadzhik S.S.R.
- BT Soviet Union
- NT Dushanbe (Tajik S.S.R.)

TALES [Here are entered collections of traditional narratives that are for the most part fictitious and are told primarily for entertainment. Works that deal with shorter narratives passed on by word of mouth about common or illiterate people are entered under *Folk literature*. Works of traditional narrative that are shorter than epics but still purport to have some basis in reality are entered under *Legends*. Works of traditional narrative that are shorter than epics but deal more with the supernatural and less with the historical are entered under *Mythology*. Broad and lengthy works that recount the deeds of a legendary or historical hero are listed under *Epic literature*. Collections of relatively short works of fiction with a definite formal development and unity whose intent is to reveal characters or situations using only a few actions or events are entered under *Short stories*.]
- UF Stories
- BT Fiction
- RT Epic literature
  Folk literature
  Legends
  Mythology
- NT Sagas
  Short stories

TALL TALES [Here are entered tales and short stories as well as novels and novellas (short novels) characterized by bragging and exaggeration of the truth. Works that stretch the limits of probability yet fall outside the conventions of readily identifiable genres such as *Science fiction*, *Magic realistic fiction*, etc., are entered under *Improbable fiction*\.]
- UF Exaggeration
- BT Fiction
- RT Improbable fiction\

TALLAHASSEE (FLA.)
- BT Florida

TALLINN (ESTONIA)
- BT Estonia

TASHKENT (UZBEK S.S.R.)
- BT Uzbek S.S.R.

TASMANIA
- UF Van Dieman's Land
- BT Australia
- NT Hobart (Tas.)

TBILISI (GEORGIAN S.S.R.)
- BT Georgian S.S.R.

TEACHERS
- UF Instructors
  School teachers
- BT Schools
- RT Students
  Tutors and tutoring

TEENAGE BOYS [Here are entered works dealing with boys from 13 to 17 years of age inclusive. The age of the boy may be added to this heading (for example, *Teenage boys—13*\; *Teenage boys—14*\) although this is not a Library of Congress practice. Works dealing with males in the general age range from 18 to 25 years inclusive are entered under

Young men. Works dealing with boys generally or with boys up to 12 years of age are entered under *Boys.*]
  BT Boys
       Men
  RT Young men

TEENAGE GIRLS [Here are entered works dealing with girls from 13 to 17 years of age inclusive. The age of the girl may be added to this heading (for example, *Teenage girls—13*; *Teenage girls—14*, etc.) although this is not a Library of Congress practice. Works dealing with females in the general age range from 18 to 25 years inclusive are entered under *Young women.* Works dealing with girls generally, or with girls up to 12 years of age are entered under *Girls.*]
  BT Girls
       Women
  RT Young women

Teenage runaways
  USE Runaway teenagers

TEENAGERS [Here are entered works dealing with persons from 13 to 17 years of age inclusive. Works dealing with persons from 13 to 25 years of age inclusive are entered under *Youth.* Works dealing with persons in the general age range from 18 to 25 years inclusive are entered under *Young adults.*]
  BT Children
  RT Young adults
       Youth
  NT Juvenile delinquents
       Maturation (Psychology)
       Problem children

Teenagers, Mentally handicapped
  USE Mentally handicapped teenagers

TELEPATHY [Here are entered works dealing with communication between one mind and another without the use of ordinary senses. Works dealing with communication with the dead are entered under *Spiritualism.* Works dealing with persons who have telepathic powers are entered under *Psychics.*]
  BT Extrasensory perception
  RT Spiritualism
  NT Psychics

Telephone counseling
  USE Hotlines (Counseling)

TELEVISION BROADCASTING

TELEVISION JOURNALISTS
  RT Reporters and reporting

**TELEVISION JOURNALISTS AS DETECTIVES **
  UF Reporters as detectives
  BT Journalists as detectives \

**TELEVISION STORIES ** [Here are entered works of fiction based on programs originally written for television broadcasting.]
  UF Television tie-in fiction
  BT Fiction
  RT Radio stories

Television tie-in fiction
  USE Television stories \

TENNESSEE
  NT Nashville (Tenn.)

TERENGGANU
  BT Malaysia

TERMINALLY ILL
  BT Sick
  RT Cancer—Patients

TERMINALLY ILL CHILDREN

TERRORISM
  UF International intrigue
       Intrigue
  RT Adventure stories
       Conspiracies
       Irish Republican Army
       Thrillers \

TERRORISTS

Tetralogies
  USE Sequels (Literature)
        Series (Publications)

Tetraplegics
  USE Quadriplegics

TEXAS
  NT Dallas (Tex.)
       Houston (Tex.)

TEXAS RANGERS
  UF Rangers, Texas

TEXTILE INDUSTRY
  RT Clothing trade

THEATER
  UF Theater life
  RT Drama
       Dramatists
  NT Actors
       Actresses
       Vaudeville

Theater life
  USE Theater

THEOLOGIANS
  RT Religion

THIEVES [Here are entered works dealing with persons who commit theft or take another's property without permission. Works dealing with the ethical and psychological aspects of theft are entered under *Stealing*. Works dealing with stealing as a crime are entered under *Larceny*. Works dealing with taking another's property using violence or the threat of violence are entered under *Robbery*. Works dealing with robbery committed on the street and involving a beating or other physical assault are entered under *Mugging*. Works dealing with persons who commit robbery are entered under *Brigands and robbers*. Works dealing with breaking and entering for the purpose of theft or robbery are entered under *Burglary*. Works dealing with persons who steal, profiteer, or kill, especially in a merciless manner, are entered under *Outlaws*.]
  RT Kleptomania
      Larceny
      Outlaws
      Stealing
  NT Brigands and robbers
      Burglary
      Embezzlement
      Horse stealing
      Mugging
      Robbery
      Shoplifting

THREE-DECKER NOVELS [Here are entered single novels which are published in three separate volumes. Do not confuse with trilogies, which are three separate novels that are sequels to one another.]
  BT Fiction
  RT Series (Publications)

THRILLERS\ [Here are entered works designed to hold the reader's interest by the use of swift and continuous action, intrigue, suspense and adventure.]
  UF International intrigue
      Intrigue
  BT Fiction
      Light fiction\
  RT Conspiracies
      Kidnapping
      Terrorism
  NT Adventure stories
      Crime
      Detective and mystery stories
      Disasters
      Fantastic fiction
      Gothic revival fiction\
      Horror tales
      Larceny
      Natural disasters
      Romantic suspense fiction\
      Science fiction
      Spy stories
      Suspense fiction\
      War stories

TIBET (CHINA)
  BT China

TIME
  RT Clocks and watches

Time machines
  USE Time travel

TIME TRAVEL
  UF Time machines
  RT Science fiction

TITOGRAD (MONTENEGRO)
  BT Montenegro

TOPEKA (KAN.)
  BT Kansas

TORONTO (ONT.)
  BT Ontario

TOURIST CAMPS, HOSTELS, ETC.
  UF Hostels
  RT Resorts

TOURIST TRADE
  RT Vacations

TRACK-ATHLETICS
  RT Marathon running

TRADE SCHOOLS
  UF Schools, Vocational
      Vocational schools

TRADE-UNIONS
  NT Industrial Workers of the World
      Strikes and lockouts

Traders
  USE Merchants

Traitors
  USE Betrayal\
      Defectors
      Informers
      Spy stories
      Treason

TRAMP SHIPPING [Here are entered works dealing with ships that do not make regular voyages between the same ports but

that will take cargo, when and where it is offered, to any other port.]
   BT Ships
TRAMPS [Here are entered works dealing with traveling beggars who will not work. Works dealing with the legal charge of being a tramp are entered under *Vagrancy*. Works dealing with aimless persons who wander from place to place and job to job are entered under *Drifters*. Works dealing with persons who travel as a way of life are entered under *Wayfaring life*. Works dealing with wandering, disorderly, or dissolute but not necessarily displeasing persons are entered under *Rogues and vagabonds*. Works that are episodic in the detailing of the adventures of a rascal, rogue, or vagabond getting by on his or her wits are entered under *Picaresque fiction*.]
   RT Drifters
      Homelessness
      Picaresque fiction \
      Rogues and vagabonds
      Vagrancy
      Wayfaring life
TRAMPS IN LITERATURE [Here are entered nonfiction works on the history and criticism of tramps as portrayed in literature.]
TRAPPERS
   RT Fur trade
TREASON [Here are entered works dealing with overt acts of betrayal or of resistance to a government. Works dealing with conduct leading to resistance to a government are entered under *Sedition*.]
   UF Traitors
   RT Betrayal \
      Sedition
      Spy stories
TRIALS [Here are entered works dealing with a judicial examination and determination of issues between parties to an action. Works dealing with a suit brought in court are entered under *Actions and defenses*.]
   UF Courtroom fiction
   BT Legal stories
   RT Actions and defenses
      Witnesses
TRIALS (HOMICIDE) [Here are entered works dealing with trials in which it has not yet been determined that the death which occurred was a crime. Works dealing with trials in which the death that occurred was definitely a crime are entered under *Trials (Murder)*.]
   RT Trials (Murder)
TRIALS (IMPOSTORS AND IMPOSTURE) [Here are entered works that deal with trials of someone accused of either false personation or impersonating an officer. Works that deal with assuming an identity with the intent to deceive are entered under *Impostors and imposture*. Works that deal with imposture as a legal charge are entered under *False personation*. Works that deal with imposture of a public official as a legal charge are entered under *Impersonating an officer*. Works that deal with assuming the personality, behavior, or appearance of someone for other than deceitful intent are entered under *Impersonation*. Works dealing with who one is or who one is known as are entered under *Identity*. Works dealing with persons who are innocently mistaken for someone else are entered under *Mistaken identity*. Works dealing with someone who has two separate identities, each of his own invention, are entered under *Double identity*.]
   RT Double identity \
      False personation
      Impersonating an officer
      Impostors and imposture
      Mistaken identity \
TRIALS (MURDER) [Here are entered works dealing with trials in which the death that occurred was definitely a crime. Works dealing with trials in which it has not yet been determined that the death which occurred was a crime are entered under *Trials (Homicide)*.]
   RT Trials (Homicide)
Trilogies
   USE Sequels (Literature)
      Series (Publications)
TRIPLETS
   RT Brothers
      Sisters
TROJAN WAR [Thought to have been fought sometime between 1399 and 1000 B.C.]

Truck hijacking
　USE Hijacking of trucks
TRUTHFULNESS AND FALSEHOOD
　UF Lies
Tsars
　USE Soviet Union—Kings and rulers
TSUNAMIS [Here are entered works dealing with an unusually large sea wave or a tidal wave associated with high winds.]
　RT Hurricanes
　　Storms
　　Typhoons
TUCSON (ARIZ.)
　BT Arizona
Tudor England
　USE Great Britain—History—Tudors, 1485-1603
TUGBOATS
　BT Boats and boating
TURKEY
　NT Dardanelles Strait (Turkey)
TURKMEN S.S.R.
　BT Soviet Union
　NT Ashkhabad (Turkmen S.S.R.)
TUTORS AND TUTORING
　RT Teachers
TWINS
　RT Brothers
　　Sisters
Tycoons
　USE Capitalists and financiers
　　Millionaires
TYPHOONS [Here are entered works dealing with cyclonic storms of the China Seas and the Philippines. Works dealing with cyclonic storms of the West Indies are entered under *Hurricanes*. Works dealing with an unusually large sea wave or tidal wave associated with high winds are entered under *Tsunamis*.]
　RT Hurricanes
　　Tsunamis

U-boats
　USE Submarine boats
U.F.O.s
　USE Unidentified flying objects
U.S.
　USE United States

U.S.S.R.
　USE Soviet Union
UKRAINE
　BT Soviet Union
　NT Kiev (Ukraine)
ULSTER (IRELAND AND NORTHERN IRELAND) [Although sometimes popularly used as a synonym for Northern Ireland, Ulster as a subject heading applies only to the former province of Ulster in the north of Ireland. In 1920, the counties of Antrim, Armagh, Down, Fermanagh, Londonderry, and Tyrone were joined to form the new state of Northern Ireland. The remaining counties of Cavan, Donegal, and Monaghan became the province of Ulster in Eire, the Republic of Ireland.]
　NT Irish
　　Scots-Irish
UNCLES
　RT Aunts
　　Domestic fiction
　　Nephews \
　　Nieces
UNDERGROUND MOVEMENTS IN LITERATURE [Here are entered nonfiction works on the history and criticism of underground movements as portrayed in literature.]
UNDERGROUND RAILROAD
　RT Slavery
UNDERWATER COLONIES \
　UF Colonies, Underwater
　RT Manned undersea research stations
Underworld, Criminal
　USE Crime
　　Organized crime
UNFINISHED BOOKS [Here are entered incomplete works or works not completed by the original author.]
　UF Novels, Unfinished
　BT Fiction
UNIDENTIFIED FLYING OBJECTS
　UF U.F.O.s
Unidentified Victims
　USE Victims, Unidentified \
Union of South Africa
　USE South Africa
Union of Soviet Socialist Republics
　USE Soviet Union
United Kingdom
　USE Great Britain

UNITED STATES
  UF U.S.
  NT Atlantic states
     Middle Atlantic states
     Middle West
     New England
     Northeastern states
     Northwestern states
     South Atlantic states
     Southern states
     Southwest, New
     Southwest, Old
     Southwestern states

UNITED STATES—ARMED FORCES—WOMEN
  BT United States. Air Force—Military life
     United States. Army—Military life
     United States. Marine Corps—Military life
  NT United States. Navy—Women

United States—East
  USE Atlantic states [Includes Connecticut, Delaware, Florida, Georgia, Maine, Maryland, Massachusetts, New Hampshire, New Jersey, New York, North Carolina, Rhode Island, South Carolina, and Virginia]
     Middle Atlantic states [Includes Delaware, Maryland, New Jersey, New York, Pennsylvania, and Washington, D.C.]
     New England [Includes Connecticut, Maine, Massachusetts, New Hampshire, Rhode Island, and Vermont]
     Northeastern states [Includes that part of the U.S. north of the Ohio and Potomac rivers, and east of the Mississippi River]
     South Atlantic states [Includes Florida, Georgia, North Carolina, South Carolina, and Virginia]

UNITED STATES—FOREIGN RELATIONS—SOVIET UNION
  UF American-Russian relations
     Russian-American relations

United States—Middle West
  USE Middle West [Includes Illinois, Indiana, Iowa, Kansas, Michigan, Minnesota, Missouri, Nebraska, North Dakota, Ohio, South Dakota, and Wisconsin]

United States—New England
  USE New England

United States—Northeast
  USE Atlantic states [Includes Connecticut, Delaware, Florida, Georgia, Maine, Maryland, Massachusetts, New Hampshire, New Jersey, New York, North Carolina, Rhode Island, South Carolina, and Virginia]
     Middle Atlantic states [Includes Delaware, Maryland, New Jersey, New York, Pennsylvania, and Washington, D.C.]
     New England [Includes Connecticut, Maine, Massachusetts, New Hampshire, Rhode Island, and Vermont]
     Northeastern states [Includes that part of the U.S. north of the Ohio and Potomac rivers, and east of the Mississippi River]

United States—Northwest
  USE Northwestern states [Includes Idaho, Montana, Oregon, Washington, and Wyoming]

United States—Northwest, Old
  USE Northwest, Old

United States—Pacific Northwest
  USE Northwestern states [Includes Idaho, Montana, Oregon, Washington, and Wyoming]

United States—South
  USE Southern states [Includes Alabama, Arkansas, Florida, Georgia, Kentucky, Louisiana, Mississippi, North Carolina, South Carolina, Tennessee, Virginia, and West Virginia]

United States—Southeast
  USE South Atlantic states [Includes Florida, Georgia, North Carolina, South Carolina, and Virginia]
     Southern states [Includes Alabama, Arkansas, Florida, Georgia, Kentucky, Louisiana, Mississippi, North Carolina, South Carolina, Tennessee, Virginia, and West Virginia]

United States—Southwest
  USE Southwestern states [Includes Arkansas, Arizona, California, Colorado, Kansas, Louisiana, Missouri, Nevada, New Mexico, Oklahoma, Texas and Utah]

United States—Southwest, New
  USE Southwest, New

United States—Southwest, Old
  USE Southwest, Old
United States—West
  USE West (U.S.) [Before the 20th century, this region included all states west of the Mississippi River. In current popular usage, it now generally excludes Minnesota, Iowa, Missouri, Arkansas, and Louisiana.]
UNITED STATES. AIR FORCE—MILITARY LIFE [Here are entered works dealing in a general way with life in the United States Air Force. Works dealing specifically with members of the United States Air Force, whether male or female, officers or enlisted personnel, are entered under *United States. Air Force—Airmen*. Works dealing primarily with officers is entered under *United States. Air Force—Officers*. Works dealing primarily with non-commissioned officer are entered under *United States. Air Force—Noncommissioned officers.*]
  NT United States—Armed Forces—Women
    United States. Air Force—Non-commissioned officers
    United States. Air Force—Officers
UNITED STATES. AIR FORCE—NON-COMMISSIONED OFFICERS
  BT United States. Air Force—Military Life
UNITED STATES. AIR FORCE—OFFICERS
  BT United States. Air Force—Military Life
UNITED STATES. ARMY—MILITARY LIFE
  RT United States Military Academy
  NT United States—Armed Forces—Women
UNITED STATES. ARMY. SPECIAL FORCES
  UF Green Berets
    Special Forces
UNITED STATES. CENTRAL INTELLIGENCE AGENCY
  UF C.I.A.
    Central Intelligence Agency
  RT Spy stories
UNITED STATES. CONGRESS
  UF Congress
UNITED STATES. CONGRESS. HOUSE
  UF House of Representatives
    United States. House of Representatives

  NT Legislators—United States
    Women legislators—United States
UNITED STATES. CONGRESS. SENATE
  UF Senate
    United States. Senate
  NT Legislators—United States
    Women legislators—United States
UNITED STATES. FEDERAL BUREAU OF INVESTIGATION
  UF F.B.I.
    Federal Bureau of Investigation
  RT Spy stories
United States. House of Representatives
  USE United States. Congress. House
UNITED STATES. MARINE CORPS
  BT Marines
UNITED STATES. MARINE CORPS—MILITARY LIFE
  NT United States—Armed Forces—Women
United States. Military Academy, West Point
  USE United States Military Academy
UNITED STATES. NATIONAL AERONAUTICS AND SPACE ADMINISTRATION
  UF N.A.S.A.
    NASA
United States. Naval Academy, Annapolis
  USE United States Naval Academy
UNITED STATES. NAVY—MILITARY LIFE [Here are entered works dealing with U.S. Navy military life on land-based installations.]
  RT United States. Navy—Sea life
  NT United States Naval Academy
United States. Navy—Noncommissioned officers
  USE United States. Navy—Petty officers
UNITED STATES. NAVY—PETTY OFFICERS
  UF United States. Navy—Noncommissioned officers
UNITED STATES. NAVY—SEA LIFE [Here are entered works dealing with U.S. Navy life at sea.]
  RT United States. Navy—Military life [Land-based installations]
    United States—Navy—Women
  BT United States—Armed Forces—Women
UNITED STATES. NAVY SEA AIR LAND TEAM
  UF Seals
UNITED STATES. NAVY—WOMEN
  BT United States—Armed Forces—Women

UNITED STATES. SECRET SERVICE
  UF Secret service
United States. Senate
  USE United States. Congress. Senate
United States congressmen
  USE Legislators—United States
United States congresswomen
  USE Women legislators—United States
UNITED STATES MARSHALS [Here are entered works dealing with marshals serving in American federal courts. Note that the heading *Marshals* is used for works dealing with air marshals or field marshals in the military. Works dealing with peace officers who are elected county officials or who work as police in a department headed by such an official are entered under *Sheriffs*. Works dealing with municipal peace officers are entered under *Police*. Works that deal with various kinds of law enforcement officers or law enforcement officers generally are entered under *Peace officers*. Works dealing with peace officers charged with both keeping the public peace and certain petty judicial matters are entered under *Constables*. Westerns that deal with law enforcement officers are entered under *Peace officers* if it cannot be readily determined if the officer is a marshal or sheriff. The heading *Police* is not used with westerns unless specifically so used in the text. It would usually be superfluous to use any of the peace officer headings with detective and mystery fiction.]
  BT Peace officers
  RT Constables
       Marshals
       Police
       Sheriffs
UNITED STATES MILITARY ACADEMY
  UF United States. Military Academy, West Point
  RT United States. Army—Military life
       West Point (N.Y.)
UNITED STATES NAVAL ACADEMY
  UF United States. Naval Academy, Annapolis
  BT United States. Navy—Military life
  RT Annapolis (Md.)

United States senators
  USE Legislators—United States
        Women legislators—United States
Universities and colleges
  USE College stories
UNIVERSITIES AND COLLEGES—ALUMNI
  UF College alumni
  NT Class reunions
University life
  USE College stories
UNIVERSITY OF CAMBRIDGE
  UF Cambridge University
  RT Cambridge (England)
UNIVERSITY OF OXFORD
  UF Oxford University
  RT Oxford (England)
Unjust accusation
  USE Malicious accusation
UNMARRIED COUPLES [Here are entered works dealing with couples who are not married. This term implies nothing about sexual relationships, sexual orientation, or living arrangements. Works dealing with unmarried couples living together as husband and wife are entered under *Cohabitation*. Works dealing with a woman who fornicates with a particular man but does not sell herself are entered under *Mistresses*.]
  RT Cohabitation
  NT Mistresses
UNMARRIED MOTHERS
  BT Mothers
  RT Single-parent family
UPPER CLASSES [Here are entered works dealing with persons considered of the highest class of people either because of wealth or prestige. Works dealing with persons who are so wealthy that they do not work are entered under *Leisure class*. Works dealing with persons of an ideally superior caste, either because of breeding, education, wealth, or philosophy, not necessarily a fixed or definite group, are entered under *Aristocracy*. Works dealing with persons whose rank is inferior to royalty but superior to all others and whose rank is either directly granted by a ruler or inherited are entered under *Nobility*. Note that *Nobility* includes baronets even though British popular usage does not. Works dealing with persons who are not nobility but

who are entitled to bear a coat of arms, and hence, are considered gentlemen or ladies in the technical sense, and are landed proprietors are entered under *Gentry*.]
- UF Society life
- RT Aristocracy
  Gentry
  Knights and knighthood
  Love stories, Regency\
  Millionaires
  Nobility
- NT Leisure class

USURY
- UF Juice loans
  Loan sharks

UTAH
- NT Salt Lake City (Utah)

UTOPIAS
- RT Dystopias [The reverse of utopias]
  Fantastic fiction
  Science fiction

UXORICIDE [Here are entered works dealing with the murder of a wife by her husband. Works dealing with the murder of a husband by his wife are entered under *Mariticide*\.]
- BT Crime passionel [Killing for sexual motives]
  Husbands
  Murder [Killing with malice aforethought]
  Wives
- RT Mariticide\

UZBEK S.S.R.
- BT Soviet Union
- NT Tashkent (Uzbek S.S.R.)

VACATIONS
- UF Summer vacations
- RT Camps
  Health resorts, watering places, etc.
  Resorts
  Tourist trade

VACCINES
- BT Drugs

VAGRANCY [Here are entered works dealing with the legal charge of being a tramp. Works dealing with traveling beggars who will not work are entered under *Tramps*. Works dealing with aimless persons who wander from place to place and job to job are entered under *Drifters*. Works dealing with persons who travel as a way of life are entered under *Wayfaring life*. Works dealing with wandering, disorderly, or dissolute but not necessarily displeasing persons are entered under *Rogues and vagabonds*. Works that are episodic in the detailing of the adventures of a rascal, rogue, or vagabond getting by on his or her wits are entered under *Picaresque fiction*\.]
- RT Drifters
  Homelessness
  Picaresque fiction\
  Rogues and vagabonds
  Tramps
  Wayfaring life

VAMPIRES
- RT Horror tales
  Monsters

VAMPIRES IN LITERATURE [Here are entered nonfiction works on the history and criticism of vampires as portrayed in literature.]

Van Diemen's Land
- USE Tasmania

VANCOUVER (B.C.)
- BT British Columbia

VATICAN CITY
- BT Catholic Church
- RT Popes

VAUDEVILLE
- BT Entertainers
  Theater

VENDETTA [Here are entered works dealing with taking revenge for the murder of a kin on the person or kin of the person who was murdered.]
- UF Family feuds
- BT Revenge
- RT Quarreling

VER SACRUM [Here are entered works dealing with the Greek and Italian custom of sacrificing animals born in the spring and of sending away 20-year-old humans in times of distress or overpopulation.]
- BT Human sacrifice

VERMONT
- NT Burlington (Vt.)

VETERANS
   SA subdivision *Veterans* under specific wars, for example, *World War, 1939-1945—Veterans*
VETERANS—UNITED STATES
VICTIMS, UNIDENTIFIED \
   UF Unidentified victims
   BT Identity
   RT Murder
VICTORIA [Here are entered works dealing with the Australian province of Victoria.]
   BT Australia
   NT Melbourne (Vic.)
Victorian England
   USE Great Britain—History—Victoria, 1837-1901
VIENNA (AUSTRIA)
   BT Austria
VIETNAM
   NT Saigon (Vietnam)
VIETNAMESE CONFLICT, 1961-1975
VIETNAMESE CONFLICT, 1961-1975—PROTEST MOVEMENTS
VIETNAMESE CONFLICT, 1961-1975—VETERANS
   RT Post-traumatic stress disorder
VIGILANTES
   UF Regulators (Vigilantes)
VIKINGS
   RT Danes
VILLAGES [Here are entered works dealing with rural villages. Works dealing with life in rural areas, including rural villages, are entered under *Country life*. Works dealing with villages and small towns in suburban areas are entered under the name of the suburban area, for example, *Chicago suburban area*, unless the suburb is known. Works presenting a generally idealized version of rustic life and expressing complex ideas through supposedly simple characters, such as shepherds who speak in courtly language, are entered under *Pastoral fiction*.]
   UF Provincial and rural life
       Small town life
   BT Country life
   RT City and town life
       Pastoral fiction
       Suburban life
VILLEINAGE [Here are entered works dealing with peasants who are slaves to their feudal lord but free in other respects. Works dealing with agricultural laborers bound to the land in service to its owner are entered under *Serfdom*. Works dealing with laborers bound in servitude by prison sentence or indebtedness are entered under *Peonage*. Works dealing with agricultural laborers or owners of very small plots of farm land, especially in Europe, Asia, or South America, are entered under *Peasantry*. Works dealing with the laboring classes are entered under *Working class*.]
   BT Farm life
       Peasantry
       Working class
   RT Peonage
       Serfdom
VILNIUS (LITHUANIA)
   BT Lithuania
VINEYARDS [Here are entered works dealing with fields of grapes. Works dealing with the science of growing grapes are entered under *Viticulture*. Works dealing with places where wine is made are entered under *Wineries*. Works dealing with the making of wine are entered under *Wine and winemaking*.]
   BT Viticulture
   RT Wine and winemaking
       Wineries
VIOLENCE [Here are entered works that deal with the motivation for or effects of the exertion of physical force to injure or abuse someone. Works that deal with the disposition to inflict pain or suffering or with a person who has no humane feelings are entered under *Cruelty*. Works that contain the explicit portrayal of violent acts are entered under *Violent fiction* \ .]
   UF Brutality
   BT Cruelty
   NT Violent fiction \
VIOLENCE IN LITERATURE [Here are entered nonfiction works that deal with the history and criticism of violence as portrayed in literature.]
VIOLENT FICTION \ [Here are entered works that contain the explicit portrayal of violent acts.]
   UF Explicit violence in fiction
   BT Fiction
       Violence
   RT Gloomy fiction \

NT Detective and mystery stories, Hard-boiled\
VIRGIN ISLANDS
  NT British Virgin Islands
     Charlotte Amalie (V.I.) [Capital of the Virgin Islands of the United States]
     Road Town (V.I.) [Capital of the British Virgin Islands]
     Virgin Islands of the United States
VIRGIN ISLANDS OF THE UNITED STATES
  BT Virgin Islands
  NT Charlotte Amalie (V.I.)
VIRGINIA
  NT Richmond (Va.)
VIRGINITY
  RT Celibacy [Not marrying]
     Chastity [Refraining from sexual relations]
Visitors from outer space
  USE Extraterrestrial beings\
VITICULTURE [Here are entered works dealing with the science of growing grapes. Works dealing with fields of grapes are entered under *Vineyards*. Works dealing with places where wine is made are entered under *Wineries*. Works dealing with the making of wine are entered under *Wine and winemaking*.]
  RT Wine and winemaking
     Wineries
  NT Vineyards
Vocational schools
  USE Trade schools
VOODOOISM
  RT Magic
     Satanism
     Supernatural
VOYAGES, IMAGINARY [Here are entered works dealing with voyages and travels imagined by a character within a story. Works dealing with voyages and travels imagined by the author are entered under *Voyages and travel*.]
  BT Voyages and travel
VOYAGES AND TRAVELS [Note that this term also includes land travel.]
  NT Automobile travel
     Road fiction\
     Voyages, Imaginary

Wagon trains\
  USE Caravans

WALES [If a place is located in Wales, add the identifier *(Wales)*, for example, *Cardiff (Wales)*. For further information, see 23.4D2 in *AACR2R*.]
  BT Great Britain
WALL STREET [Here are entered works dealing with the financial activities in the Wall Street district of New York City.]
  BT Finance
  RT Manhattan (New York, N.Y.)
     New York (N.Y.)
WANDERING JEW
  BT Folk literature
     Legends
WAR [Here are entered works dealing with war in a general, abstract, or philosophical way. Works dealing with the specific effects of war or with the actions taking place in a war are entered under *War stories*.]
  RT War stories
War of the Roses, 1455-1485
  USE Great Britain—History—Wars of the Roses, 1455-1485
WAR STORIES [Here are entered novels and stories about unspecified wars or wars imagined by the author and about the specific effects or actions of that war. Works dealing with a specific war or battle are entered under the specific heading for that war or battle, for example, *World War, 1939-1945*; *Wounded Knee Creek, Battle of, 1890*. Works of nonfiction on the history and criticism of imaginary wars are entered under *Imaginary wars and battles*. Works dealing with war in an abstract or philosophical way are entered under *War*.]
  BT Adventure stories
     Fiction
     Thrillers\
  RT War
  NT Battles
     Imaginary wars and battles
     Space warfare
Warlocks
  USE Wizards
WARSAW (POLAND)
  BT Poland
WARSHIPS
  SA subdivision *Sea life* under the names of navies, for example, *United States. Navy—Sea life*; also headings for

specific kinds of warships, for example, *Aircraft carriers*; *Destroyers (Warships)*; *Submarine Boats*, etc.
WASHINGTON (D.C.)
WASHINGTON (STATE)
  NT Seattle (Wash.)
Wastrels
  USE Degeneration
       Picaresque fiction \
       Prodigals
WAYFARING LIFE [Here are entered works dealing with persons who travel as a way of life. Works dealing with wandering, disorderly, or dissolute but not necessarily displeasing persons are entered under *Rogues and vagabonds*. Works that are episodic in the detailing of the adventures of a rascal, rogue, or vagabond getting by on his on her wits are entered under *Picaresque fiction*\. Works dealing with traveling beggars who will not work are entered under *Tramps*. Works dealing with the legal charge of being a tramp are entered under *Vagrancy*. Works dealing with aimless persons who wander from place to place and job to job are entered under *Drifters*.]
  RT Drifters
      Homelessness
      Picaresque fiction \
      Rogues and vagabonds
      Tramps
      Vagrancy
WEALTH
  RT Leisure class
WEATHER
  RT Meteorologists
WEDDINGS
  RT Betrothal
      Honeymoon
      Newlyweds \
Wehrmacht
  USE Germany. Heer
WELFARE RECIPIENTS
  BT Poor
WELSH
  BT British
WELSH FICTION [Here are entered works written in the Welsh or English languages by Welsh authors. Works written in English by Welsh authors or collections of works written exclusively in English by Welsh authors are also entered under *English fiction—Welsh authors*.]
  RT English authors—Welsh authors
WEREWOLVES
  RT Horror tales
      Monsters
WEST (U.S.) [Prior to the 20th Century, this region included all states west of the Mississippi River; in current popular usage, it now generally excludes Minnesota, Iowa, Missouri, Arkansas, and Louisiana.]
  UF United States—West
  RT Frontier and pioneer life
  NT Northwestern states [Includes Idaho, Montana, Oregon, Washington, and Wyoming]
      Southwestern states [Includes Arkansas, Arizona, California, Colorado, Kansas, Louisiana, Missouri, Nevada, New Mexico, Oklahoma, Texas and Utah]
      Western stories
WEST POINT (N.Y.)
  RT United States Military Academy
WEST VIRGINIA
  NT Charleston (W. Va.)
WESTERN AUSTRALIA [Here are entered works dealing with the province of Western Australia.]
  BT Australia
  NT Perth (W.A.)
WESTERN STORIES [Here are entered novels and stories of the adventure genre that take place in the American West.]
  BT Fiction
      Light fiction \
      West (U.S.)
  RT Caravans [Used for wagon trains]
      Coaching [Used for stage coaches]
      Cowboys
      Cowgirls
      Frontier and pioneer life
      Gunfighters \
      Outlaws
      Ranch life
WIDOWERS
  BT Men
      Single men
WIDOWS
  BT Wives
WIDOWS AS DETECTIVES \
  BT Women detectives

WIFE ABUSE
   BT Cruelty
      Problem marriages \
Wife swapping
   USE Adultery
Wight, Isle of
   USE Isle of Wight (England)
WILDERNESS SURVIVAL
   UF Survival in the wilderness
   RT Robinsonades [Nonfiction works on the literature of survival]
WILDLIFE CONSERVATION
   BT Nature stories
WILDLIFE REFUGES
   RT National parks and reserves
WILMINGTON (DEL.)
   BT Delaware
WINE AND WINEMAKING [Here are entered works dealing with the making of wine. Works dealing with fields of grapes are entered under *Vineyards*. Works dealing with the science of growing grapes are entered under *Viticulture*. Works dealing with places where wine is made are entered under *Wineries*.]
   RT Vineyards
      Viticulture
   NT Wineries
WINERIES [Here are entered works dealing with places where wines are made. Works dealing with fields of grapes are entered under *Vineyards*. Works dealing with the science of growing grapes are entered under *Viticulture*. Works dealing with the making of wine are entered under *Wine and winemaking*.]
   BT Wine and winemaking
   RT Vineyards
      Viticulture
WINNIPEG (MAN.)
   BT Manitoba
WIRETAPPING
   RT Spy stories
WISCONSIN
   NT Milwaukee (Wis.)
WIT AND HUMOR [Here are entered works of fiction dealing with wit and humor as a topic or theme. Works of fiction employing wit and humor as a device are entered under *Humorous stories*.]
   NT Humorous stories
WITCHCRAFT [Here are entered works dealing with a woman who practices witchcraft or who is exceptionally skilled in the occult arts or who can achieve the seemingly impossible. Works that deal with a man who practices witchcraft, or who is exceptionally skilled in the occult arts, or who can achieve the seemingly impossible are entered under *Wizards*.]
   UF Black magic
   BT Demonology
   RT Satanism
      Supernatural
      Witchcraft
      Wizards
WITNESSES
   BT Trials
WIVES
   RT Husbands
   NT Mariticide \ [Murder of a husband by his wife]
      Uxoricide [Murder of a wife by her husband]
      Widows
WIZARDS [Here are entered works dealing with a man who practices witchcraft or who is exceptionally skilled in the occult arts or who can achieve the seemingly impossible. Works that deal with a woman who practices witchcraft or who is exceptionally skilled in the occult arts or who can achieve the seemingly impossible are entered under *Witchcraft*. Works dealing with people who use charms and spells and are believed to have supernatural powers as well as works dealing with conjurers who perform tricks are entered under *Magicians*. The heading *Magic* is confined to works dealing with the use of charms and spells and supernatural powers, while the heading *Conjuring* is used for works dealing with entertainment that uses tricks to simulate the supernatural.]
   UF Black Magic
      Mages
      Warlocks
   BT Occultism
   RT Conjuring
      Fantastic fiction, Sword and sorcery \
      Magic
      Magicians
      Witchcraft

Wobblies
  USE Industrial Workers of the World
Womanhood
  USE Femininity (Philosophy)
        Femininity (Psychology)
        Maturation (Psychology)
WOMEN
  SA headings such as *Actresses*; *Governesses*; *Nuns*; etc.
  NT Daughters
      Girls
      Mistresses
      Prostitutes
      Sexual harassment of women
      Teenage girls
      Young women
Women—Relations with men
  USE Female-male relationships \
WOMEN—SOCIAL CONDITIONS
Women—Success
  USE Success—Women \
       Success in business—Women \
Women, Relations between
  USE Female-female relationships \
WOMEN ARTISTS
WOMEN ATHLETES
WOMEN AUTHORS
WOMEN CLERGY
  RT Nuns
WOMEN COLLEGE TEACHERS
WOMEN DETECTIVES
  BT Policewomen
  NT Actresses as detectives \
      Daughters as detectives \
      Governesses as detectives \
      Husband and wife detectives \
      Lesbian detectives \
      Mothers as detectives \
      Nuns as detectives \
      Nurses as detectives \
      Sisters as detectives \
      Widows as detectives \
      etc.
WOMEN HEADS OF STATE [If a woman who is a head of state is also the president, the heading *Presidents* may also be used.]
  UF Women presidents
  BT Women in politics
  RT Presidents
WOMEN IN AGRICULTURE
  BT Farm life
WOMEN IN BUSINESS
  RT Businessmen
      Success in business—Women \
  NT Executives
WOMEN IN POLITICS
  BT Political fiction
      Presidents
  NT Women heads of state
Women in the military
  USE Women soldiers
WOMEN JOURNALISTS
WOMEN LAWYERS
WOMEN LEGISLATORS—UNITED STATES
  UF United States congresswomen
      United States senators
  BT United States. Congress. House
      United States. Congress. Senate
WOMEN LEGISLATORS AS DETECTIVES \
  UF Congresswomen as detectives
      Senators as detectives
WOMEN MUSICIANS
WOMEN POETS
Women presidents
  USE Presidents
       Women heads of state
WOMEN RANCHERS
  RT Cowgirls
WOMEN SOLDIERS
  SA subdivision *Armed Forces—Women* under names of countries, for example, *United States—Armed Forces—Women*; and subdivision *Participation, Female* under individual wars, for example, *Vietnamese Conflict, 1961-1975—Participation, Female*
WOMEN SPIES [Here are entered works dealing with or featuring women spies. Works dealing with the operations of women agents would also be entered under the heading *Spy stories*.]
  BT Spies
      Spy stories
WORK ENVIRONMENT
  UF Industrial conditions
  RT Industrial relations
WORKING CLASS
  UF Labor and laboring classes
      Lower classes
  RT Industrialization
  NT Children—Employment
      Factories
      Peasantry
      Peonage
      Proletarian fiction \
      Proletariat [The working class considered from an economic standpoint]
      Serfdom

Strikes and lockouts
Villeinage
WORLD POLITICS
  UF Foreign relations
    International intrigue
    Intrigue
    Politics, International
  BT Political fiction
  NT Diplomatic and consular service
WORLD WAR, 1914-1918
WORLD WAR, 1914-1918—ENGLAND
  BT World War, 1914-1918—Great Britain
World War, 1914-1918—Espionage
  USE World War, 1914-1918—Secret service
WORLD WAR, 1914-1918—FRANCE
WORLD WAR, 1914-1918—GERMANY
WORLD WAR, 1914-1918—GREAT BRITAIN
  NT World War, 1914-1918—England
WORLD WAR, 1914-1918—SECRET SERVICE
  UF World War, 1914-1918—Espionage
  BT Spy stories
WORLD WAR, 1914-1918—UNITED STATES
WORLD WAR, 1939-1945—CONCENTRATION CAMPS
  RT Holocaust, Jewish (1939-1945)
  NT Japanese Americans—Evacuation and relocation, 1942-1945
WORLD WAR, 1939-1945—ENGLAND
  BT World War, 1939-1945—Great Britain
  NT Bombing, Aerial—England, 1940-1941
World War, 1939-1945—Espionage
  USE World War, 1939-1945—Secret Service
WORLD WAR, 1939-1945—FRANCE
WORLD WAR, 1939-1945—GERMANY
WORLD WAR, 1939-1945—GREAT BRITAIN
  NT World War, 1939-1945—England
World War, 1939-1945—Japanese internment, 1942-1945
  USE Japanese Americans—Evacuation and relocation, 1942-1945
WORLD WAR, 1939-1945—NAVAL OPERATIONS
  SA headings such as *World War, 1939-1945—Atlantic Ocean*, etc.
WORLD WAR, 1939-1945—POLAND
World War, 1939-1945—Russia
  USE World War, 1939-1945—Soviet Union
WORLD WAR, 1939-1945—SECRET SERVICE
  UF World War, 1939-1945—Espionage
  RT World War, 1939-1945—Underground movements
  BT Spy stories
WORLD WAR, 1939-1945—SOVIET UNION
  UF World War, 1939-1945—Russia
WORLD WAR, 1939-1945—UNDERGROUND MOVEMENTS
  RT World War, 1939-1945—Secret Service
WORRY [Here are entered works dealing with the mental activity of fretting or stewing over a problem. Works dealing with apprehensive uneasiness of mind, often involving self-doubt, and with doubt concerning the nature and reality of the uneasiness are entered under *Anxiety*. (Anxiety involves the anguish of fear with the anticipation or uncertainty of failure and may have physiological symptoms.) Works dealing with a loss of courage that may amount to cowardice are entered under *Fear*.]
  RT Anxiety
    Fear
WYOMING
  NT Cheyenne (Wyo.)

Y.A. accessible fiction
  USE Young adult accessible fiction\
YACHTS AND YACHTING [Here are entered works dealing with large sailboats or powerboats with closed cabins and built for pleasure or private cruising. Works dealing with other large seagoing vessels are entered under *Ships* or *Sailing ships*. Works dealing with smaller craft operated on inland bodies of water or near the shore on oceans and usually powered by oars, paddles, poles, or outboard motors are entered under *Boats and boating*. Works dealing with small boats using sail power are entered under *Sailboats*.]
  BT Ocean travel
    Sea stories
  RT Boats and boating
    Sailboats

Sailing ships
Ships
YAKUZA
UF Mobsters
RT Japan
YELLOWKNIFE (N.W.T.)
BT Northwest Territories
YEREVAN (ARMENIAN S.S.R.)
BT Armenian S.S.R.
Yeshiva
USE Jewish religious education
YEZIDIS [Here are entered works dealing with a Middle Eastern sect that worships an angel believed to have formerly been the author of evil but who now is the chief angel of good.]
RT Satanism
YIDDISH FICTION [Here is entered fiction originally produced in the Yiddish language. Fiction produced by Israelis in Hebrew or in several languages collectively is entered under *Israeli fiction*. Fiction originally written in the Hebrew language by non-Israelis is entered under *Hebrew fiction*. Collections of fiction produced by individual Jews of an unspecified nationality and in an unspecified language are entered under *Jewish fiction*. Works of fiction produced by individual Jews are entered only under the fiction of their nationality.]
RT German fiction
Hebrew fiction
Israeli fiction
Jewish fiction
Polish fiction
YOUNG ADULT ACCESSIBLE FICTION [Here are entered adult works that can be read by junior high through high school readers; approximate ages are 11 through 17 years.]
UF Adult fiction for young adult readers
Y.A. accessible fiction
BT Fiction
YOUNG ADULT FICTION [Here are entered collections of fiction for young adults in the 6th through 12th grades.]
BT Children's stories [Collections of fiction for children up through the 5th grade]
Fiction
YOUNG ADULTS [Here are entered works dealing with persons in the general age range from 18 to 25 years. Works dealing with persons in the general age range of 13 to 25 years are entered under *Youth*. Works dealing with persons from 13 to 17 years of age inclusive are entered under *Teenagers*.]
BT Children
RT Teenagers
Youth
YOUNG MEN [Here are entered works dealing with men 18 to 25 years of age inclusive. The age of the young man may be included here (for example, *Young men—18*; *Young men—19*, etc.) although this is not a Library of Congress practice.]
BT Men
RT Boys
Teenage boys [13 to 17 years inclusive]
YOUNG WOMEN [Here are entered works dealing with women 18 to 25 years of age inclusive. The age of the young woman may be included here (for example, *Young women—18*; *Young women—19*, etc.) although this is not a Library of Congress practice.]
BT Women
RT Teenage girls [13 to 17 years inclusive]
YOUTH [Here are entered works dealing with persons in the general age range of 13 to 25 years. Works dealing with persons from 13 to 17 years of age inclusive are entered under *Teenagers*. Works dealing with persons in the general age range from 18 to 25 years are entered under *Young adults*.]
BT Children
RT Teenagers
Young adults
YOUTH HOSTELS
UF Hostels
RT Hotels, taverns, etc.
YUGOSLAV AMERICANS [Here are entered works dealing with Americans of Yugoslavian ancestry.]
BT Yugoslavs—United States
YUGOSLAVIA (REPUBLIC) [There are six constituent republics in Yugoslavia. They are Bosnia and Hercegovina; Croatia; Macedonia; Montenegro; Serbia; Slovenia. Do not add any geographic identifier to the name of a republic of

Yugoslavia. See 23.4C in *AACR2R* for further information.]
- NT Bosnia and Hercegovina
  Croatia
  Dalmatia
  Macedonia
  Montenegro
  Serbia
  Slovenia

YUGOSLAVS—UNITED STATES [Here are entered works dealing with Yugoslavs visiting in or living in the United States.]
- NT Yugoslav Americans

YUKON TERRITORY
- BT Canada
- NT Klondike River Valley (Yukon)

YUPPIES \
- BT Middle classes

ZAGREB (CROATIA)
- BT Croatia

ZIMBABWE

ZIMBABWEAN FICTION

Appendix A

Guidelines on Subject Access to Individual Works of Fiction, Drama, Etc.

Introduction

The following guidelines, prepared and endorsed by the American Library Association's Subject Analysis Committee, constitute a recommendation for national standard practice in the provision of subject access to individual works of fiction, drama, poetry, humor, and folklore in all formats.* At the time of publication, these guidelines differ in some respects from Library of Congress practice. The Committee is concurrently recommending these guidelines to the Library of Congress. For improved national access to fiction, we urge the guidelines acceptance by other libraries, even if the Library of Congress is not able to adopt them. They provide an opportunity for libraries that are committed to better subject access to fiction for their users, and that are willing to undertake the extra file maintenance this entails, to provide this access in a standard way, and, thus, to share the cataloging effort among themselves. . . .

The guidelines are intended to apply only to *individual* works of fiction, drama, poetry, humor and folklore. For collections by one or several authors, or for literary criticism, consult the Library of Congress subject manual.[1]

The Subject Analysis Committee recommends the provision of four kinds of subject access: form/genre, access for characters or groups of characters, access for setting, and topical access. The following guidelines consist of instructions for providing these kinds of access. . . .

Extracted from *Guidelines on Subject Access to Individual Works of Fiction, Drama, Etc.* (Chicago: American Library Association, 1990). Some prefatory information, the thesaurus, MARC information, and the bibliography are not quoted.

*Note that OLDERR'S FICTION SUBJECT HEADINGS is designed only for use with fiction.

[1]Library of Congress, Subject Cataloging Division, *Subject Cataloging Manual: Subject Headings*, 3rd ed. (Washington, D.C.: The Library, 1988), Section H 1430 (Comics and Comic Characters), H 1610 (Fictitious Characters), H 1627 (Folklore Materials), H 1720 (Legends and Stories about Animals), H 1780 (Drama), H 1790 (Fiction), H 1795 (Legends and Romances), H 1800 (Poetry).

I. Form/genre access

Form/genre headings indicate what the work is, rather than what it is about. **Western stories,** for example, is used for the westerns themselves, rather than for works about westerns. Assign as many form/genre headings as appropriate. . . .

[Here follows a list of form and genre headings. They are not included here for reasons discussed on page xv.]

II. Character access

Introduction

As indicated in the general introduction, the guidelines below are not designed to apply to works *about* characters, which is out of our scope, but rather to provide subject access for characters in works of fiction, drama, etc.

Fictitious characters

Assign headings for fictitious and legendary characters and groups to individual works of fiction, drama, poetry, humor, folklore, and music, providing that they appear prominently in three or more different works. Add an appropriate parenthetical qualifier from the following list:

(Fictitious character)
(Legendary character)
([Nationality] deity), e.g. (Greek deity)
([Nationality] mythology), e.g. (Greek mythology)

Use more specific qualifiers only when needed to resolve a conflict or when ambiguity might result from use of a more general qualifier.

EXAMPLES: **Thor (Cartoon character)**
Thor (Norse deity)

. . . .

[The form subdivisions —*Fiction* or —*Juvenile fiction* may be added if desired.]
EXAMPLE: Sherlock Holmes (Fictitious character)—Fiction. . . .

Use the form of name that appears in *LCSH* [or LC's name authorities*]. If the name is not an LC heading, accept the form in the Hennepin County (Minnesota) Public Library authority file.** If it is not there, establish it as follows.

If the name varies, consult other works featuring the character or group, and then appropriate reference works, to determine the commonly used form. Prefer a commonly known form of name in English, if there is one. If there is not, prefer the commonly used form of name in English language reference sources. If the name cannot be found in reference sources, establish the name based on the work in hand.

---

*CDMARC Names (Washington, D.C.: Library of Congress, 1990; three CD-ROM disks).
Name Authorities Cumulative Microform Edition (Washington, D.C.: Library of Congress, 1990; 48X microfiche). There are two separate cumulations: 1977–1986 and 1987–1990. Both of these versions have the same coverage.
***Hennepin County Library Cumulative Authority List* (Minnetonka, Minn.: Hennepin County Library, quarterly, 1977–   ). Available only on microfiche. Contact the Bibliographic Products Librarian, Hennepin County Library, 12601 Ridgedale Drive, Minnetonka, MN 55343.

A bibliography of appropriate reference works is attached as an Appendix [not included in this extract]. Follow practices in *AACR2*, Chapter 22–24, to determine forms of name for fictitious persons with terms of nobility, corporate bodies with subdivisions, and other such special problems.

Character with surname. Establish in inverted form all characters whose names include a surname. Add as a final element of the name any titles of address associated with the name.

EXAMPLES: **Shore, Jemima (Fictitious character)**
Wimsey, Peter, Lord (Fictitious character)
Collins, Mr. (Fictitious character)
Boop, Betty (Fictitious character)
Bunyan, Paul (Legendary Character)

Character with a forename or nickname. Establish a character known by forename only or by nickname directly under that name. Add an appropriate parenthetical qualifier from the same list as for characters with surnames.

EXAMPLES: **Fabiano (Fictitious character)**
Little Orphan Annie (Fictitious character)
Bugs Bunny (Fictitious character)
John Henry (Legendary character)
Scheherazade (Legendary character)
Aphrodite (Greek deity)
Achilles (Greek mythology)

Named groups of characters. Establish named groups of fictitious or legendary characters according to the same pattern as individual characters. Use plural parenthetical qualifiers.

EXAMPLES: **Hardy Boys (Fictitious characters)**
Sartoris family (Fictitious characters)
Muses (Greek mythology)

Corporate bodies. Establish fictitious corporate bodies using the parenthetical qualifier (Imaginary organization).

EXAMPLES: **SMERSH (Imaginary organization)**
Great Britain. Circumlocution Office (Imaginary organization)

References. Make UF (see) references from other names by which the character or group may be known, including uninverted forms for characters entered under surname.

EXAMPLE: **Shadow (Fictitious character)**
UF **Cranston, Lamont (Fictitious character)**
Lamont Cranston (Fictitious character)
The Shadow (Fictitious character)

Make BT (Broader term, or see also) references from the appropriate medium to which the character is related. For literary characters, make a BT reference from **Characters and characteristics in literature.**

EXAMPLES: **Snoopy (Fictitious character)**
BT   **Comic books, strips, etc.**

Pantaloon (Fictitious character)
BT   **Commedia dell'arte**
      Pantomime

Cock Robin (Fictitious character)
BT   **Characters and characteristics in literature**

Real persons

Assign headings for real persons who appear as characters in individual works of fiction, drama, poetry, humor, folklore, and music. Following LC practice, assign the name as found in the name authority file, with appropriate form subdivision. However, if the person is best known as a literary author, use the following form instead: [Name], in fiction, drama, poetry, etc.* . . .

III. Setting access

When appropriate, bring out location and time period (setting) by means of subject headings. For settings that correspond to real places, assign the place name as found in the name authority file. . . .

For fictitious places which appear in at least three different works, assign the name as it appears in *LCSH* [or LC's name authorities**]. . . . If the name is not an LC heading, accept the form in the Hennepin County (Minnesota) Public Library authority file. If it is not there, establish the name as indicated below. Fictitious places use the parenthetical qualifier (Imaginary place). . . .

If the fictitious place name varies, consult other works featuring the place, and then appropriate reference works to determine the commonly used form. Prefer a commonly known form of name in English, if there is one; if there is not, prefer the commonly used form of name in English language reference sources. If the name cannot be found in reference sources, establish it based on the work in hand. A bibliography of appropriate reference works is attached as the Appendix [not included in this extract]. Use *AACR2*, Chapter 23, for jurisdictional names, or the subject cataloging manual for other place names to determine the form in which a place name should be established.

EXAMPLES: . . .
Grand Fernwick (Imaginary place)—Fiction.
Middle-Earth (Imaginary place)—Fiction.

---

*Note, though, that the LC rule is "Use the free-floating phrase heading **[name of author], in fiction, drama, poetry, etc.,** as (1) a form heading for biographic belletristic works, including musical dramatic work such as opera, ballets, musical comedies, etc., about an individual literary author; or (2) a topical heading for works which discuss an individual literary author as a theme in belles lettres, including musical dramatic works." (*Subject Cataloging Manual: Subject Headings,* Section 1155.4, p. 1, rev. 2/28/91).
Therefore, you should use only the subdivision —**Fiction.**
EXAMPLES: **Lincoln, Abraham, 1809-1865—Fiction.**
Veronica, Saint, 1st century—Fiction.

**CDMARC Names* (three CD-ROMs) and *Name Authorities Cumulative Microform Edition* (48X microfiche).

Narnia (Imaginary place)—Fiction.
Yoknapatawpha County (Imaginary place)—Fiction.

IV. Topical access

Assign as many topical subject headings as necessary to bring out the topic(s) covered, as determined after a superficial review of the publication in hand. Do not attempt to discern topics which have not been made explicit by the author or publisher, or which could be interpreted as representing value judgments. . . .

Appendix B

Subject Headings

Fictitious Characters

Background:

Fictitious characters may have names which resemble personal names or may have names which are descriptive phrases or nicknames. This instruction sheet provides guidelines for establishing and assigning subject headings for fictitious characters. For more specific instructions on comic and cartoon characters, see H 1430; for lengendary characters, see H 1795.

Procedures:

1. **Form of heading**

   a. **Character with surname.** Establish in inverted form all characters whose names include a surname. Add as a final element of the name any titles of address associated with the name. Add the parenthetical qualifier (**Fictitious character**). *Examples:*

   Shore, Jemima (Fictitious character)
   Wimsey, Peter, Lord (Fictitious character)
   Collins, Mr. (Fictitious character)

   b. **Character with forename or nickname.** Establish a character known by forename only or by nickname directly under that name. Add the parenthetical qualifier (**Fictitious character**). *Examples:*

   Fabiano (Fictitious character)
   Operator 5 (Fictitious character)
   Little Orphan Annie (Fictitious character)

Fictitious Characters is reprinted from *Subject Cataloging Manual: Subject Headings*, section H 1610 (Washington, D.C.: Library of Congress, 1988).

2. **References**

    a. **UF references.** Make UF references from other names by which the character may be known, including uninverted forms for characters entered under surname. *Examples:*

    Shadow (Fictitious character)
    UF Cranston, Lamont (Fictitious character)
    UF Lamont Cranston (Fictitious character)
    UF The Shadow (Fictitious character)

    Marple, Jane (Fictitious character)
    UF Marple, Miss (Fictitious character)
    UF Miss Marple (Fictitious character)

    b. **BT references.** Make BT references from the appropriate medium to which the character is related. For literary characters, make a BT reference from **Characters and characteristics in literature.** *Examples:*

    Snoopy (Fictitious character)
    BT **Comic books, strips, etc.**

    Pantaloon (Fictitious character)
    BT **Commedia dell'arte**
    BT **Pantomime**

    Cock Robin (Fictitious character)
    BT **Characters and characteristics in literature**

3. **Named groups of characters.** Establish named groups of fictitious characters according to the same pattern as individual characters. Use as a qualifier the term **(Fictitious characters).** *Examples:*

    Hardy Boys (Fictitious characters)
    BT **Characters and characteristics in literature**

    Sartoris family (Fictitious characters)
    BT **Characters and characteristics in literature**

4. **Assignment of headings**

    a. **Literary texts.** Assign a heading for a fictitious character to collections of literary texts about the character, using the subdivisions —**Fiction,** —**Drama,** —**Poetry** or —**Literary collections** as appropriate.

    For individual plays or poems, assign a heading only if the character has been borrowed by the author from another author or source and used in the creation of a new work. Do not assign a heading for works that are simply adaptations of another author's work.

    Do not assign a heading for a fictitious character to an individual work of fiction.

b. **Works about the character.** Assign a heading without further subdivision to general works on a fictitious character.

For works limited to specific media, use the heading with an appropriate qualifying phrase such as: **. . . in art, . . . in literature, . . . in mass media.**

EXCEPTION: Do not use **. . . in literature** for literary characters. Use the phrase **. . . in literature** only for characters borrowed from other media, e.g. **Snoopy (Fictitious character) in literature.**

For works on the use of a fictitious character by an individual author, also assign a heading of the type **[name of author]—Characters—[name of character]** (cf. H 1155.4).

Fiction

Procedures:

1. **General rule**

    For collections of fiction, assign as many headings as necessary to bring out both the form and the topic(s). For single works of fiction, assign headings to bring out topic(s) and form only as noted in section 4, below.

2. **Designating the form of collections**

    a. Bring out the form of a collection by assigning headings of the type **American fiction—20th century; Short stories, American; Epistolary fiction;** etc., as in the first heading in the following example:

    Title: Golf story omnibus
    Short stories, American
    Golf—Fiction

    Certain phrase headings combine both form and topical aspects into a single heading, e.g. **Detective and mystery stories, American; Science fiction, American**; etc. These headings are used to designate both the form and the topic of collections, and no additional heading is usually required.

    Do not use a phrase heading of this type if a more specific **[topic]—Fiction** heading can be formulated to designate the topic of the collection. Instead, assign the more specific heading in conjunction with a *broader, nontopical* form heading. For example, assign the following headings to a collection of American stories about jungle warfare:

    1. American fiction
    2. Jungle warfare—Fiction

    [*not* **1. War stories, American**]

    [*not* **1. War stories, American**
    2. Jungle warfare—Fiction]

Fiction is reprinted from *Subject Cataloging Manual: Subject Headings,* section H 1790 (Washington, D.C.: Library of Congress, 1988).

b. **Collection of fiction by one author.** As a general rule, assign form headings (a) if the form heading includes a topical aspect, e.g. **Western stories**, or (b) if it is readily apparent from a cursory examination of the work that it comprises fiction of a highly specific form and that this form is an essential point of the collection, e.g. **Allegories; Fairy tales; Radio stories; Children's stories, English;** etc.

>Do not assign nonspecific form headings to collections of fiction by one author, e.g. **American fiction; Short stories, American;** etc.

c. **Collections of children's fiction.** Assign the headings **Children's stories** or **Children's stories, American, [English**, etc.] to collections of children's fiction, whether by one author or several authors, in addition to the other required form and topical headings. Do not assign this heading to collections of fiction for young adults.

3. **Designating the topic(s) of collections by one or several authors**

   Bring out identifiable topics, using one of the following types of headings:

   a. **[topic]—Fiction or [topic]—Juvenile fiction.** Use headings of this type as the standard means of designating topics in fiction, e.g. **Slavery—United States—Fiction; Parent and child—Fiction; Horses—Fiction; Paris (France)—Fiction; Voodooism—Fiction.**

   > NOTE: The subdivision **—Stories,** which had formerly been used under some topics, is no longer to be used. Use only **—Fiction.**

   b. **Phrase headings with topical aspects.** If a phrase heading has both form and topical aspects, assign only the one heading to designate both form and topic, as described in sec. 1.a, above. **Sea stories, Western stories,** and **Love stories** are examples of such headings.

   c. If the collection of fiction features as its theme an individual character, real or imaginary, bring out the character, e.g. **Lincoln, Abraham, 1809–1865—Fiction; Tarzan (Fictitious character)—Fiction; Holmes, Sherlock (Fictitious character)—Fiction.**

   > If the featured character is a literary author, assign the heading **[name of author], in fiction, drama, poetry,** etc.

4. **Individual works of fiction**

   Bring out topic(s) only for the following types of individual works of fiction:

   a. **Biographical fiction.** Assign the heading **[name of biographee]—Fiction.** For biographical fiction about literary authors, assign the heading **[author's name], in fiction, drama, poetry,** etc.

   b. **Historical fiction.** Assign headings for specific historical events, periods, etc., with the subdivision **—Fiction,** e.g. **World War, 1939–1945—Fiction; Earthquakes—California—San Francisco—Fiction.**

Do not assign a heading of this type when the event or period is merely the backdrop to a story. Assign it only when the event or period is the principal focus of the work.

Interpret the term historical fiction broadly to include works about entities such as movements, corporate bodies other than jurisdictions, camps, parks, structures, geographical features other than regions, ethnic groups, disasters, categories of events, etc.

c. **Animal stories.** Assign the heading **Animals—Fiction** to individual novels or stories about animals in general. For a work about a specific type of animal, assign a heading for the type of animal with the subdivision **—Fiction,** e.g. **Horses—Fiction.**

Assign no form headings to individual works of adult fiction, children's fiction, or young adult fiction.

5. **Limitations on assigning headings**

Assign topical and form headings, especially to single works of fiction or to collections by one author, only as they come readily to mind after a superficial review of the work being cataloged.

Do not attempt to assign a form heading to a collection of fiction by one author if the form is not stated on the title page or in another prominent location.

Do not attempt to discern topics which have not been made explicit by the author or publisher, or which could be interpreted as representing value judgments.

6. **History and criticism**

a. **General rule.** For works about particular themes in fiction, assign as many headings as necessary to bring out the form (use subdivision **—History and criticism**) and the topic(s) (normally using headings of the type **[topic] in literature**), e.g.

1. **American fiction—20th century—History and criticism.**
2. **Politics in literature.**

If a heading has both form and topical aspects, assign only the single heading with the subdivision **—History and criticism,** e.g. **Detective and mystery stories, American—History and criticism.**

b. **Fiction about individual persons.** For criticism of fiction about particular individuals, including individual literary authors, assign **[name of person], fiction, drama, poetry, etc.** as a topical heading.

c. **Fiction about imaginary persons.** For criticism of fiction about particular imaginary individuals, assign the name of the person. Also assign, if appropriate for the work, the name of the author with the subdivision **—Characters— [name of person]** (cf. H 1610). *Example:*

1. **Doyle, Arthur Conan, Sir, 1859–1930—Characters—Sherlock Holmes.**
2. **Holmes, Sherlock (Fictitious character).**

d. **Fiction about wars and similar events.** For works of fiction about a specific war, revolution, uprising, etc., assign **[name of event]—Literature and the war, [revolution, uprising, etc.]** as a topical heading (cf. H 1200).

e. **Single works of fiction.** For works about an individual novel or story in one of the categories described in sec. 4.a–4.c, above, assign a heading for the individual work as well as a heading for the theme, e.g.

1. **Mitchell, Margaret, 1900–1949. Gone with the Wind.**
2. **United States History—Civil War, 1861–1865—Literature and the war.**

Selected and Annotated Bibliography

American Library Association. Resources and Technical Services Division. Subject Analysis Committee. Subcommittee on Subject Access to Individual Works of Fiction, Drama, Etc. *Guidelines on Subject Access to Individual Works of Fiction, Drama, Etc.* American Library Association, 1990.
    Required reading for the cataloging of fiction, but the thesaurus is poor.

Anglo-American Cataloguing Rules, second edition, 1988 Revision. American Library Association, 1988.
    Commonly referred to as *AACR2R*. You shouldn't catalog without it.

Benet's Readers Encyclopedia. 3rd ed. Harper, 1977.
    Useful as a source for literary definitions.

CDMARC Names. Library of Congress, 1990.
    2.4 million records on three CD-ROM disks; cumulated quarterly. See entry under *Name Authorities Cumulative Microform Edition.* for a fuller description.

Cuddon, J. A. *A Dictionary of Literary Terms.* Doubleday, 1977.
    Generally a good source for definitions, but the coverage can be uneven. For example, it gives more than four pages to something as vague and unlikely to be looked up as "Fancy and imagination" but only a short paragraph to "Beat literature."

Fiction Catalog. New edition every four years. H. W. Wilson, 1960– .
    Uses its own thesaurus, which can vary unaccountably from that of LC. No subject headings are listed with the main entries, and so it is of little use as a cataloging aid. Strong on older fiction, but weak on current works. The bulk of the titles indexed are the same from one edition to the next.

Free-Floating Subdivisions: An Alphabetical Index. 2nd ed. Library of Congress, 1990.
    A finding aid for information contained in LC's *Subject Catalog Manual: Subject Headings* (listed below). A great time-saver and well worth the price.

Holman, C. Hugh. *A Handbook to Literature.* 5th ed. Macmillan, 1986.
    Frequently described as *the* authoritative source for literary definitions, but it is not comprehensive and a second source is often necessary.

Hennepin County Library Cumulative Authority List. Issued in quarterly microfiche cumulations. Hennepin County (Minn.) Library, 1977– .
    Occasionally idiosyncratic, with even fewer scope notes than in *LCSH*, but it fearlessly plunges in where LC fears to tread. An excellent backup source for anyone doing large amounts of original cataloging.

Library of Congress Filing Rules. Library of Congress, 1980.
> LC has its own way of filing, which unfortunately does not conform to ALA rules. *Olderr's Fiction Subject Headings* uses LC rules to make it congruent with *LCSH.*

Library of Congress Name Authorities, Cumulative Microform Edition, 1977–1986. Library of Congress, 1986.
> Doesn't always seem to follow LC filing rules, or any rules at all sometimes, which can make it confusing and difficult to use. Unfortunately, there is no other readily available source nearly as thorough. Updated microfiche cumulations are now available on CD-ROM.

Library of Congress Subject Headings. Issued annually. Library of Congress.
> Too often maligned for containing occasionally dated or awkward headings, this magnificent and utterly necessary work of librarianship categorizes and cross-references nearly every topic in the universe.

Name Authorities Cumulative Microform Edition. Library of Congress, 1990. 48X microfiche; in two separate cumulations: 1977–1986 and 1987–1990.
> Also available in a CD-ROM version, listed above under *CDMARC Names.* Both versions have the entire 2.4 million LC name authority file, including personal and corporate names, conference headings, uniform titles, series entries, and geographic names of political and civil jurisdictions. The microform version can be difficult to use because the alphabetization procedure is not readily apparent.

Olderr, Steven. *Olderr's Fiction Index.* Issued annually. St. James Press, 1988– .
> A full index of all American fiction reviewed in the major library journals each year. Also lists subject headings and characters with the main entries; very useful as a cataloging aid. Since 1989, the cataloging has been fully congruent with LC headings.

Olderr, Steven. *Mystery Index: Subjects, Settings, and Sleuths of 10,000 Titles.* American Library Association, 1987.
> Does not list subject headings with main entries. Includes some specialized terms for mysteries not found elsewhere. Includes a character index with names of authors.

Olderr, Steven. *Young Adult Fiction Index.* Issued annually. St. James Press, 1989– .
> The young adult version of *Olderr's Fiction Index,* described above. Covers fiction intended for readers from sixth grade through high school.

Oxford English Dictionary. Oxford University Press, 1933.

Sears, Minnie Earl. *Sears List of Subject Headings.* H. W. Wilson, 1986.
> It's hard to understand why it is necessary for these headings to vary at all from *LCSH,* but they sometimes do. In researching the meaning of LC terms, this source is occasionally useful because of its different cross references and scope notes.

Subject Cataloging Manual: Subject Headings. Library of Congress, 1988.
> Explains LC cataloging practices. After *LCSH* and *AACR2R,* this is the next most important resource for catalogers.

Subject Guide to Books in Print. Issued annually. R. R. Bowker.
> The use of newsprint makes this extremely difficult to read and there are a number of errors. Not all of the headings are LC, but it is still useful for gaining an understanding of how subject headings are being used.

The Chicago Manual of Style. 13th ed., rev. University of Chicago Press, 1982.
> In the preparation of *Olderr's Fiction Subject Headings,* this manual was relied upon when there was no guidance from LC. There are too many style manuals in the world, but if they are ever reduced in number, this one should remain. Comprehensive, reasonable in its judgments, and well indexed.

Webster's New Dictionary of Synonyms. Merriam Webster, 1968.
>Very useful in distinguishing between synonyms. It would be a service to researchers if an expanded version were produced.

Webster's New Geographical Dictionary. Merriam Webster, 1988.
>This excellent resource would be even better if it had more entries for regions.

Webster's Third New International Dictionary of the English Language, Unabridged. Merriam Webster, 1986.
>The best American dictionary available, but the relatively recent copyright is a smokescreen to hide the fact that the work is overdue for a complete updating.

A Women's Thesaurus. Harper, 1987.
>More than just a thesaurus, it's a different way of looking at the world. Interesting, but of no use in fiction cataloging.

Steven Olderr is the author of *Olderr's Fiction Index, Olderr's Young Adult Fiction Index* (annual publications, St. James Press), *Mystery Index* (ALA, 1987), and *Symbolism: A Comprehensive Dictionary* (McFarland, 1986). From 1974–88 he served as head librarian at the Riverside Public Library in Illinois. Steven Olderr holds an M.A.L.S. from Rosary College and is presently a self-employed writer.